Maurice Angus Oudin

Standard polyphase Apparatus and Systems

Maurice Angus Oudin

Standard polyphase Apparatus and Systems

ISBN/EAN: 9783743337206

Manufactured in Europe, USA, Canada, Australia, Japa

Cover: Foto ©ninafisch / pixelio.de

Manufactured and distributed by brebook publishing software (www.brebook.com)

Maurice Angus Oudin

Standard polyphase Apparatus and Systems

CONTENTS.

CHAPTER		PAGE
I.	Definitions of Alternating-Current Terms	1
II.	Generators	17
III.	Generators (*Concluded*)	38
IV.	Induction Motors	60
V.	Synchronous Motors	92
VI.	Rotary Converters	106
VII.	Static Transformers	120
VIII.	Station Equipment and General Apparatus	140
IX.	Two-Phase System	166
X.	Three-Phase System	180
XI.	Monocyclic System	194
XII.	Choice of Frequency	207
XIII.	Relative Weights of Copper for Various Systems,	214
XIV.	Calculation of Transmission Lines	221

STANDARD POLYPHASE APPARATUS AND SYSTEMS.

CHAPTER I.

INTRODUCTORY.

DEFINITIONS OF ALTERNATING-CURRENT TERMS.

Alternating Currents. — On account of the limitation imposed by the space of this book, mathematical demonstrations of alternating-current phenomena have been omitted in the following pages, and the chapter will be found to consist mainly of elementary explanations and statements which partake of the nature of definitions. It is hoped that these definitions will be found useful in aiding the uninformed reader to obtain a clearer understanding of the principles underlying polyphase apparatus and methods. For a more comprehensive treatment of alternating-current phenomena, the reader is referred to the many works on the subject.

The alternating-current generator was one of the earliest applications of the principles of induction. Unlike the current from the direct-current generator, which came at a later date, the alternating current rapidly changes its value and direction, the fluctuations being periodical. Such a current reaches a maximum in one sense, declines to zero, reverses, and then attains a maximum in the other sense, as often as the pressure of the generator follows this variation. This variation of current, or of pressure in its simplest and ideal form, follows the law of simple harmonic motion, and may be represented by the projection of a point moving in a circle, with a constant velocity, upon a perpendicular diameter.

The development of this motion and its application to the variation of the current or the induced pressure of an ideal alternating-current generator is illustrated in Fig. 1. The point P on the circle is considered as moving with a

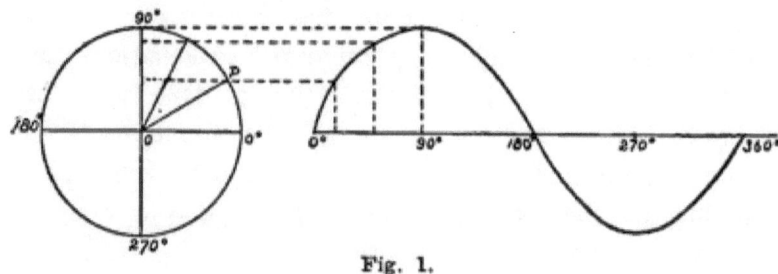

Fig. 1.

constant velocity. Its projection on the diameter is the value of the pressure at any instant of time. The circle represents a complete revolution or cycle of change of current or pressure. The straight line to the right is the development of the circle expressed in degrees, 360 of which constitute one complete period. On this line the instantaneous values of the current or the pressure derived from the projection of P are plotted. It is seen that a line drawn through these points, obtained for the complete revolution, gives a sine-curve.

On account of the irregular magnetic field, in practice few alternating-current generators give rise to pressures following a simple sine-law. The variation from a sine-curve is not so great, in the majority of alternating-current generators, but that, for purposes of most commercial calculations, their electro-motive forces can be considered as simple harmonic quantities.

The formula for the flow of current in an alternating system of conductors is, in its general form, similar to that used for determining the flow in a direct-current system. It differs from Ohm's law only in the introduction of certain factors, which, however, may become so complex as to conceal the simple quantities of the equation resistance and *E.M.F.* The value of these factors depends on three well-known properties of a conductor. These are:

1. Inductance.
2. Capacity.
3. Virtual Resistance.

Inductance. — The magnetic field, surrounding a circuit through which a current is flowing, exerts no influence on the circuit in the case of a direct current of constant value. In the case of an alternating current it is of far greater practical importance, and gives rise to a variety of phenomena. The magnetic flux then varies periodically with, and in the same manner as, the current and *E.M.F.* The setting up of this magnetic flux — or lines of force, as they are sometimes called — produces an *E.M.F.* in the circuit, in opposition to the induced *E.M.F.* This counter *E.M.F.*, or *E.M.F.* of self-induction, is stronger when the magnetic flux is changing most rapidly; therefore arriving at a maximum, 90° later than the flux and the current producing the flux. The result of this counter *E.M.F.* is that, when an external $E.M.F.$ is applied, the current does not immediately attain its maximum, and, when the $E.M.F.$ is withdrawn, the current persists for awhile. The current reaches its maximum later in point of time than the $E.M.F.$, — i.e., is always lagging behind the $E.M.F.$ It would seem as if a current of electricity possessed a quality of the nature of the inertia of matter.

The strength of this flux, or the induction as Faraday called it, is determined by the current. The extent to which a gixen flux affects a circuit in a non-magnetic medium — i.e., the magnitude of the counter $E.M.F.$ — depends solely upon the geometry of the circuit. If the circuit is wound in a coil, or so arranged that in the periodic variation of the flux the same lines of force encircle more than one portion of the conductor, the counter $E.M.F.$ will be increased.

That constant quality of a circuit which determines its inductive effects is called inductance. The inductance may be either self or mutual inductance, according as the circuit is isolated or acted on by an adjacent circuit, also carrying a current. Inductance is frequently called the co-efficient of induction. The symbol L is used to designate self-inductance, — the unit of measurement of which is the henry.

Capacity. — Like inductance, the capacity of a circuit depends upon its geometry and its surroundings. It is the quality which a conductor possesses of being able to hold a quantity of electricity. A combination of conductors or conducting surfaces, advantageously placed to hold the greatest possible quantity of electricity, is called a condenser. All insulated lines act more or less like condensers. The charging or discharging current of a condenser is greatest when the rate of change of effective pressure is greatest; that is, when the *E.M.F.* is at zero at the moment of passing from negative to positive, or *vice versa*. The effect of capacity, then, is opposite to the effect of inductance, and may neutralize it, or even overcome it, when existing in the same circuit. In a circuit having capacity, the current may lead the *E.M.F.* in phase. Fig. 2 shows the lead produced by capacity. The curve *V* represents the curve of *E.M.F.*, and *I* the current curve leading the *E.M.F.* The unit of measurement of capacity is the farad, and is usually represented by the symbol *K*.

Impressed E.M.F. — The more frequently an alternating current is reversed, the less time is there available for it to reach the value it would have in a direct-current system. To drive this maxi-

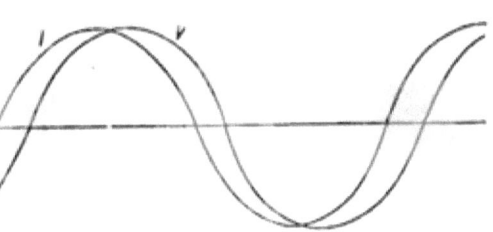

Fig. 2.

mum current through an alternating system of conductors having inductance, requires a greater *E.M.F.* than is needed in a direct-current system to produce this same current. The inductance of a circuit, as explained, determines the counter *E.M.F.*; and it must be overcome by an added amount to the *E.M.F.* required to produce the same current in a direct-current system. The name of impressed *E.M.F.* has been given to this resultant. The counter *E.M.F.* acts at right angles to the current, and is greatest when the current is reversing its sign, or when the rate of change of the lines of force is greatest. The values and direction of the impressed $E.M.F.$ and its components may be considered in a diagram. In Fig. 3 the impressed $E.M.F.$ is shown as the hypotenuse of a right-angled triangle. That component of the $E.M.F.$ which would drive the same current through a circuit without inductance, being necessarily in phase with the current, is shown as lagging behind the impressed $E.M.F.$ by an angle, Φ, and by a length equal to its magnitude. In quadrature with the component is the $E.M.F.$ of self-induction, the magnitude of which determines the length of the line in the diagram. The magnitude of the impressed $E.M.F.$ is then readily found. The name of energy $E.M.F.$ has been given to that component in phase with the current, and which is effective in doing any work in a circuit. As all the quantities in the diagram must follow the law of simple harmonic motion, the curve of self-inductive $E.M.F.$ will be shown in the same way as the curve of impressed $E.M.F.$ The effect of this inductive component, in increasing the impressed volts needed to cause a given current to flow, is shown in Fig. 4. The curve RI represents the energy component of the impressed $E.M.F.$ which would drive the current if there were no inductance. It is equal in value to the product of the current and the resistance. In quadrature with it, is the inductive $E.M.F.$, designated by the curve pLI, p being equal to $2N$, where N is the number of complete cycles per second, and L the inductance. This is the component required to offset the effect of the inductance. By adding the ordi-

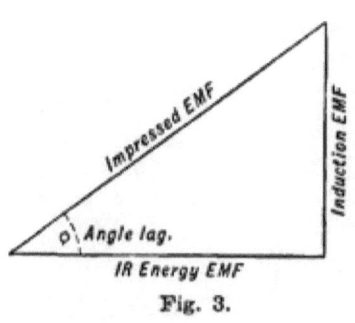

Fig. 3.

nates of the two curves, we obtain a third curve, V, also following the sine-curve law. This is the curve of the

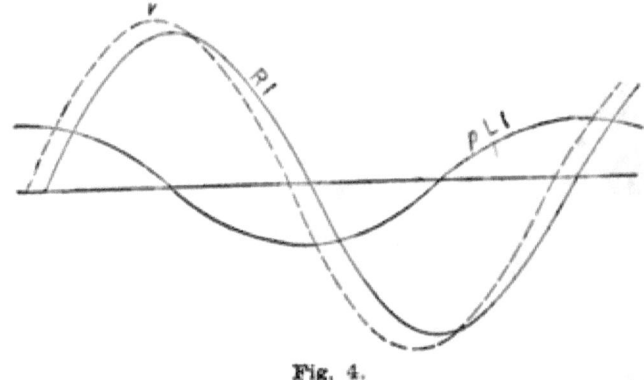

Fig. 4.

impressed $E.M.F.$ required to produce the given current in this particular circuit.

Impedance; Reactance. — Impedance is the total opposition in a circuit to the flow of current. It determines the maximum current that can flow with a given impressed $E.M.F.$ It is made up of a resistance component and another component to which the name of reactance has been given. The relations of resistance, reactance, and impedance are shown in Fig. 5. As there may be energy

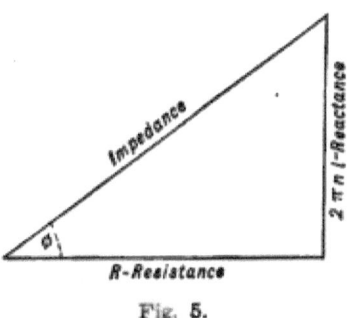

Fig. 5.

losses external to a circuit, and yet dependent on that circuit, which require a flow of current that cannot be determined by a calculation based upon the ohmic resistance alone, it is not correct to designate the resistance component as the ohmic resistance. Such losses are those due to hysteresis in transformers and iron cores, which have the effect of a small transformer interposed in the circuit. This component of impedance is termed energy resistance, and the other, reactance which has sometimes been called the inductive resistance.

Reactance is the effect of self-induction expressed in ohms. It becomes prominent in lines of large cross-section. The relative value of reactance to resistance can be reduced by selecting a number of conductors of small areas having a combined equal resistance. For instance, when for one No. 000 wire two No. 1 wires are substituted, the resistance will remain the same, but the reactance will be almost halved.

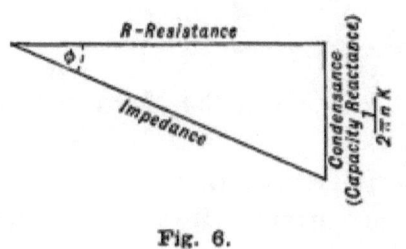

Fig. 6.

When capacity is introduced into the circuit, the current may lead in phase. Fig. 6 illustrates the effect of capacity on the circuit. The reactance due to capacity, or condensance as it is designated, acts in the opposite direction to the reactance of inductance. The impedance in Fig. 6 is the resultant of the resistance and the capacity reactance. When capacity and inductance are both present, the impedance is the resultant of the resistance component and a component equal to the difference between the numerical values of the condensance and reactance. In Fig. 7 the magnetic reactance is laid off above the line of resistance and in quadrature with it. The capacity reactance, or condensance, is represented as having a greater numerical value, and acting in opposing direction. The resultant impedance is readily found. When the inductance is equal to the **capacity, the** current is in phase with the impressed volts, **and follows** Ohm's law.

In aërial **conductors of** low resistance, **the reactance is** often prominent, **and the** distribution of *E.M.F.* may be seriously affected by it. It becomes important, **then,** in selecting **conductors** for transmission lines, that **those** of large **cross-section, and** correspondingly low resistance, be avoided as **much as** possible, except in special cases, as, for instance, in the employment of rotary converters supplied by its **own set of con-**ductors, where **some** reactance is desirable.

Virtual Resistance. — If the cross-section of **a con-**ductor carrying an alternating **current is** resolved into many elements, it will

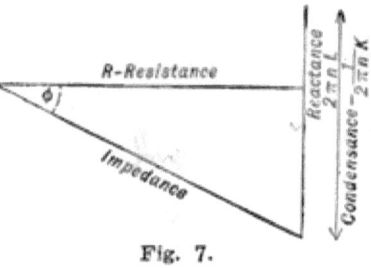

Fig. 7.

be seen that the internal portions are subject to greater inductive effects than the elements **nearer the** surface. The outer streams **of current** suffer less opposition, and reach a maximum sooner than those centrally located. In large conductors, **carrying heavy currents of high** frequency, there **may not only be no** current flowing **in the** central portion of the conductor, **but a** condition may exist where a current will flow in the opposite direction. The central core **is** then not only valueless as a conductor, but had **better be** omitted.

As a result **of** the reduction of **the** effective cross-section **of a** conductor carrying an alternating current, the resistance **is increased,** and slightly **less** current **will flow** than would if the **specific** resistance **and the** inductance of the wire are alone **considered.** This increment of resistance of a conductor is called its virtual resistance. The phenomenon is also called the skin effect.

The best shape for conductors of large cross-section, carrying heavy alternating currents, is that of a tube or flat strip.

In common practice the sizes of wire and the rapidity of current reversals are not such as to appreciably produce this effect. The ratio of the resistance of a conductor carrying an alternating current, to its resistance when a direct current is flowing, can be readily computed for different sizes of conductors and reversals of current.

In Fig. 8 the ordinates represent the product of area and cycles per second. Corresponding factors for the virtual or apparent resistance of cylindrical copper conductors are read off the horizontal scale. The factor for a conductor of any other non-magnetic metal will vary in the ratio of its conductivity to that of copper. In the case of magnetic materials, especially iron, the factor for the virtual resistance is greater than that in the curve.

Energy in a Circuit. — The work done in a circuit will always be some product of the current and the quantities in phase with it. In a direct-current system the product of measured volts and amperes will give the energy of the circuit. In an alternating-current system the product of the measured amperes, and the component of impressed $E.M.F.$ in phase with the current, — i.e., the energy $E.M.F.$, — will give the energy. The component of $E.M.F.$ in quadrature with the current — i.e., the induction component — drives a wattless current, and consequently adds nothing to the energy of the circuit. The product of the impressed $E.M.F.$ and the current will be easily understood to give too large results. This product is the apparent watts of the circuit. The error in calculating the power by the measured amperes and volts will depend upon the extent of the displacement in phase of the impressed *E.M.F.* and the current, or the angle of the lag, usually denoted as Φ. The energy in the circuit can be

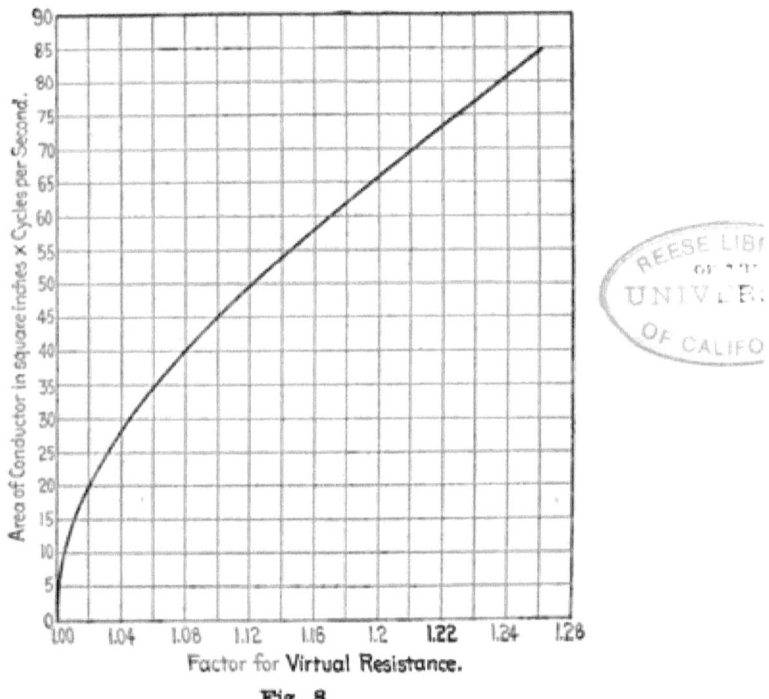

Fig. 8.

found by multiplying the product of volts and amperes by the cosine of this angle of lag.

Power Factor — Induction Factor. — The ratio of the true watts in the circuit, as measured by an indicating wattmeter, to the apparent watts, — the volt-amperes, — is called the power factor. The power factor is useful in determining the true energy in a circuit when the apparent energy is known, the resistance when the impedance is known, the energy volts when the total impressed volts are given, and the energy current when the total current is known.

The quantities in quadrature with the energy values of current and $E.M.F.$, and with the resistance, may be determined in the same way, from the resultants by a multiplier or factor, called the induction factor. As the power factor is proportional to the energy quantities, and the induction factor to the components in quadrature with them, it follows that the former must be numerically equal to the cosine, and the latter to the sine of the lag angle. Accordingly, a table of cosines and sines for all angles will give the corresponding power and induction factors.

Wattless Current. — The component of the total current in quadrature with the energy current is called the wattless current. It should be understood that the current and other quantities of a circuit are resolved into components for the sake of a better understanding of the phenomena taking place in the circuit. There is actually but one current flowing, as there is but one $E.M.F.$, in any one part of a circuit. The presence of reactance, either in the transmission circuit or in the apparatus connected to it, increases the lag-angle, and consequently the wattless current. This component does no work in a circuit, but increases the total current, and thereby the heating of conductors. The wattless current required to balance the reactance may become sufficiently great to practically tax the full capacity of generators and of conductors, although very little energy is being generated or transmitted. If it were possible to have conductors without resistance, a true wattless current could then, in fact, actually exist in an alternating-current circuit. In such a case the current would be in quadrature with the impressed E.M.F., and the circuit would give back as much energy as it received, the sum being zero.

Relative Values. — Designating the current as I, resistance as R, reactance as S, and impedance as U, from what has preceded, the following relations will be understood:

1. $\begin{matrix}\text{The reactance} \\ \text{of a line, } S,\end{matrix} \Big\} = \dfrac{\text{Induction } E.M.F. \text{ consumed in line}}{I}$.

2. The impedance, $U, = \dfrac{\text{Impressed } E.M.F. \text{ consumed in line}}{I}$.

3. The energy component of $E.M.F.$ consumed by the resistance, R, of a conductor is IR, and is in phase with the current.

4. The inductive component of $E.M.F.$ consumed by the reactance, S, of a conductor is IS, and is in quadrature with the current.

5. The impressed $E.M.F.$ consumed by the impedance, U, of a conductor, is IU.

5. The energy loss in a conductor is I^2R, and depends on the current and resistance only.

Voltage Drop Due to Power Factor. — The $E.M.F.$ consumed by the impedance, IU, does not represent the voltage drop in a conductor, as it is usually out of phase with the impressed $E.M.F.$ as well as with the current. This voltage drop, as will be shown, can be anything between IR and IU. It will depend upon the difference in phase between the current and the impressed $E.M.F.$, or the lag angle, and can be easily determined when the power factor is known. In Figs. 9 to 14, let OE' be the $E.M.F.$ at the receiving end of a transmission line. For various power factors at the receiving end of the line, there will be corresponding phase differences, Φ. Let OI be the current out of phase with the E.M.F. by Φ. IU, IR, and IS have the relations heretofore assigned to them, IR being in phase with OI, and IS in quadrature with OI. Where these quantities are small relatively to the impressed E.M.F., as they usually are in practice, the drop of voltage is IA, equal to $OE - OE'$, OE being equal to the generator voltage, A the apparent resistance of the line.

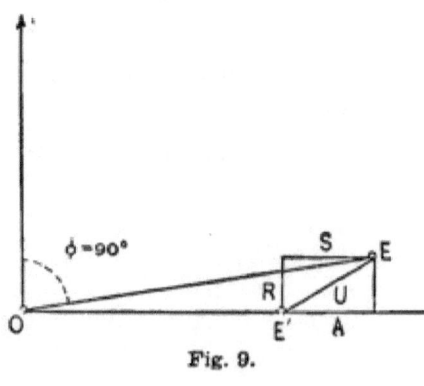

Fig. 9.

Assume a given E.M.F. at the end of the line, and a constant resistance and reactance. If the phase displacement Φ, or what is the same, if the power factor of the receiving system, is varied, the triangle of electromotive forces will revolve around E' as center. The projection of IU, or its components, upon the E.M.F. will give the voltage drop. With a lag angle of 90° (Fig. 9), the drop of voltage is due to the reactance alone. As the lag angle decreases, the drop IA becomes less than the impressed E.M.F. consumed in the line IU until it reaches 60° (Fig. 10), when with the given values of IU and IS the drop is seen to be equal to the

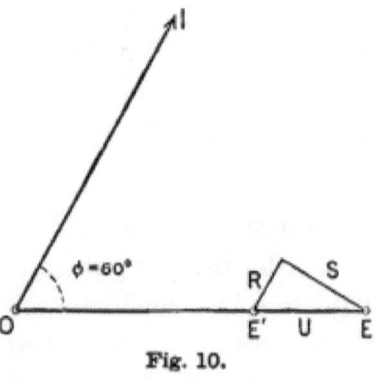

Fig. 10.

impedance IU, and has the greatest value it can have. As the phase displacement grows less, the effect of the reactance decreases until $\Phi = 0$ (Fig. 11), when the drop is due to resistance alone, a case of a non-inductive load.

If, now, capacity is introduced into the line by the use of long cables, synchronous motors, rotary converters, or condensers, the phase displacement Φ becomes negative. Up to 30° the projection of the reactance is in opposition to the projection of the impedance, i.e., negative (Fig. 12), and as a result the drop IA is less than the resistance drop. Finally, at 30° (Fig. 13) there is no drop of voltage in the line; for the reactance raises the voltage as much as the resistance lowers it, and the line apparently has no resistance. As the phase displacement increases, the voltage at the receiving end becomes higher than the generator $E.M.F.$, due to the predominating effect of the capacity reactance over the resistance. This is the greatest at 90° (Fig. 14). For the sake of simplicity we have assumed in the foregoing that the projection of E determines the apparent resistance.

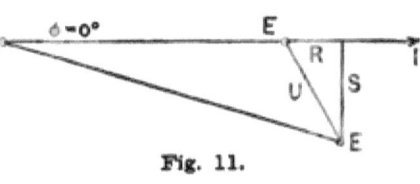

Fig. 11.

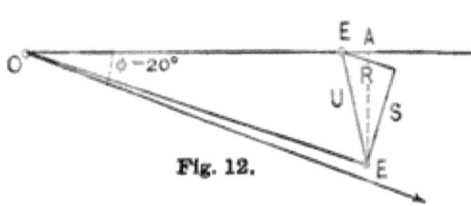

Fig. 12.

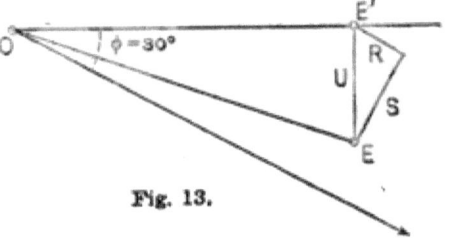

Fig. 13.

This is not strictly accurate, but in practice the error involved will be found to be insignificant.

Frequency. — The number of complete reversals of alternating quantities in any given time is called their frequency. Each complete reversal is a period or cycle, and is measured in degrees. An alternation is a half period or cycle, and in the curve of impressed $E.M.F.$ (Fig. 1) is measured by the value of the $E.M.F.$ from 0° to 180°, and from 180° to 360°. In a bipolar generator every revolution of the armature corresponds to one cycle. In multipolar generators there will be as many cycles for every revolution as there are pairs of poles. Frequency is usually denoted in cycles per second. In a twenty-four polar generator of 300 $R.P.M.$, the number of alternations per minute is 7,200. The number of cycles per minute is one-half of this, or 3,600, and in one second is 60. Applying this, —

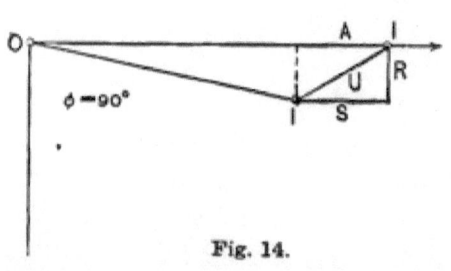

Fig. 14.

$$\text{Frequency, or Cycles per sec.} = \frac{\text{Poles} \times R.P.M.}{60 \times 2}.$$

CHAPTER II.

GENERATORS.

Elementary Forms. — The simplest form of polyphase generator consists of two single-phase alternators coupled together on one shaft in such a manner that the electromotive forces at the terminals of the armature conductors arrive at a maximum 90°, or one-fourth of a period, apart. The currents from this machine will therefore have a two-phase relationship. An arrangement of three such armatures, with similar coils one-third of a pole arc, or 60

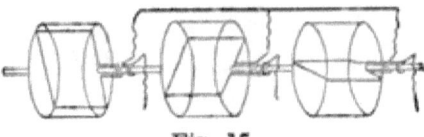

Fig. 15.

electrical degrees, apart, will generate three-phase currents. Fig. 15 illustrates the armature connections of an ideal three-phase unit, made up of three single-phase alternators arranged in this manner.

This combination of two or more independent alternators, forming one polyphase unit, facilitates the regulation of the circuits in case of unbalancing, as the fields (not shown in this diagram) are separate. This form of generator is not commercially manufactured, as it is naturally expensive. Being made up of smaller machines, the cost would be greater than that of a single unit of the same output. Polyphase generators are smaller, and consequently cheaper to build, than single-phase alternators of the same capacity. Most types of polyphase generators have one field and one armature, with as many sets of windings as there are phases. Irregularities in the voltage of the different phases — if any exist — must be overcome in some other manner than by a variation of the field strength. In some inductor types of generators, this regulation is obtained by varying the number of armature turns in the unbalanced phase.

The principles of construction and operation of single-phase generators apply equally well to polyphase machines. The requirements of recent alternating-current practice, involving the transmission and utilization of power to an extent that is already beginning to overshadow the purely lighting branch of the art, have necessitated vast improvements in machinery and methods. Not the least improvement has been in polyphase generators.

Revolving Armature Type. — The type of alternating-current generator most commonly employed in the United States is that in which the armature is the moving member. For some time past in Europe, and more recently in this country, another type has been in use, in which the armature is stationary, and the field structure is the revolving part. All modern generators, including what is known as the inductor generator, are modifications of either the revolving armature or the stationary armature type.

Fig. 16 illustrates a standard form of belt-driven generator of the revolving armature construction, designed by the Westinghouse Electric and Manufacturing Company. The frame has graceful, dignified lines, the bearings form-

GENERATORS. 19

ing one casting with the lower yoke and base. The pole-
pieces project inwardly from the frame, and are made up

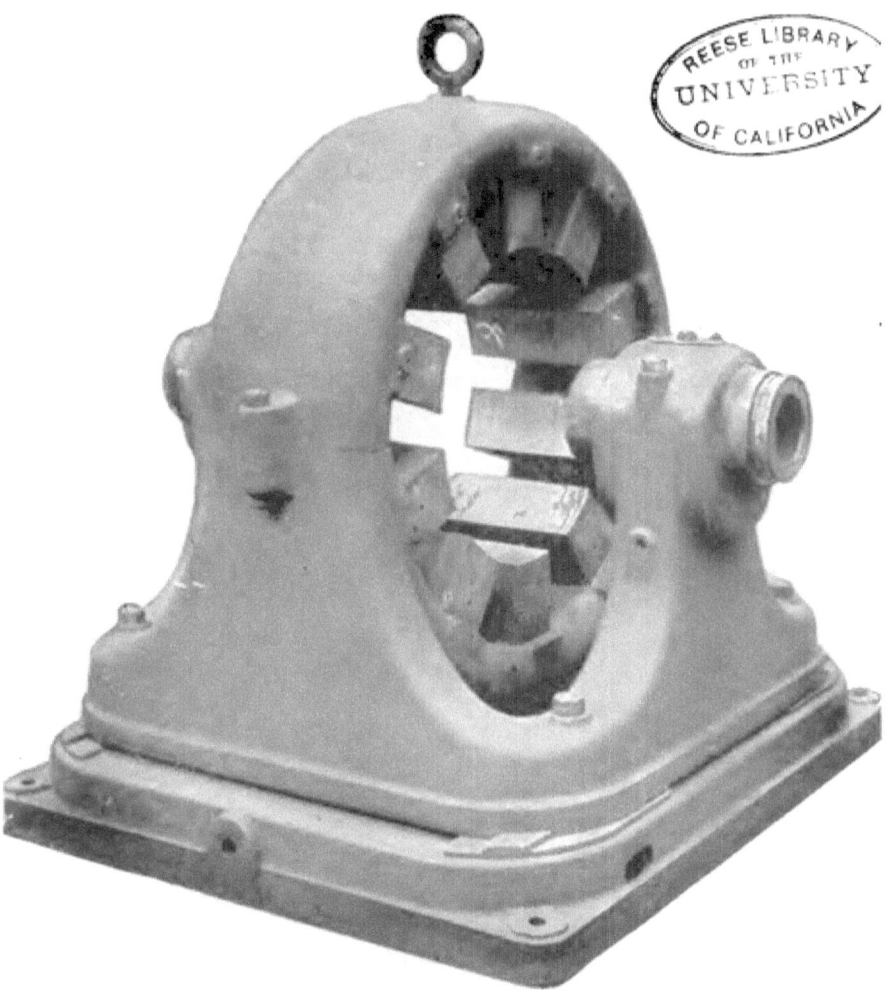

Fig. 16.

of steel laminations cast into the yoke. The field coils are
wound upon insulated spools, and are removable. When

these generators are built for automatic compounding, two field windings, one for the separate and one for the self-exciting current, are required. The armature is of the iron-clad type, and is built up of laminations, slotted to admit the coils. These are usually machine-wound, and held firmly in place by seasoned wedges of wood. This armature winding construction, and the arc and shields of an arma-

Fig. 17.

ture of the General Electric make, are shown in Fig. 17. An injury to the insulation, from lightning or other causes, is usually limited to one or a few adjacent coils, which can be easily replaced without disturbing the rest of the winding. All the standard belted polyphase generators of the revolving armature type conform to the general lines of the generator shown in Fig. 16. Generators of an output

GENERATORS. 21

greater than 200 K.W. are usually provided with a third, or outboard, bearing to sustain the weight of the pulley and strain of the belt. Generators of 500 K.W., and over, are almost invariably built for direct connection to either engine or water-wheel. If built for connection to the former, the base is ordinarily omitted, while generators for coupling to water-wheels are provided with base and two bearings, and in small sizes are self-contained as a rule, the base and two bearings comprising one casting. When-

Fig. 18.

ever possible, a generator, irrespective of its size, should be direct-connected, on account of saving of space and of belt losses.

Revolving Field Type.—The revolving field type of generator is one of a number of forms of the stationary armature machine. The rotating member, or field, consists of a heavy cast-steel wheel, into which are bolted or keyed pole-pieces, projecting radially outward. These are usually built up of laminated sheet-iron. Fig. 18 illustrates a rotating field magnet of a 200 K.W. generator made by the

22 POLYPHASE APPARATUS AND SYSTEMS.

Walker Company. The laminated construction prevents formation of eddy currents, which would occur if the pole-pieces were solid castings. The coils are wound on spools, placed on the poles, and held in place by the pole-tips. The field coils on large machines are made of a single spiral of strip-copper, wound on edge. Fig. 19 shows the construction of the field-spools of a 750 K.W. General Electric Company's generator. On small machines wire is used. The revolving field acts like a fan, forcing the air out-

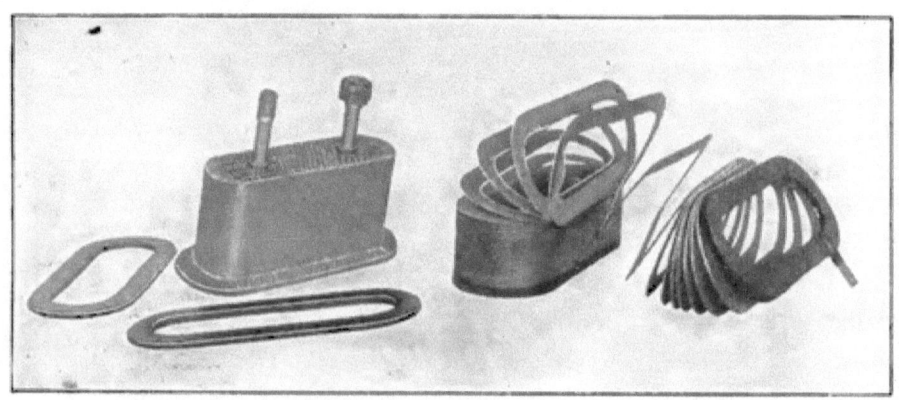

Fig. 19.

wardly through the openings between the armature laminations. The shields of the circular armature structure prevent undue loss through windage of the revolving field. Direct current for excitation is carried to the field by means of a small two-ring cast-iron or copper collector, equipped with carbon brushes, requiring practically no attention in operation.

The stationary armature consists of a circular cast-iron frame or spider, inside of which are dove-tailed sheet-iron disks, with slots to receive the coils. Ventilating

GENERATORS. 23

spaces are left between laminations, through which the air flows rapidly when the generator is running. Fig. 20 shows the construction of a stationary three-phase armature of 750 K.W. capacity.

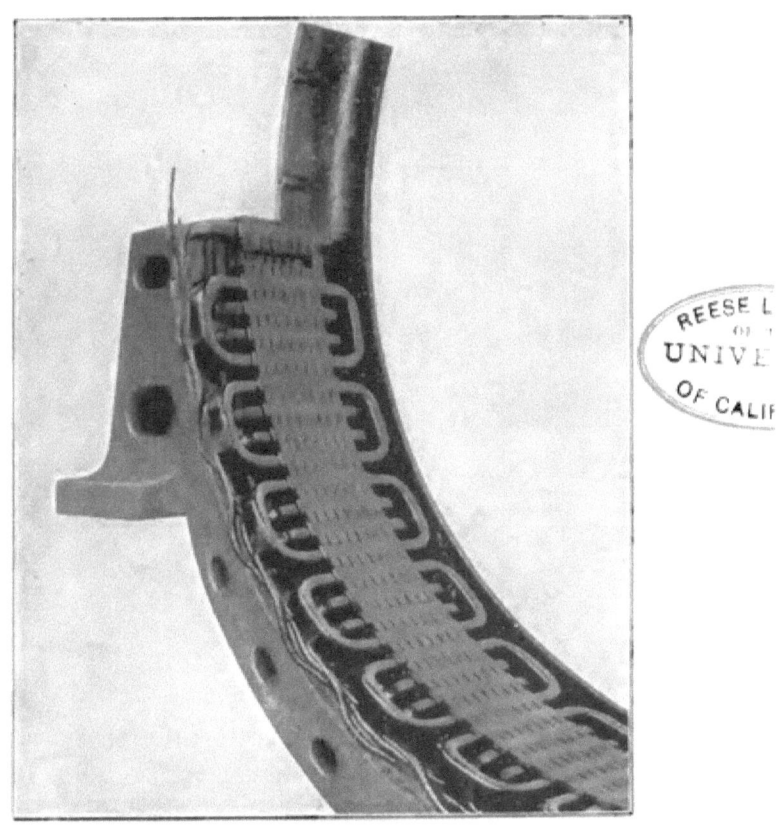

Fig. 20.

Fig. 21 is a sectional view of the field and armature of a typical revolving field three-phase generator. The relation of the magnetic circuit to the armature coils is clearly shown.

The generator shown in Fig. 22 is one of a number installed near Redlands, Cal. It has 20 poles, and runs at 300 $R.P.M.$, giving a current of 50 cycles. The driving-power of each generator is supplied by Pelton water-wheels, keyed to the shaft, and mounted and housed on the generator base, as indicated. The machine is wound for 750 volts, no load, and generates in each branch 525 amperes. The commercial efficiency at full load is

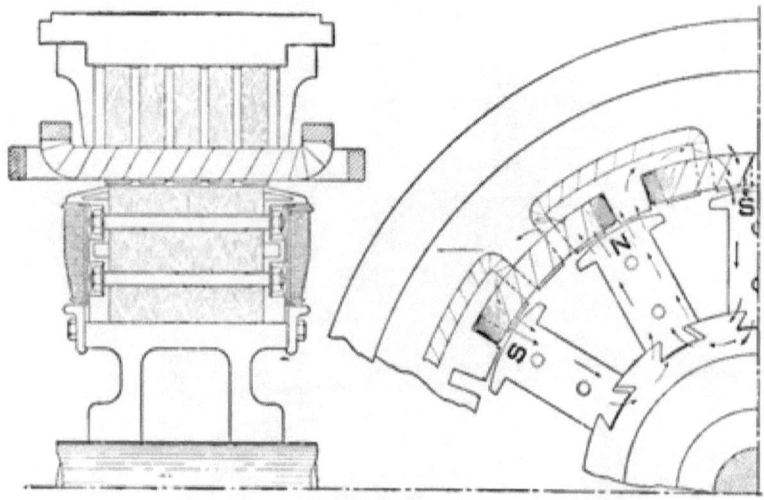

Fig. 21.

95.6 per cent. The regulation on non-inductive load is 7.1 per cent. The cut shows the armature, slid along on its base to permit ready inspection of the field and other parts.

Fig. 23 shows a Ganz & Co. 80 K.W. revolving field generator. The armature winding used in this machine is in the form of spools bolted to the outer ring. This arrangement has the advantage of accessibility for inspection and repair. The field construction is practically the

GENERATORS.

Fig. 22.

same as that of the generator described above. It is claimed that these machines have a moderate armature reaction, and at the same time, when short-circuited, will

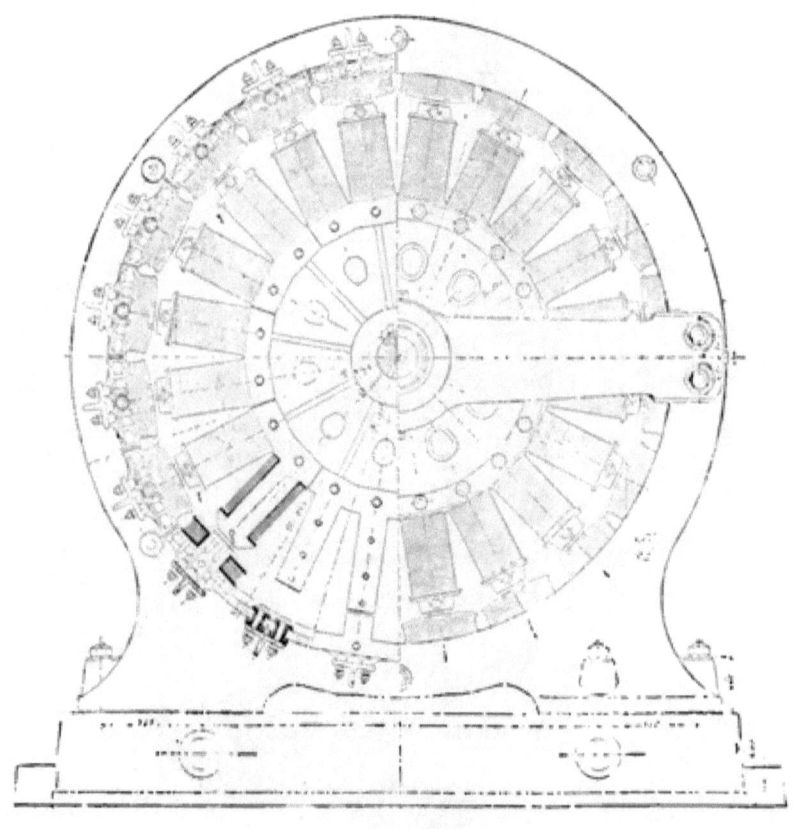

Fig. 23.

not deliver more than two and one-half times the normal full-load current.

Another form of the stationary armature type of generator is one in which the field winding is a single coil. The exciting coil is wound on a bobbin, occupying a channel on the periphery of a cast-iron wheel. Two steel rims are bolted to this, the laminations being formed into poles. This is one of the original forms of polyphase generators; and this construction, which has considerable merit, was adopted, in the early days of power transmission apparatus, by European manufacturers.

Inductor Type. — Another modification of the stationary armature type is the inductor machine, manufactured to some extent abroad by Mordey, Thury, and the Allgemeine Elektricitats Gesellschaft, and in this country chiefly by the Stanley Electric Company. The distinguishing characteristic of this type is, that any one set of armature coils, or portion of the armature conductors, is subjected to a magnetic flux of one polarity only. The magnetism fluctuates from zero to maximum, and back again, and does not reverse its sign. Most generators of this type have both fixed armature and fixed field-windings, the only moving part being the inductor, — a laminated iron core, with polar projections. The exciting winding, wound into an annular coil, is sometimes placed centrally on the internal surface of the armature spider, embracing the revolving element, as in the Stanley machine. This is usually a ring of iron, with a double row of laminated polar projections. In some machines, notably those made by Thury abroad and by the Warren Company of Sandusky, Ohio, and the Westinghouse Company, the armature has a single set of coils, and the inductor is provided with a single row of laminations. The annular exciting coil may be part of the revolving element, and revolve with it.

Reference to Fig. 24 will show the general arrangement of the magnetic circuit of the Stanley inductor generator.

28   POLYPHASE APPARATUS AND SYSTEMS.

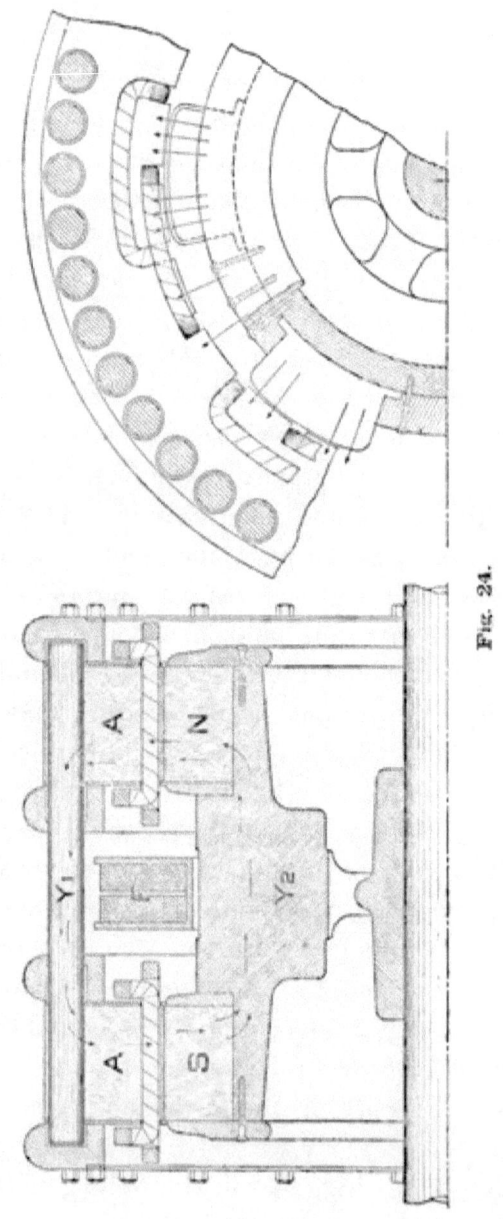

Fig. 24.

The annular field coil, F, is surrounded by the magnetic circuit, made up of the laminated cores AA, the armature yoke Y_1, and the laminated poles N and S, and the field yoke Y_2. The armature windings, consisting of two complete sets, are laid in grooves in the armature cores in a manner similar to the revolving field-machine. It will be seen that the North and South poles do not alternate, but the magnetic flux simply pulsates in one direction. Only one-half of each turn of the armature winding is in an active field at one time, the other half of the coil being between the poles in an inactive field. The $E.M.F.$ generated is one-half as great as it would be if the polarity of the flux were reversed. In order to obtain a given $E.M.F.$ with the inductor type of machine, either the armature windings or the total magnetic flux must be doubled. The essential characteristics, therefore, of an inductor generator are a rather high density of the magnetic circuit, and a short air gap, the latter in order to reduce the magnetic leakage to a minimum. The stationary element of the Stanley inductor machine consists of two series windings, forming two separate armatures. The currents in the coils are usually in quadrature with each other, thus giving a two-phase current. A three-phase relationship can be established by means of a symmetrical three-phase winding, or by making one set of coils with .86 the number of turns of the other, and connecting the end to the middle of the larger coil. By the theory of the resultant of electromotive forces, the currents in the three circuits will be equal, and the impulses will follow one another at intervals of 60°. Fig. 25 shows a 600-K.W. Stanley inductor generator.

Fig. 26 shows a sectional view along the shaft of an

30   POLYPHASE APPARATUS AND SYSTEMS.

inductor generator manufactured by the Warren Electric Manufacturing Company. *GG* is the frame, or spider, of

Fig. 25.

the stationary armature, into which are dovetailed the laminated polar projections *AA*. *CC* are the armature

GENERATORS.

coils surrounding the poles. The revolving element is made up of the spider H carrying the laminated polar projections DD. F is a single magnetizing coil. The magnetic circuit is from G, through A, to D, and thence from H to G. It will be seen that there are two air gaps, one between A and D, and the other between G and H. As in all inductor generators, the magnetism pulsates only, and the revolving polar projections have one polarity.

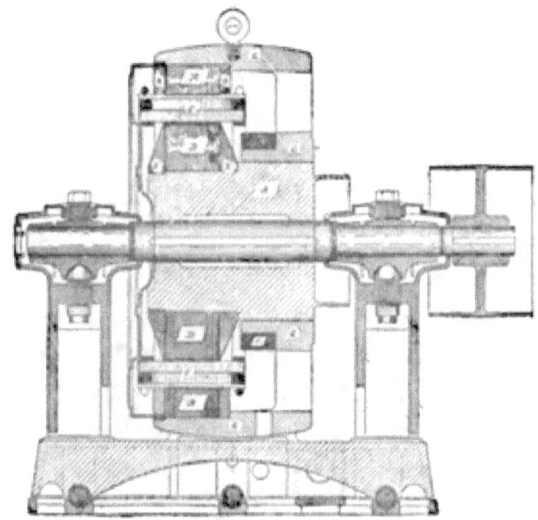

Fig. 26.

The armature of the inductor machine made by the Westinghouse Company is illustrated in Fig. 27. This is a 150 K.W. generator, designed for belt-driving. The larger machines of this type have much the same general appearance as the revolving field machines.

The type of generator, with revolving armature, is particularly desirable for general power and lighting distribution where only a moderate voltage is required. Machines of this type are cheap to build. They can be automatically compounded, without any complication of parts, which is not the case in the revolving field or inductor generator.

Fig. 27.

This construction is not suitable for high or for low voltages, on account of the difficulties of insulating the collector rings in the first case, and of collecting a large current in the second case.

The stationary armature can be easily insulated to withstand a testing pressure of 25,000 volts; and, as no collecting device is required, currents of any volume can be cared for.

Generators with stationary armatures are now wound for pressures up to 12,000 volts.

Armature Windings. — The armature windings of modern alternators are laid in slots or grooves, below the surface of the armature punchings. The shape and number of the slots have a material effect upon the performance of a generator, as we will proceed to show. The old-fashioned ironclad armature had one coil for each pole, or pair of poles, laid in deep slots. On account of this grouping of the conductors into a coil of many turns, this generator possessed great armature reaction, and could be short-circuited with no bad effects. This construction is sometimes carried out in those modern polyphase generators whose armatures have one slot for each phase and each pole, and are called unitooth machines. Thus the armature of an eight-pole two-phase generator has 8 coils; a three-phase generator of the same number of poles has 12 groups of conductors. The shape of the armature punchings of a 12-pole unitooth three-phase generator is shown in Fig. 28. The advantage of safety, in case of short circuits, is a doubtful one, as most

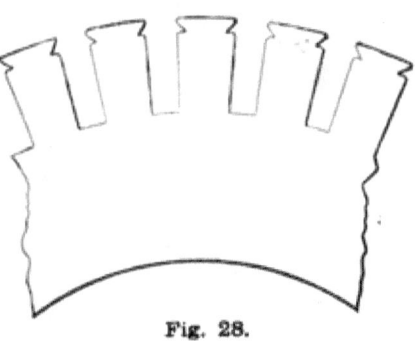

Fig. 28.

plants are provided with protective devices which render a short circuit more inconvenient than dangerous. Armature reaction deforming the wave-shape of the $E.M.F.$, and high inductance, requiring large exciting currents at full load, are often characteristic of the unitooth winding. As will be shown, these generators can be designed so as in a great measure to overcome these objections.

Many modern polyphase armatures have two or three slots per pole per phase. The slots are open, which, with the distributed form of winding, gives a very low inductance (Fig. 29). This necessitates only a slight increase of exciting current at full load. Generators with multitooth armatures are built, for the most part, for low potentials and for low frequencies. They are most suitable for long-distance transmission, where step-up transformers are employed. The regulation is good, and the wave-shape approaches a sine-curve, — the best shape for this work, as it reduces the possibility of resonance, or rise of voltage, at a distant point in the transmission circuit, above that at the generating end.

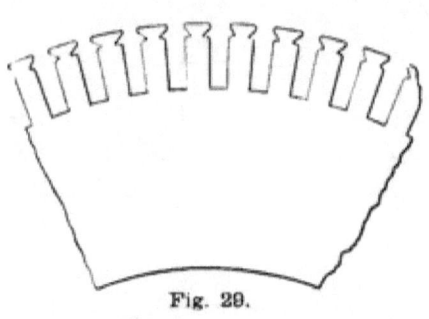

Fig. 29.

The various connections of generator armature windings will be found explained in chapters on polyphase systems.

Electromotive Force. — The drop at the terminals of a direct-current generator, as the output is increased, is principally due to the armature resistance and reaction. In alternators the IR drop is generally not so prominent as that

GENERATORS.

due to **inductance and to** armature **reaction.** The counter
$E.M.F.$ **of** self-induction lowers the terminal pressure, **and**
armature reaction **by** opposing its **flux to** the field magnetism reduces the effective number of lines of force, passing
through the **armature conductors, with** the like result.

The inductance **of** unitooth **armatures can be** lessened
by widening the opening of **the** slots, which, at the same
time, increases the resistance to the magnetic flux, — i.e.,
the reluctance of the air gap. As inductance varies, directly, **with the square of the number of** turns, by using
fewer **turns per slot and more slots,** — in **other** words, **the**
distributed **form of** winding, — this disagreeable property
can **be** much reduced, without **sacrificing** efficiency, **or**
increasing **the cost** of the generator.

Armature reaction **is greatest**
when **the** load is
inductive, as then
the current lags
behind the $E.M.F.$,
and brings the maximum armature
magnetism in the most favorable position for demagnetizing the field. The distributed winding minimizes the evil
effect of a lagging current. As armature reaction produces
a distortion of the field, a curve **of** $E.M.F.$, that may be **a**
sine-curve **at** no **load,** will often depart widely from **this**
form **when** the generator **is** loaded. **The** distortion of
the wave-shape **in unitooth** machines may be overcome,
in great **part, by careful** shaping **of** the pole pieces.

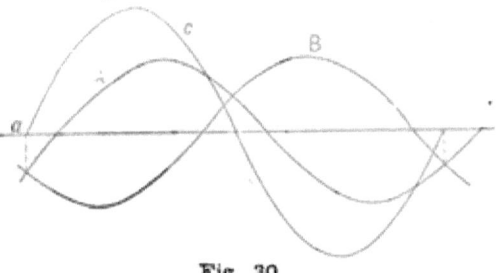

Fig. 30.

While the armature reaction, due **to a** lagging **current,**
lowers the terminal $E.M.F.$ of a generator, **a** leading cur-

rent may have the opposite effect, by adding its flux to that of the field.

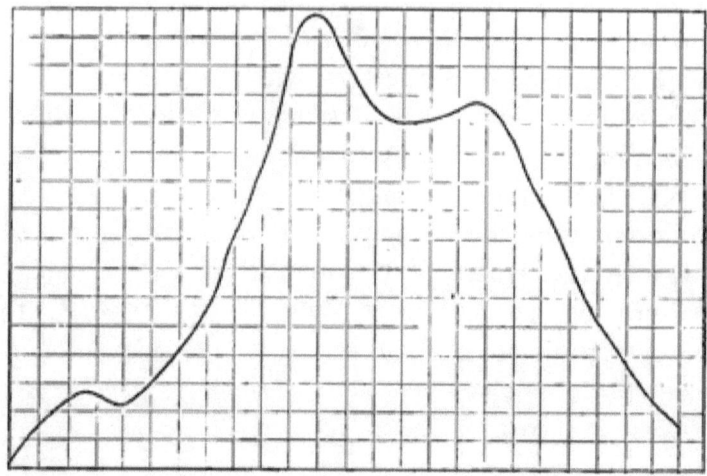
Fig. 31.

The relation between the induced *E.M.F.* in the armature windings and the terminal *E.M.F.* of a three-phase

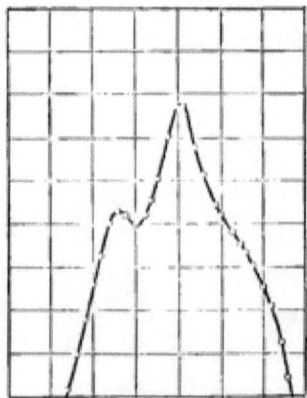
Fig. 32.

machine is shown in Fig. 30. Curves *A* and *B* represent the voltages measured between the common center and end of the armature coils. Curve C, formed by uniting these Y electro-motive forces, is the Δ $E M.F.$ or pressure between the terminals of the armature coils, and therefore the measured line voltage. In this way, if the line voltage is found to be 1,732 volts, the voltage of any conductor with respect to the common center is $\dfrac{1,732}{\sqrt{3}} = 1,000$.

The Y $E.M.F.$ of a standard three-phase unitooth machine under full load is shown in Fig. 31.

The "delta" $E.M.F.$, or curve of pressure between any two of the line wires under the above condition of load, is shown in Fig. 32. This last curve can be readily obtained by uniting the Y curves for any particular condition of load, displaced 60°.

CHAPTER III.

GENERATORS (CONCLUDED).

Field Excitation and Compounding. — The voltage of a generator may be maintained uniform, under all normal conditions of load, by varying the strength of the field excitation. For local lighting and power distribution where the circuits have fairly equal loads, an automatic or compounding arrangement, as it is called, is generally desirable. The same results are obtained, in a measure, by using generators of good regulation and proper frequency, and sufficient line-copper to keep the loss down to within a very few per cent. Generators of greater capacity than 300 K.W. are not, as a rule, automatically compounded, on account of the difficulty of commutating heavy currents. Generators for long-distance transmission work are also without this device; for, besides being usually of large capacity, they are required to take care of heavy voltage drops in the transmission apparatus, and of pressure variations due to gradually changing loads. These voltage changes can best be overcome by hand regulation of the field excitation.

The usual method for producing automatic compounding by variation of the field excitation requires two sets of field windings, — a shunt winding for the current from an outside source, and a series winding for the current obtained from the commutation of the alternating currents

GENERATORS.

of the various phases. Fig. 33 shows the connections of a General Electric three-phase generator with composite field windings. A three-part commutator rectifies the currents from each of the three-phase circuits, so that unbalancing in any one line has a minimum effect on the regulation. The rotating shunt is practically the common center of the coil, giving a current in the series field, due to about 1 per cent of the terminal voltage. The stationary shunt is adjustable, and can be varied for loads of different power factors. It also serves to prevent sparking at the commutator. The connections of the monocyclic generator are similar, except that the commutator rectifies the current of the main circuit only. In the Westinghouse polyphase generator (Fig. 34), the low potential current for the series field is derived from a series transformer within the armature. All phases are represented in the primary. The compounding field current depends upon the sum of the currents flowing in the circuits supplied by the armature.

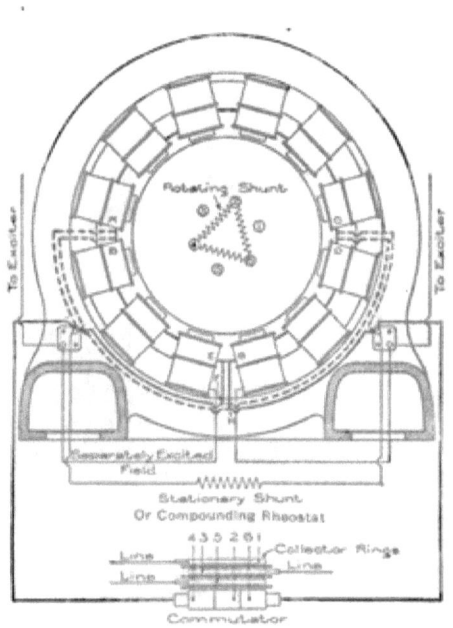

Fig. 33.

The demagnetizing effect, and consequent reduction of voltage, due to a load of poor power factor, has been explained. A generator so loaded requires a greater field excitation than when running on non-inductive load. The comparative voltages with loads of varying power-factor, and the same excitation is shown in Fig. 35. Curve *a* is the compounding when lights are the chief load, and *b* the curve when the load consists chiefly of motors.

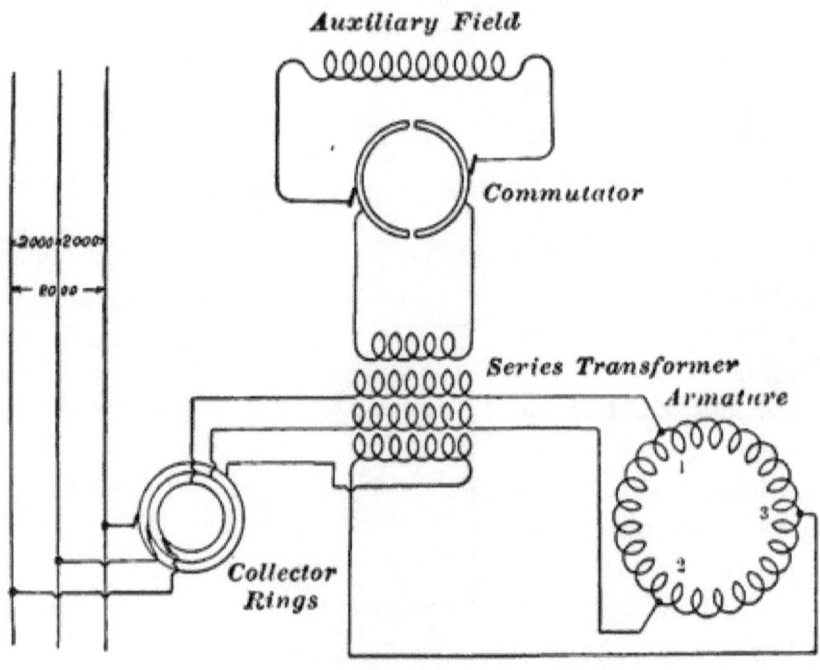

Fig. 34.

It will be seen that a generator properly over-compounded for a night load of lamps will not give the proper voltage for a day load of motors. The stationary shunt in Fig. 33 will then have to be adjusted for the varying character of the load. The monocyclic generator is an exception, in that this adjustment is not necessary, as will be shown later. Automatic compounding may also be attained by variation of the current in the shunt windings alone. In this method the exciter $E.M.F.$ is varied by an arrangement of solenoids and magnetic plungers, acting on the exciter rheostat.

The energy required to excite the fields of good commercial generators on a non-inductive load varies from about 1 per cent, in the case of generators of 500 K.W. capacity and over, to 2, and sometimes 3, per cent in

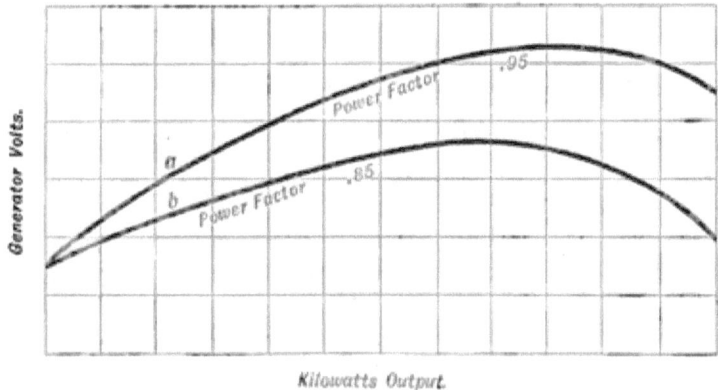

Fig. 35.

smaller machines. The dynamo supplying the separate exciting current must, of course, be of greater capacity when the alternating generator is non-compounded, and does not furnish a portion of the exciting current.

The exciting dynamos are usually driven from a pulley on the shaft of the alternating generator. In large water-power plants the best practice is to drive the exciters from separate water-wheels, and in steam plants from separate engines. By this method any variation in the generator speed is without effect on the exciting current.

Regulation. — Inherent regulation is defined in four or five different ways; but the now commonly accepted definition is the percentage rise of the voltage when full non-inductive load is thrown off, the generator speed and the field excitation remaining constant. From what has been said in connection with armature windings, it follows that, as a rule, generators with unitooth armatures will not have as good a regulation as the multitooth type. However, good regulation in these machines can be obtained at a slight sacrifice of efficiency, or by using more copper in the construction of the generator, and thus increasing its cost, or by the use of a high magnetic saturation of the iron. A certain three-phase unitooth machine of large output gave a regulation of $6\frac{1}{4}$ per cent, from full load to 10 per cent of the load. The same generator, when the load in one circuit was reduced 50 per cent, did not rise in voltage more than $5\frac{1}{2}$ per cent; and with no load on one of the circuits, the others being fully loaded, the greatest variation was 8 per cent. The standard belt-driven machines of the unitooth construction regulate within 10 per cent, which is close enough for satisfactory results to be obtained, even without automatic compounding. Generators of the multitooth construction require less compounding. The standard machines of this type have a regulation of 6 per cent or less.

On inductive loads the regulation, of course, is not so good. The generator mentioned above as having a non-inductive regulation of $6\frac{1}{4}$ per cent, will require nearly 1,200 more ampere turns in the field to give full-load voltage when it is supplying current to motors, the power factor of the circuit being 80 per cent. The regulation under these conditions is about 16 per cent. These results are immensely superior to those obtained with the old iron-clad alternators, which often required 30 to 50 per cent increase in exciting current on non-inductive loads to maintain constant pressure.

The construction, resulting in poor regulation, is sometimes used in generators designed for special purposes; for instance, in alternating arc lighting where a constant current is required. Generators of a high inherent regulation are sometimes used in certain kinds of electric smelting, where a constant watt output is required. The process is started at a certain voltage; and, as the resistance decreases, the voltage falls in inverse ratio to the increase of current.

Efficiency and Losses. — Fig. 36 gives the efficiency curves of a 750 K.W. three-phase generator, and shows the individual losses in the machine. It will be noted that the highest efficiency is reached a little above full load, the losses being only about 5½ per cent of the total output. The efficiency at half load, 91 per cent, is most excellent, while 84 per cent for one-fourth load is almost as high as can be expected. This generator was designed for direct-coupling to a water-wheel; so the friction loss is mainly due to two bearings, and is constant at about 1 per cent for all loads. The I^2R loss in the field varies little from no to full load, showing that the generator is easy to regulate. The copper loss in the armature is the smallest loss. The core loss varies from 19 K.W., at no load, to 24 K.W., at full load. Generators for engine connection will have an apparently higher efficiency, especially at light loads, as the friction losses are, as a rule, reduced by the omission of all bearing losses, these being considered as among the engine losses.

44 POLYPHASE APPARATUS AND SYSTEMS.

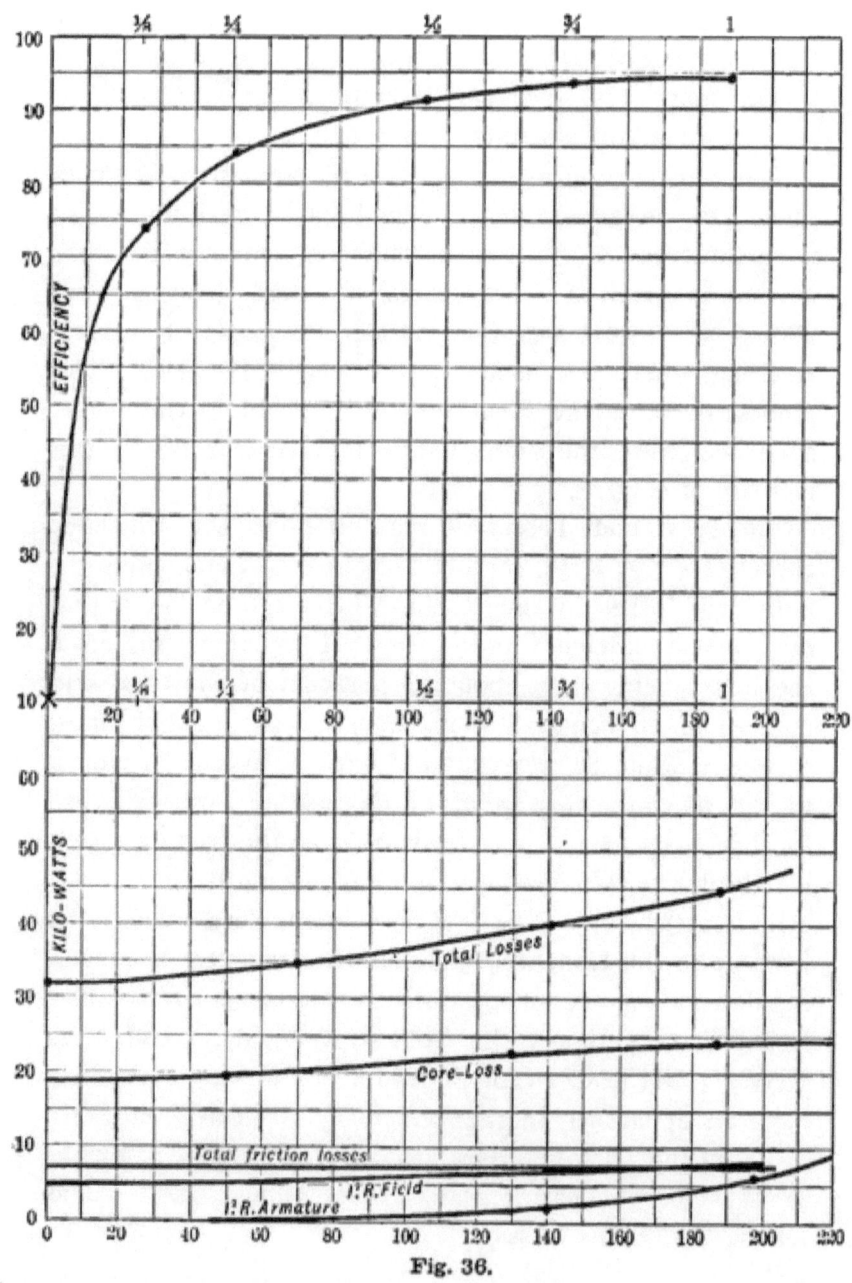

Fig. 36.

The efficiencies of generators, as usually given, do not include the losses in the exciter. As the exciter efficiency is from 80 to 90 per cent, and the I^2R loss in the fields is about 1 per cent, the reduction of the generator efficiency due to this source will seldom be greater than .2 per cent, almost outside the range of commercial accuracy.

Speed. — As the frequency of an alternating-current generator, with a given number of revolutions per minute, determines its number of poles, it follows that a high-frequency generator, operating at a normal speed of from, say, 300 to 600 *R.P.M.*, requires numerous poles. The old-style alternators of moderate output, and of frequencies of 125 to 133 cycles, ran at from 1,500 to 2,000 revolutions, and had 10 to 8 poles. To maintain this high frequency, and reduce the speed, thereby increasing the number of poles, results in an expensive and inefficient machine. A much better machine, having a speed of 300 or 600 revolutions, is obtained by reducing the poles to 24, or 12, giving a frequency of 60 cycles. The majority of polyphase belt-driven generators in actual operation are wound for 60 cycles. Standard belt-driven generators of this frequency have the following number of poles and speeds for the respective outputs:

K.W.	Poles.	*R.P.M.*
50	8	900
75	8	900
100	8	900
100	10	720
150	12	600
250	16	450
500	24	300

The alternating-current generator is far from being like a direct-current machine,— a flexible piece of apparatus in respect to speed. The speed cannot be altered more than 10 per cent either way from that for which it was designed, without appreciably affecting the constants of the generator and the apparatus to which the generator is supplying current.

Parallel Running. — In modern alternating-current plants of large capacity, especially long-distance power transmission plants, parallel operation is necessary in order to effect a reduction in the number of circuits and transmission lines. Other advantages are economy, simplicity, and reliability of operation. Polyphase generators, as now designed, can be operated in multiple without any difficulty.

The principal requirement in the generators is that they shall have a moderate armature impedance. Too small an impedance permits an excessive exchange of current with slight inequality of the field excitation of the machine, and a dangerous flow if the generators are connected up when they are not quite in step. Generators having a large armature impedance will operate in parallel; but, owing to the small synchronizing current that can be exchanged, the condition is not stable, and the generators are liable to alternately lead in speed or "hunt." When a number of generators are to be run in parallel the excitation of each one should be separately adjusted to give the same current, otherwise there will be an exchange of current.

The requirements of the prime mover are uniform speed and uniform angular rotation. In belt-driven generators the pulleys must all have the same dimensions. The belts must be watched to see that they do not slip. These two points must be especially observed in generators driven from the same shaft. The speed regulation of engines operating direct-connected alternators in parallel is discussed in the following section. Water-wheels have an absolutely uniform angular rotation, and are the best prime movers for parallel running.

Synchronism of two polyphase generators is determined by some form of phase indicator. The commonest arrangement consists of two transformers, the primaries of which are connected to each generator, care being taken that the connections are made to similar phases. The secondaries are connected in series with one or two lamps in circuit. The machines are in synchronism when the lamps cease to glow. They may then be thrown in parallel by the main switches. With composite field machines the commutators must be connected by an equalizer to place the series windings in multiple. The connections and station instruments required for the process of throwing generators in parallel, and operating them continuously, as used extensively in this country, are shown in Fig. 37.

It does not follow that, because one phase of a polyphase circuit is synchronized, the other phases are ready for parallel connection. It is quite important that when a number of machines are first installed for operating in parallel, the connections should correspond throughout in all the machines. The circuits can be tested out, for proper connection, by means of two sets of phase lamps.

In the diagram (Fig. 38) temporary transformers are shown connected to a different phase of the circuit than that in which are the permanent lamps. Connection should first be made with the outside blades, as shown by the dotted lines, to prove that the two sets of lamps will operate together. By the separate connections of the temporary transformers, it can be ascertained if the machines are properly connected to the synchronizing

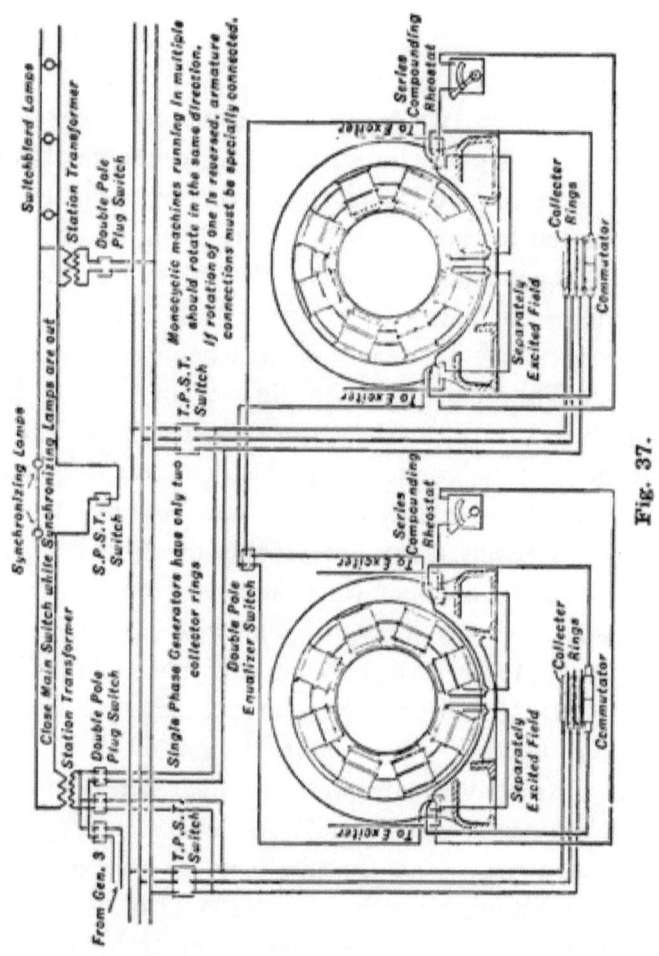

Fig. 37.

switches. The connections are correct when both sets of lamps are simultaneously dark.

Speed Regulation of Engines. — Steam-engines intended for direct connection to alternators, especially such as

GENERATORS. 49

supply current to rotary converters, or are operated in parallel, should have such a rotation that the maximum deviation from the position of absolutely uniform speed of which never exceeds $1\frac{1}{4}°$ in phase, — that is, $1\frac{1}{4}°$ when counting two complete poles as 360°.

This means, that, in an engine direct-connected to an alternator of $2n$ poles, the position of the revolving part should never differ more than $\frac{1\frac{1}{4}°}{n}$ in circumference from the position it would have at absolutely uniform rotation.

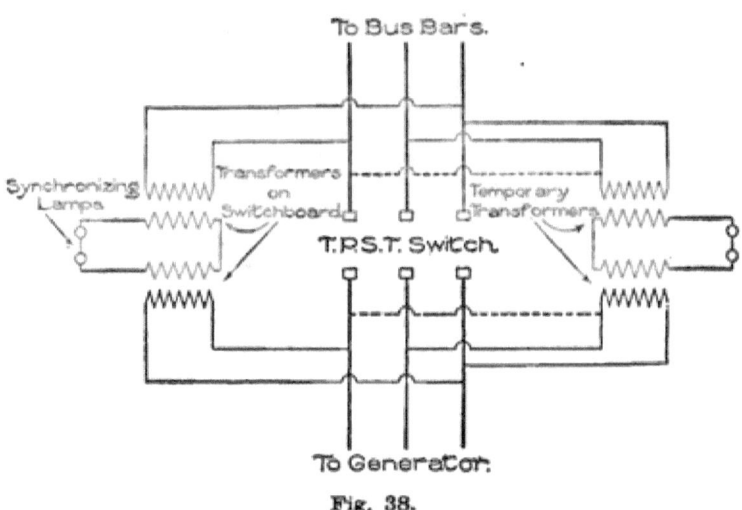

Fig. 38.

Thus, in a 40 polar alternator, the maximum deviation from the position of uniform rotation would be $\frac{1\frac{1}{4}}{20}$, or $\frac{1}{16}$ electrical degrees.

The above expresses the regulation of the engine as a deviation in position from that of absolutely uniform rotation in degrees of total circumference, measured, for example, on the circumference of the fly-wheel or revolving member of the direct-connected alternator. It is called the "variation" of the engine when expressed in degrees circumference, the "variation" of the alternating circuit when expressed in degrees of phase.

The regulation of the engine can be expressed as a percentage of variation from that of an absolutely uniform rotative speed. A close solution of the general problem shows that $1\frac{1}{4}°$ of phase displacement corresponds to a speed variation, or "pulsation," with an alternator of two n poles, as follows:

In the case of a single cylinder or tandem compound
engine . . . . $\frac{2.75\%}{n}$

A cross compound . . . . $\frac{5.5\%}{n}$

A working out of the problem also shows that the momentum of the reciprocating parts and the distribution of load between the various engine cylinders predominate so much that no better results are obtained from a three-crank engine than from a two-crank.

From the above formula it will be seen that a 40-polar alternator, driven by a cross-compound engine or three-cylinder engine, gives a permissible pulsation of .275 per cent (a little over ¼ of 1 per cent). This is relatively easy to secure in a modern well-designed engine.

Methods of Driving Generators. — The mechanical coupling of a generator to the prime mover is determined mainly by the size of the generator and the type and speed of the prime mover. Polyphase units up to 200 K.W. are usually belted, unless the prime mover consists of a waterwheel of high speed, or special conditions favor direct connection to an engine. The mechanical arrangement of the generator parts is shown by Fig. 39. The yoke rests on, and is sometimes an integral part of, the bedplate, which also supports two bearings. The pulley is overhung.

The method of belt-driving larger units is shown in Fig. 40. The bedplate is extended, and carries a third or outboard bearing which partly relieves the inner bearing of the belt strain and the weight of the pulley.

Generators designed for water-wheel connection are usually provided with bedplate shaft and two bearings. These machines are self-contained for the more perfect alignment of the bearings. Fig. 41 illustrates the general arrangement of generators of 500 K.W. capacity and above. A half-coupling is provided, which is machined to a close fit with the other half furnished with the water-wheel.

Generators for direct connection to engines are built without bedplate, shaft, or bearings. The yoke rests on a thin iron soleplate supported by a suitable foundation. The engine bearing serves also for the inner bearing of the generator. The outboard bearing rests on a separate cap. It is usually furnished with the engine, and is of a design uniform with the inner bearing. The engine shaft extended carries the revolving element of the electrical unit (Fig. 42).

Polyphase generators above 500 K.W. should preferably be direct-coupled to the prime mover. The method of driving large generators by belts or ropes necessitates a large extension of the base, and a heavy pulley, and is mechanically awkward. This method of driving may be used in exceptional cases, as, for instance; in connection with a wheel plant already installed, operating under a very low head at a low speed. The increased cost of

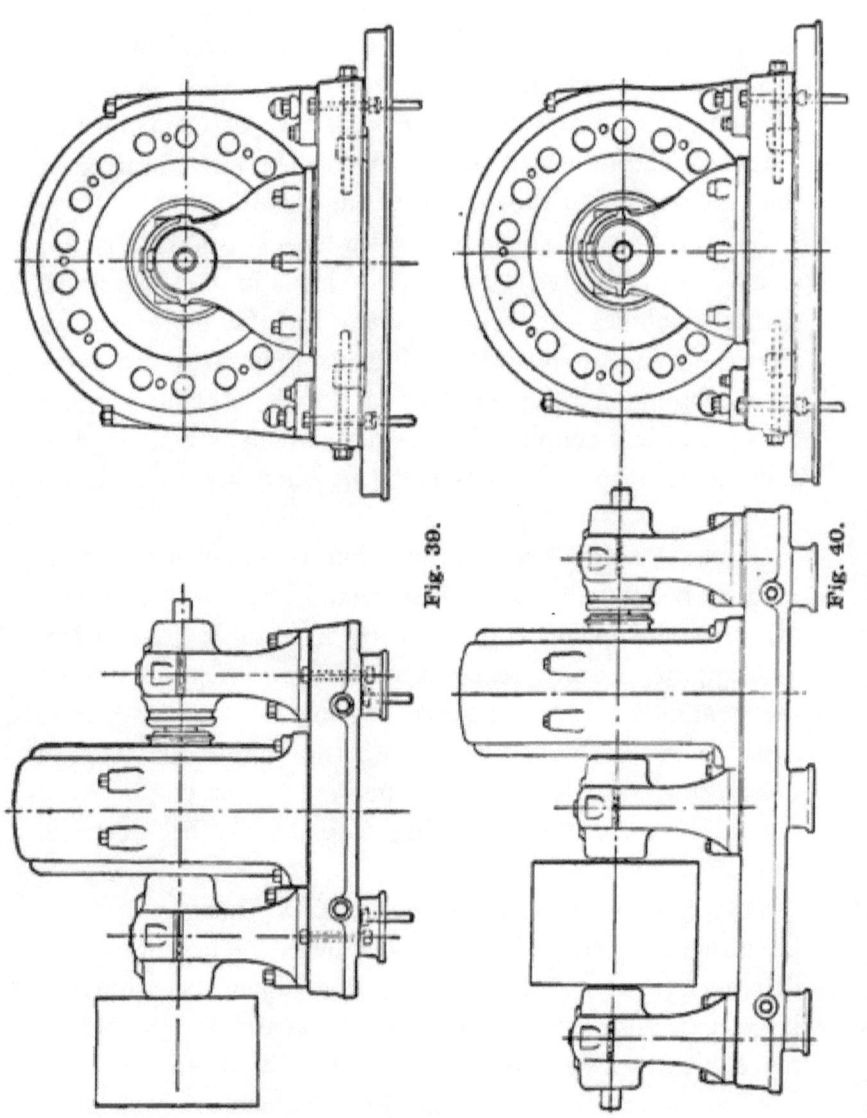

Fig. 39. Fig. 40.

GENERATORS. 53

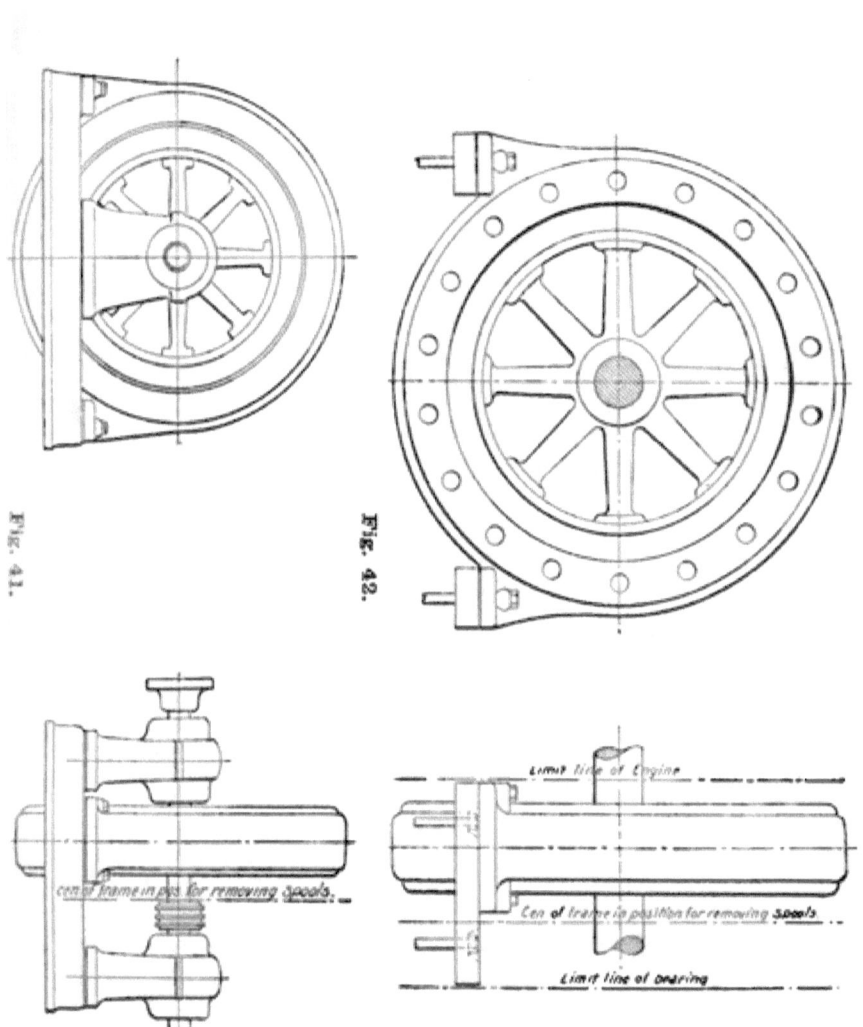

Fig. 41.

Fig. 42.

extended shaft, outboard bearing, and pulley will go far towards offsetting the increased cost of a slower speed generator, for direct connection, which does not require these parts.

Polyphase generators are direct-connected to water-wheels, either by a vertical or by a horizontal shaft. Very few generators in this country run from vertical turbines. The notable exceptions are the superb generators at Niagara Falls, and those in the station of the Portland General Electric Company at Oregon City, Oregon. The advantages of the vertical connection lie in the saving of floor-space, requiring a smaller power-house, and in more responsive wheel regulation. The shafting is out of sight, the revolving parts reduced to a minimum, and the effect, as a whole, most pleasing. The disadvantages are, the increased cost, and a possible mechanical difficulty in supporting the vertical shaft, weighted with the revolving electrical and hydraulic parts. The European practice is to almost exclusively employ the vertical generator in connection with vertical water-wheels.

Horizontal generators, for direct coupling to turbines, are usually so constructed that the lower frame forms one part of, or rests on, a base, which also supports the two standards. Sometimes, as shown in Fig. 22, an extension and third bearing is used, the water-wheel, properly housed, taking the place of the pulley. Such an arrangement is peculiarly adapted for use with impact wheels. This construction is used in the power plants of the Big Cottonwood Electric Company, the Pioneer Electric Company, Ogden, Utah, and the Southern California Power Company, Redlands, Cal. Perfect and permanent alignment of bearings is obtained by this construction.

GENERATORS. 55

A typical Westinghouse two-phase generator of the revolving armature type, for direct connection to water-

Fig. 43.

wheels, is illustrated in Fig. 43. This generator is one of four in service in the plant of the Helena Water and Electric Power Company of Helena, Montana. The machines are of 656 K.W. output, run at 150 *R.P.M.*, and generate 60 cycle current at 500 volts. Eight 325 K.W. step-up transformers raise the voltage from 500 to 10,000 volts for transmission over a distance of eleven miles.

Where engines are direct-connected to polyphase gen-

Fig. 44.

erators, it is customary for the electrical manufacturers to furnish the machine without shaft, base, or bearings. For the same speed, therefore, engine-driven generators are cheaper than those driven by water-wheels. It must not be forgotten, however, that engine speeds are limited by a number of conditions, while water-wheels are practically limited in speed only by the head obtainable.

Fig. 44 illustrates a three-phase generator of 1,200 H.P. capacity, direct-connected to an engine running at 94 R.P.M.

This generator is direct-coupled to a Corliss type of engine of 1,300 indicated H.P., running at 94 revolutions. It has 32 poles, and gives a current at 5,000 volts and a frequency of 25 cycles. The armature windings consist of 96 coils, three for each pole, or two slots per phase per pole. The windings are Y connected. The field coils are flat strip-copper, 1 in. by $\frac{1}{16}$ in., wound on edge, and insulated by intervening layers of paper. As the exciting current has a pressure of not greater than 120 volts, the potential at the terminals of each field spool is about four volts. The efficiency of the generator is $95\frac{1}{2}$ per cent at full load, $94\frac{1}{2}$ per cent at three-quarter load, $92\frac{1}{2}$ per cent at half load, and 87 per cent at quarter-load. The regulation on non-inductive load is 6 per cent, and the exciting current about 120 amperes.

Conditions Affecting Cost. — From what has preceded, it will be easily understood that the first factor in determining the cost of a polyphase generator of a given capacity and conditions of operation, is its speed. The efficiency is another factor, and likewise the regulation. A generator of high efficiency can be built at a reasonable cost, but at the expense of some regulation. The same generator may have good regulation at the sacrifice of efficiency, and cost no more. To obtain both these constants, in an eminent degree, requires a liberal use of copper and iron, and results in an expensive machine.

The frequency of the current for which a generator is

designed is another determining factor of the cost. With a given speed, changing the frequency alters the number of poles; correspondingly, a reduction in the number of poles cheapens a generator. Less exciting copper is

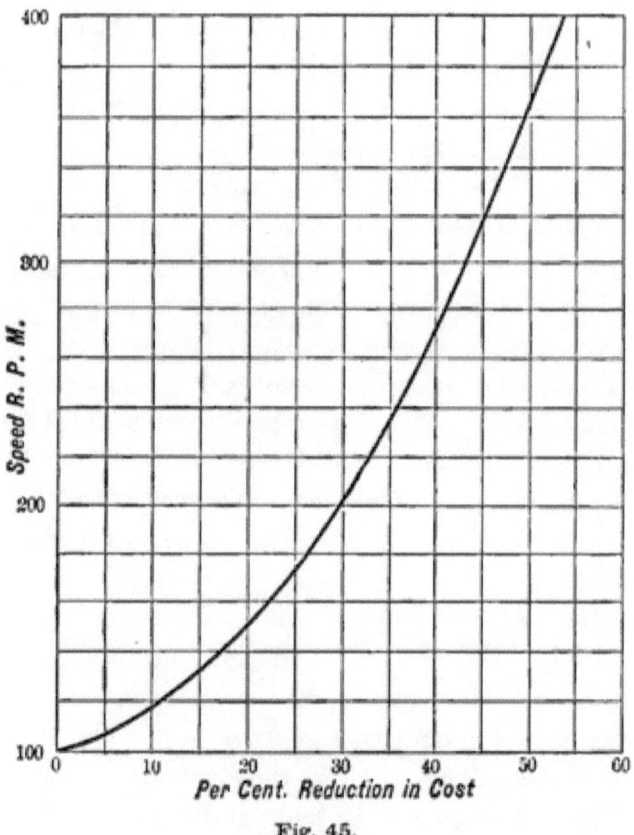

Fig. 45.

needed; for, while the polar cross-section is unchanged, the average length of turn is less. The number of operations in manufacture and handling are also considerably reduced. The effect of change of frequency on cost is most noticeable in very slow-speed direct-connected units.

GENERATORS.

Take the case of a 133 cycle generator, direct-connected to an engine, running at approximately 300 revolutions per minute. To give the proper frequency, it must have 52 poles. By reducing the frequency to 40 cycles, 16 poles are needed. It must not be forgotten, however, that lowering the frequency of any piece of alternating apparatus necessitates an increase in the iron of the magnetic circuit. Iron, however, is cheap as compared with copper and price of labor. Of course, the proportionate saving is not so noticeable in high speeds, nor when the generators are belt-driven, or provided with parts that remain the same irrespective of the frequency.

Fig. 45 shows, in an approximate degree, the relative reduction in cost with increasing speed. In using this curve for comparison of costs, it must be kept in mind that it is approximately correct only, and applies to generators of the same type, frequency, general constants, and conditions of operation.

CHAPTER IV.

INDUCTION MOTORS.

Principles of Operation. — The induction motor can be compared to a direct-current shunt motor, the essential difference being that the armature or working current of the shunt motor is led into it by brushes, while the working current of the induction motor is an induced or transformer current. The windings of the induction motor, connected to the supplying circuit, besides carrying the exciting current, have the additional function of supplying the transformer current. The principles of operation of the induction motor are thus seen to combine both those of a motor and of a transformer. Rotation may be considered as being produced by the revolving member following a shifting magnetic field which is the resultant of two or more alternating fields differing in phase. The explanation of the working of the induction motor by reference to the rotating magnetic field alone, however, is apt to mislead and to hide its true functions.

The two elements of an induction motor are preferably designated as primary and secondary, and sometimes as field and armature. Either may be indifferently the rotor or stator.

When running without load, the rotor speed is very closely that of the rotating field, and there is a very small current induced in the secondary member. The magnetic pull of this current on the field produces a feeble torque. The current, taken by the primary member, or field, is then composed of the magnetizing current and that required for overcoming magnetic and mechanical friction. As the power factor is low at light loads, being not more than 15 or 20 per cent in most commercial motors, the energy supplied is not much greater than that consumed by a shunt motor of the same capacity.

When running under load, the speed of the revolving element falls away from that of synchronism, and the $E.M.F.$ and working current induced by the relative cutting of the lines of force, increase with the difference in speeds. The pull of this increased current on the field produces a powerful torque. The variation from the speed of synchronism is called the "slip," and, within certain limits, is proportional to the total secondary resistance.

To insure high efficiency and good regulation, the resistance of the shunt motor armature must be kept as low as practicable. For the same reason, the windings of the secondary of the induction motor should have a low resistance.

Methods of Starting Motors. — On connecting an induction motor to its supplying circuit, there is an excessive rush of current, which can be prevented only by the use of some device external to the motor windings proper. There are a number of such arrangements for reducing the starting current of motors. Two of these are extensively used in this country, and will be described. The others are of less commercial importance.

The first, and probably most common device, consists essentially of a variable resistance, which can be cut in or out of circuit with the secondary winding. When the secondary element is the rotor or armature, this resistance often occupies a space within the armature spider. It may be of copper strips, or — as is usually the case — of iron cast into a compact grid form, having a number of contact points. The whole of this resistance is in series with the secondary winding at starting. As the motor

Fig. 46.

attains speed, a circular short-circuiting switch, mounted in a ring encircling the shaft, is pushed centrally by a lever, thus cutting out the resistance in as many successive steps as there are contact points. Motors provided with this starting device are usually designed to start with a torque ranging from 75 to 150 per cent of full-load torque. This motor has the desirable characteristic that

INDUCTION MOTORS. 63

the current is very nearly proportional to the torque from starting to full-load speed. Fig. 46 illustrates a motor of this construction, made by the General Electric Company.

In some motors of European make, an external rheostat is used to cut down the induced current. When the secondary revolves, collector rings are required to convey the induced current to the rheostat. When the primary is the revolving element, collector rings are also needed to supply the main current to the motor.

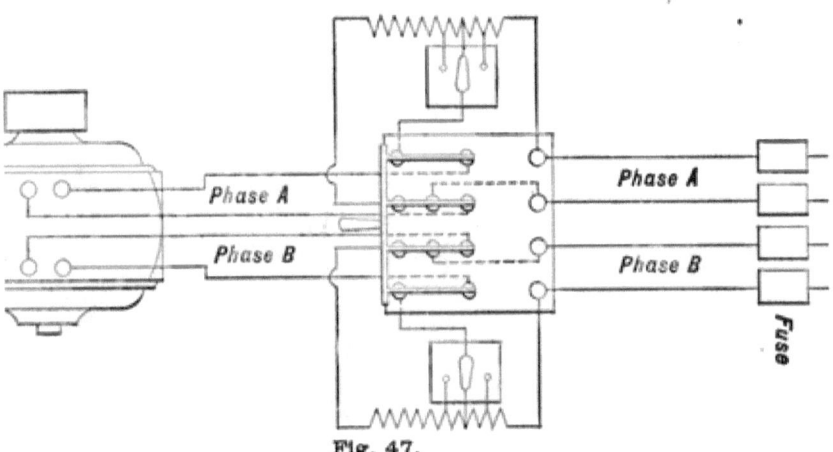

Fig. 47.

A water rheostat is sometimes employed abroad, by means of which the induced current is varied, its strength varying with the depth to which the plates are immersed. With this device, the current taken by the motor is closely proportional to the torque, from starting to full-load speed.

The second method of starting induction motors consists in reducing the impressed volts by the use of some form of reactance or of compensator coils, or of resistance in the main circuit. A compensator is the most efficient means of cutting down the voltage, and the most generally employed, one coil being required for each phase. The connections of a Westinghouse two-phase motor and starting device are shown in Fig. 47. The starter consists of two coils, sometimes called auto-converters or compensators, one in each phase. Each coil is arranged to give a number of different starting-voltages to suit different conditions of operation. Fig. 48 shows the connections of this starting device in detail. The switch is down for starting the motor, and after speed has been reached, is thrown up to its running position, thereby cut-

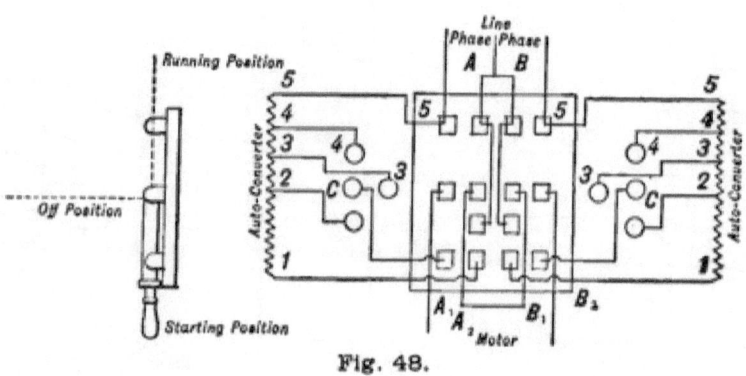

Fig. 48.

ting out the compensator. By this arrangement the motor can be started at a distance. Connections can be made from 1 to either 2, 3, or 4, giving three different starting electro-motive forces and starting torques. The maximum $E.M.F.$ and torque are obtained by connecting 1 and 4; for minimum $E.M.F.$, 1 and 2 are connected. Fig. 49 illustrates a completed Westinghouse two-phase starting device. The connections of a starting compensator for a three-phase motor, as made by the General Electric Company, is shown in Fig. 50. As in the two-phase starter, there is a coil in each phase, with a number of taps. These

INDUCTION MOTORS.

Fig. 49.

66   POLYPHASE APPARATUS AND SYSTEMS.

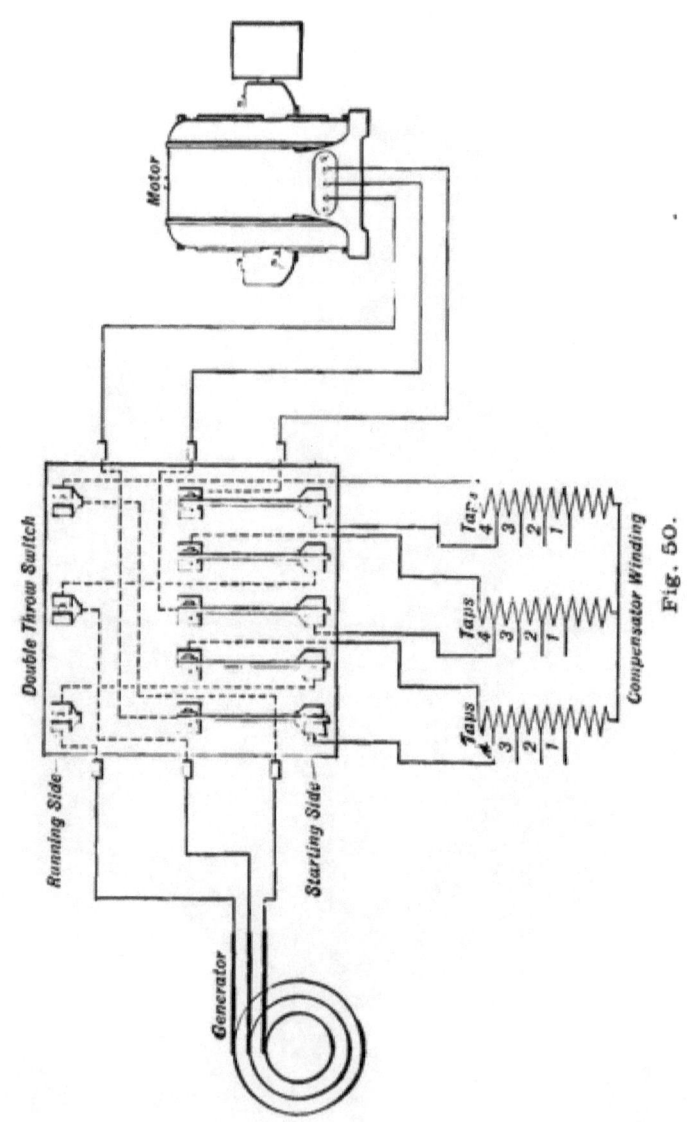

Fig. 50.

compensator starters, for use with motors of 15 H.P. and under, have three taps with voltages 40 per cent, 60 per cent, and 80 per cent of running full-load voltage. Compensators for motors above 15 H.P. have four taps, giving voltages 40 per cent, 58 per cent, 70 per cent, and 85 per cent of running full-load voltage.

Induction motors which are put in operation by the first method, may be designated as the variable resistance-in-armature type. They frequently have a higher self-induction, and require more copper and less iron. The secondary winding is definite and polar. Consequently, motors of this type are rather expensive to construct. Motors which are used with the compensator starter may be designated as the compensator or short-circuited-armature type. They are proportioned so that the primary and secondary have a low self-induction. They contain a minimum amount of copper and a considerable amount of iron in the magnetic circuit, and a short air-gap. Their distinctive feature is the short-circuited armature, which is usually of the squirrel-cage construction. They are, therefore, cheaper motors to build.

In starting an induction motor with variable secondary resistance, precaution must be taken that the resistance is all in, otherwise the flow of current may overheat the motor or overload the lines. The armature lever should be pulled out as far as it will go; then the line switch may be closed, and, finally, the short-circuiting switch may be slowly closed. The motor should be handled at starting to reach full speed in about fifteen seconds. As the secondary resistance is of a capacity only to start the motor, it never should be left in circuit or used to regulate the speed of the motor. The motor is shut down by reversing the operations of starting.

As the drop in a good transformer on a lightning load is within 3 per cent, and on an inductive load, as motors, seldom less than 5 per cent, it is advisable to always use separate transformers for lights and for motors. The exception to this rule is in a secondary system of distribution, where the motor load is a proportionately small part of the entire load.

Induction motors are sometimes started by being connected directly to the supplying circuit without the use of any form of starting device. Such a motor will, of course, take a large starting current. This can be kept down by making the resistance of the armature conductors rather high, and by confining the motor to work requiring a small starting torque. A motor started in this way should not be used on circuits where the effect of a large starting current on the potential regulation of the system is of importance.

A three-phase induction motor is reversed by changing any two of the leads, and a two-phase by changing the two leads of either phase.

Construction of Primary and Secondary. — The simple and substantial construction of the induction motor is one of its chief advantages, resulting in a minimum cost of maintenance and attendance, and offsetting its comparatively high first cost. While either element may be the rotor, by far the larger number of commercial motors are now constructed with a fixed primary and with a rotor secondary.

The fixed primary may be likened to an inverted armature. It is built up of slotted laminations mounted on a cast-iron spider. The coils are imbedded in the slots. Fig. 51 illustrates a Westinghouse primary or field ready to re-

INDUCTION MOTORS. 69

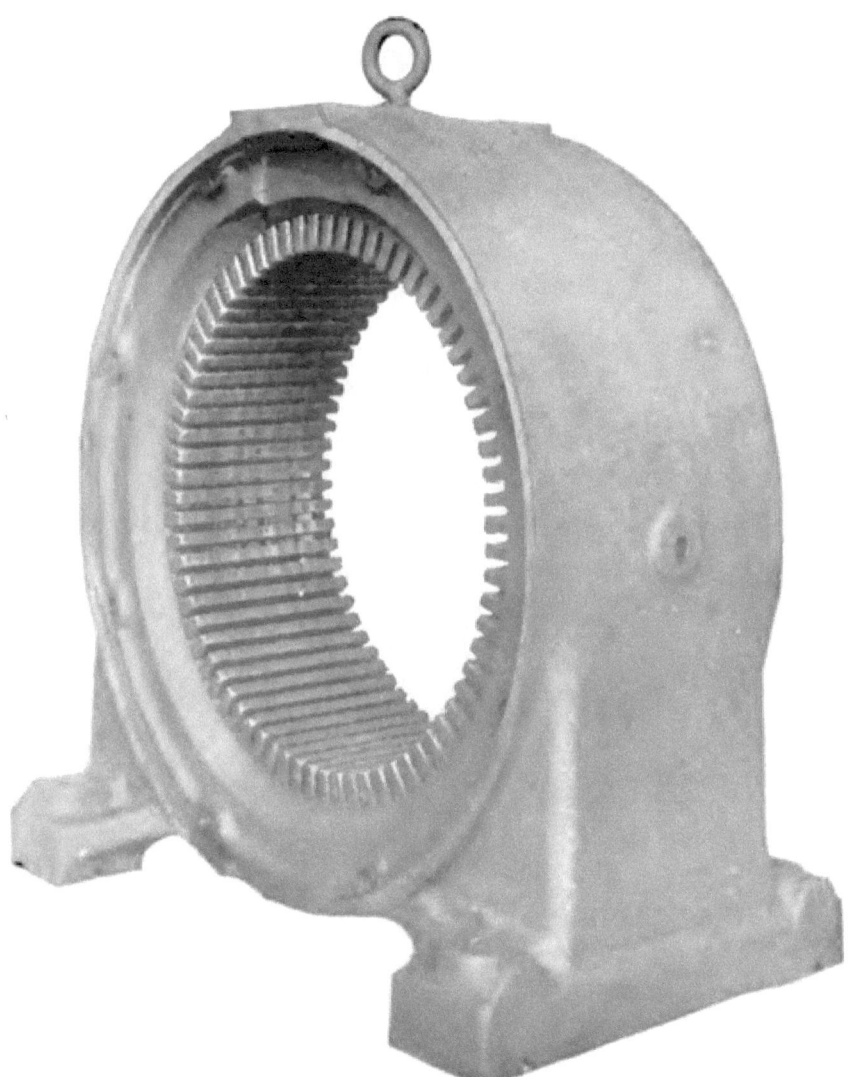

Fig. 51.

ceive its conductors. These stationary windings are usually protected from mechanical injury by end shields, which frequently support the bearings. The Westinghouse Com-

70   POLYPHASE APPARATUS AND SYSTEMS.

pany employ this form of construction in even the largest sizes, as illustrated in Fig. 52, which represents a 500 H.P. motor.

This motor is wound for three-phase current at 60 cycles

Fig. 52.

and 400 volts. It has 36 poles, running, therefore, at 200 R.P.M. The secondary has a squirrel-cage winding, bar wound as is the primary. The starting torque is two and one-fourth times the full-load rated torque. The drop in

INDUCTION MOTORS.   71

speed from no to full load is 4 per cent. The power factor at full load is given as 93 per cent. The dimensions are: Height, 10 feet 3 inches; floor space occupied, 9 feet 6 inches by 3 feet 6 inches; diameter at air gap, 7 feet. The total weight is 42,000 pounds. This motor is direct-coupled to a line shaft, driving a mill in Mexico.

The rotor armature of the standard form of motor has a laminated slotted structure similar to the primary. In motors of the variable resistance type, the secondary has a

Fig. 53.

definite series of coil windings, corresponding to the polar windings of the primary. Motors of the short-circuited type are generally wound with copper bars laid in the slots and connected at both ends by short-circuiting metal rings. Secondaries of this construction are termed squirrel-cage armatures. Fig. 53 shows an armature wound in the manner described and illustrative of this type.

In the Stanley Company's motor (Fig. 54) the field is stationary. There are in reality, two fields and two armatures. The secondary windings are connected so that the wire lying under the field poles on one armature is in series with the wire lying between the poles on the other. The field coils are staggered, each half alternately playing the part of a motor and transformer.

Starting Torque and Current. — At normal voltage certain types of motors possessing a moderate secondary resist-

Fig. 54.

ance, — as, for instance, a motor of the variable resistance type, with the resistance cut out, — will have a small starting torque due to the reaction of the excessive induced secondary current, on the primary. The starting current consumed by the motor will likewise be excessive. At nearly synchronous speed such a motor will have a pow-

INDUCTION MOTORS.

erful torque. By increasing the secondary resistance, the starting torque is raised until a critical resistance is reached, beyond which point the starting torque decreases.

The starting torque of an induction motor is also dependent upon the potential applied at its terminals. The starting current is reduced by lowering the voltage, but at

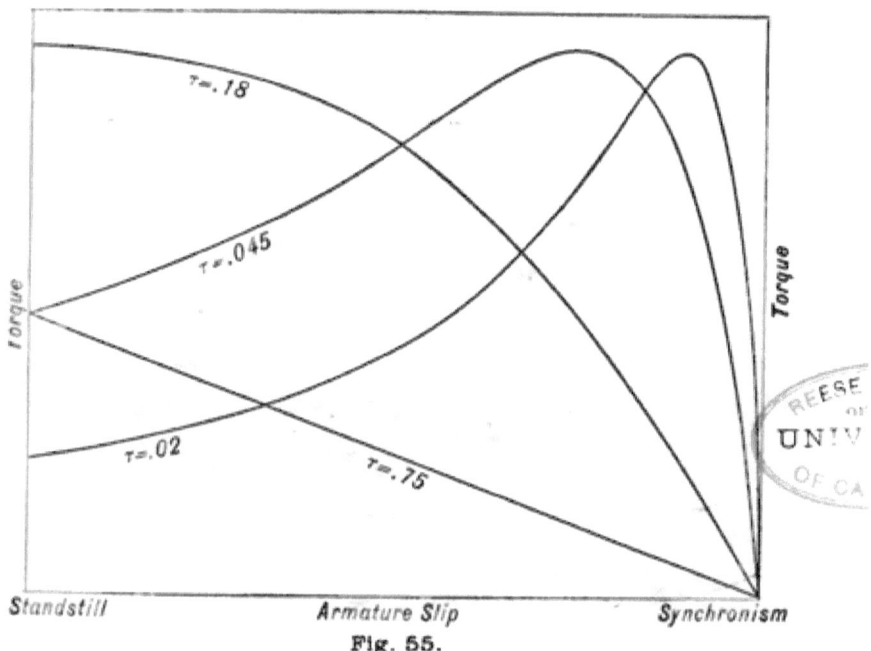

Fig. 55.

the sacrifice of the torque at starting, which varies as the square of the volts.

An inspection of the curves in Fig. 55 will show how the starting torque is influenced by varying the secondary resistance. The secondary winding of the motor is assumed to have a fixed resistance of .02 ohms. At starting, a variable resistance is connected in series, making a total of .18 ohms. The corresponding torque is about 25 pounds, or 150 per cent of full-load torque. When the motor reaches about 50 per cent of synchronism, part of the resistance is cut out, making the total .045 ohms. The torque now increases until about 85 per cent of synchronous speed is reached, when it begins to drop. At this point the remaining resistance is short-circuited, leaving only the resistance of the secondary. The torque, due to this resistance, .02 ohms, reaches its maximum at about

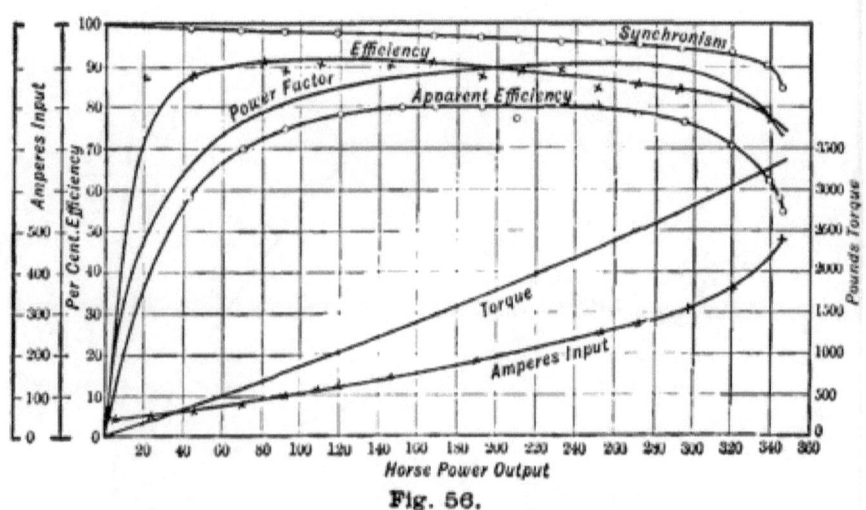

Fig. 56.

90 per cent of synchronism. The starting torque, with a secondary resistance of .02 ohms, is about seven pounds. The starting torque, due to a resistance of .75 ohms, is less than when the total secondary resistance is .18 ohms, being only 16 pounds. The current in the primary of such a motor at all speeds will be nearly proportional to the torque developed. At the moment of cutting out the successive resistances, the current will momentarily increase in strength. It can be readily seen that, by using a suf-

ficient number of resistance steps, the motor could be brought up to speed with uniform torque and current. When the motor is taxed beyond its capacity, its torque and speed rapidly diminish and a large current will flow. This break-down point is determined by the design of the motor, and is fixed at from 50 to 100 per cent greater than the rated load. The working point of such a motor is on the descending portion of the power curve, at about two-thirds of the maximum output. Curves of torque and amperes output at all loads, of a 175 H.P. motor, are given in Fig. 56.

The magnetizing current which is characteristic of most alternating-current apparatus, such as transformers, induction motors, etc., has the effect of increasing the full-load current and putting a greater demand on transformers, line, and generators. The total current is greater than that actually required in supplying the losses and doing the work of the motor. The ratio of this working or energy current to the total current gives the power factor.

As the starting current of the motor, with short-circuited armature, is reduced by lowering the voltage, it follows that, for the same starting torque as that developed by the variable resistance type, the current will be considerably greater.

The line starting current and the torque of some makes of motors with short-circuited armatures, expressed in percentages of full load, are about as follows:

E.M.F.	Starting Current.	Starting Torque.
40%	112%	32%
60%	250%	72%
80%	450%	128%
100%	700%	200%

The local current between the compensator and motor will be greater than the line starting current, as its potential is lower. The action of the compensator is similar to that of a transformer.

By increasing the resistance of the armature of these motors, the starting current for the same torque is decreased; but the result is a loss of efficiency, which may be as great as 2 or 3 per cent.

The following is a comparison of the values of torque and starting current of two 10 H.P., 220 volt, 60 cycle motors, of the high inductance and variable resistance, and of the short-circuited types:

	Variable Resistance Armature.	Short-Circuited Armature.
Running current, full load	27.6 amperes	26.7 amperes
" " no "	8.3 "	12.6 "
Starting current, maximum torque	60 "	174 "
Starting current, full-load torque	28 "	100 "
" " $\frac{2}{3}$ " "	20 "	67 "
Torque, full load	45 pounds	45 pounds
" maximum, starting	79 "	79 "
Horse-power, maximum	16 H.P.	28 H.P.
Drop in speed, full load	2.2 per cent	2.5 per cent
Rise in temperature	24° C.	20° C.
Weight with starting device	1050 pounds	943 pounds

The characteristics of the variable resistance type of high inductance, as ordinarily built, may be summed up as follows:

    Medium break-down point.
    Small magnetizing current.
    High power factor and efficiency at all loads up to and including full load.

INDUCTION MOTORS. 77

Torque proportional to the starting and running current.

Small percentage drop in speed.

The characteristics of the short-circuited armature type of low inductance are:

High break-down point.
Fairly large magnetizing current.
High power factor and efficiency at full and overloads.
Large starting-current for starting torque.
Greater percentage drop in speed.

Motors of the first type will be seen to have a special range of usefulness when operated from circuits requiring good regulation such as is demanded in central station work. They are desirable for service where the motors are apt to run considerably underloaded.

The second type is to be recommended for power circuits, and when the motors must be started from a distance and simplicity of operation is of moment. It is adapted for service, calling for low starting efforts and constant full load, and is especially advantageous when the motors are apt to run overloaded, or on circuits of varying voltage. It is not adapted for lighting circuits, where good regulation is important, unless the current at starting is small when compared with the capacity of feeders and generators. Fig. 57 represents a 75 H.P., three-phase motor of this type, made by the General Electric Company.

The fields of both types of motors may be constructed to have a low self-inductance, in which case both motors will possess the same general characteristics, except as to the relation of starting current to the starting torque.

Speed Regulation. — Absolutely synchronous speed is never attained in an induction motor, as some slip is required to furnish the current consumed by the light-load losses. Under increasing load, the speed will fall away from synchronism until the break-down point is

Fig. 57.

reached, and if the motor is not relieved of its load, it will come to a standstill. The current will then be at its maximum. The fall in speed from that at light load to that at normal rated load will vary in some types of induction motors from $1\frac{1}{2}$ per cent, as in motors of 100 H.P., to 3 per cent, as in smaller motors. Motors constructed with high and fixed secondary resistances may drop in speed as much as 9 per cent.

INDUCTION MOTORS. 79

The complaint has been made against the induction motor that it is an inflexible piece of apparatus in respect to regulation of speed. It is quite true that wide variations of speed are obtained in modern motors only at the expense of efficiency and increased cost of construction.

There are a number of possible methods of obtaining a variation of speed in an induction motor, three of which will be described; only two of which, however, are at the present time generally employed.

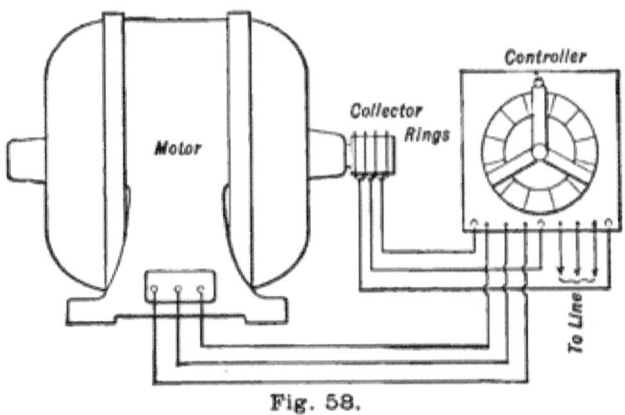

Fig. 58.

The method now most employed is that by rheostatic control. A resistance is intercalated in the secondary circuit, which can be varied by short successive steps. The range of speed usually demanded of a variable speed induction motor does not permit the use of the small resistance, such as is used in starting in some designs of motor, and which is located within the rotor armature. An external rheostat is required, of sufficient size to dissipate a considerable amount of energy. Fig. 58 shows the connections of a three-phase motor and of a rheostatic controller for variable speeds. Collector rings, as shown, must be added to motors having revolving secondaries for electrically connecting the windings and external resistance.

The main line is shown as passing through the controller. By this arrangement the circuit is closed simultaneously with the commencement of the operation of cutting out the resistance. In large motors the controller is separate from the resistance, being connected to it by cables. It is in appearance similar to the well-known street-car controller, and, like it, is reversible.

The speed of an induction motor can also be controlled by changing the impressed volts at the motor. This method requires the use of an external reactance or a compensator, and a motor possessing a high fixed armature resistance.

The controller and compensator are usually separate. By a sufficient number of taps in the latter, connected by cables to the controller, a graduated variation of the impressed volts is obtained, and a corresponding variation in speed.

The third method of controlling the speed is by changing the number of poles. When a variety of speeds is required, this method is complicated, requiring, in addition to a compensator, an elaborate switching device. It is objectionable also, as the motor can only run at full, one-half, and one-quarter speed, and at no intermediate speeds. This method has been successfully employed in cases where half speed and half full-load torque are required.

An investigation of the relative efficiencies and power factors of induction motors of 10 H.P. output, equipped with the rheostatic and with the potential, variable speed-controlling devices, gives the approximate results shown in the following table:

INDUCTION MOTORS.

Speed.*	Method of Control.	Efficiency.	P. F.	Ap. Ef.
Full	Rheostatic	83	86	72
	Potential	83	86	72
Half....	Rheostatic	41.5	86	36
	Potential	36	57	20.5
Quarter .	Rheostatic	21	86	18
	Potential	16	48	7.7

In practice it will be found that, in order to give the best all-round results, the motor for potential control will have a lower efficiency at full speed than the motor built for rheostatic speed control.

The motor with rheostatic control shows the same power factor at all speeds.

The potential control gives a lower power factor and efficiency at all but full speed.

The motor controlled by change of poles will be found to be the most efficient for half and quarter speeds, and has the highest power factor except at quarter speeds.

Of the commercial methods of obtaining speed variation, that by potential control is inferior to the rheostatic control in point of efficiency. The drawback to the rheostatic method is that the motor requires collector rings.

Frequency. — Induction motors of frequencies of from 25 to 60 cycles, as constructed at the present time, have somewhat better power factors and efficiencies than higher frequency motors. Motors of a frequency of 125 cycles or thereabouts are seldom built in sizes above 20 H.P. Motors of this frequency being somewhat difficult of construction on account of the small air gap

* The torque is assumed to be constant at all speeds.

required and the greater number of poles, are not cheaper than 25 cycle or 60 cycle motors of corresponding sizes, as might be expected. The reverse holds good with lower frequencies, 60 cycle motors costing less to build than motors of 25 cycles.

Twenty-five cycle motors have the disadvantage that on account of difficulties in the winding construction, the speeds are practically limited to 750, 500, 375, and 300 $R.P.M.$ The bipolar motor, running at 1,500 revolutions, is limited to the smallest sizes. The slow speeds of 300 and 375 revolutions make the motor, unless it be one of great capacity, an expensive piece of apparatus. These conditions limit the average practical speed of 25 cycle motors, of sizes from 5 H.P. to 75 H.P., to 750 revolutions.

Frequencies of 35 to 40 cycles are more desirable for the average conditions of motor work, as they permit a much greater range of commercial speeds.

The frequency of 60 cycles likewise permits the construction of motors with a wide range of speed, and which are comparatively cheap to build throughout the entire list.

Voltage. — Induction motors should not be run at lower voltages than that for which they are designed, as the output varies with the square of the voltage. For instance, if the volts at the motor are 10 per cent lower than normal, a motor which has a maximum output of 30 per cent greater than the full-load output will give only $\frac{(90)^2}{100}$ × 130 = 105 per cent of its rated output. The margin is too close for continuous work, as it will not take care of any sudden fluctuation of load or unusual drop in the line. The output of the motor, on a higher voltage circuit than that for which it is designed, will be increased, and the current likewise, especially at light loads. Within ordinary variation of voltages, the power factor and efficiency at full load remain practically unchanged.

In laying out the wiring of a motor which takes a heavy starting current, allowance should be made for this momentary current; otherwise the impressed volts may drop below the point where the motor will start.

Motors with stationary fields could be wound for fairly high voltage, but for the distributed form of winding required to keep down self-induction, the space necessary for high insulation being occupied by the conductor. Standard American motors below 50 H.P. are not wound above 550 volts. It is considered practical to wind larger motors up to 3,000 volts. European makers, on the other hand, build motors of 10 H.P. to 30 H.P. for pressures of 500 to 2,000 volts, motors of 50 H.P. for 3,000 volts, and those of 75 H.P. and larger for 5,000 volts.

Power Factor — Efficiency. — It has been seen that the ratio of the energy current of a motor, or the current required in supplying its losses and doing the work to the total current consumed, gives the power factor. The product of the power factor and the actual efficiency of an induction motor gives the apparent efficiency. This last quantity determines the capacity of transformers and generators required for supplying current to the motors. As has been seen, the influence of the power factor extends back in the chain of transmission with greater effect on the supplying circuit, necessitating, in the case of a poor power factor, on account of its inductive effects, an additional increase in the capacity of the transmission lines. For this reason, it is usually of importance that induction motors be designed to give the highest possible power factor. Where the generating power is expensive, it is sometimes of more importance to use motors of higher efficiency than those of high power factor. Under all circumstances, however, it is desirable to have the apparent efficiency of the motors as high as possible.

The power factors of standard commercial induction motors of American manufacture vary at full load from .75 to .92, depending upon the size and frequency of the motor. The efficiencies range from .80 to .92. The apparent efficiencies in motors above 5 H.P. output will be found, as a rule, not less than .75. This means that the transformer, supplying current to induction motors of average sizes, must have a capacity of 1 K.W. for every horse-power output of the motors.

The following table gives approximate capacities of standard transformers that should be used with two-phase and three-phase induction motors:

H. P. CAPACITY MOTOR.	THREE-PHASE.		TWO-PHASE.
	2 TRANSFORMERS.	3 TRANSFORMERS.	2 TRANSFORMERS.
1	.6 K.W.	.5 K.W.	.6 K.W.
2	1. "	.1 "	1. "
3	2. "	1.5 "	1.5 "
5	3. "	2. "	3. "
7½	4. "	2.5 "	4. "
10	5. "	3.5 "	5. "
15	7.5 "	5. "	7.5 "
20	10. "	7.5 "	10. "
30	15. "	10. "	15. "
50	25. "	15. "	25. "
75		25. "	35. "
100		30. "	45. "

INDUCTION MOTORS.

The efficiency of commercial induction motors can be somewhat increased by not sparing iron and copper, as the losses of an induction motor are of the same kind as those of a generator, consisting of copper loss, hysteresis loss, and friction loss.

The power factor can be bettered by reducing the air gap and iron density, and thereby lowering the magnetizing or "wattless" current. To do this, however, and retain high efficiency, increases the cost of the motor, and it then becomes a question whether the increased advantages are worth the extra expense. Mechanical considerations limit the clearance between field and armature. Fig. 56 shows the curves of efficiency, power factor, and apparent efficiency, as well as torque and ampere output of a 175 H.P. motor. At full load the efficiency is 91 per cent, the power factor .88, and the apparent efficiency 80 per cent. The efficiency at half load is as good as that at full load; and at one-quarter load, the efficiency is still well up, being 85 per cent. The break-down point is at over twice full load. The power factor is highest at about 260 H.P., being over 91 per cent.

In many cases it is desirable to design motors so that their maximum efficiency occurs at about three-quarters load. This is especially desirable for shop work, where the driving motors are called upon intermittently to give full load, the average demand being 15 per cent to 30 per cent less than the load for which they are rated.

The efficiency of a 10 H.P., 60 cycle motor with short-circuited armature is shown in Fig. 59, and also, for comparison, the curves of a variable resistance high inductance type. The efficiency of the variable resistance motor is the higher at all loads under full load, after which the other motor is ahead. The break-down point of the latter motor is over 200 per cent of full load.

Condensers.—Condensers are used to improve the power factor of circuits supplying current to motors by making the motors take current in proportion to the loads. The motors themselves are not improved, but the wattless current is offset by the leading current supplied by the

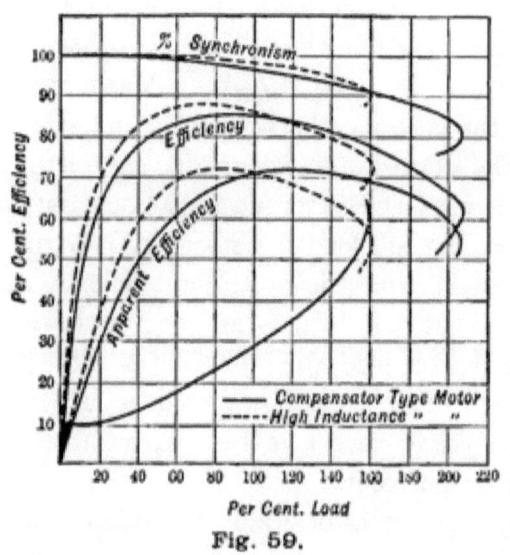

Fig. 59.

condensers, and its pernicious influence confined to the local circuit between the condenser and the motor. Fig. 60 shows the apparent efficiency of a Stanley two-phase motor with and without a condenser, and Fig. 61 the connection of motor and condensers.

The condenser consists of numerous thin sheet conductors, separated by still thinner dialectrics, the whole electrically connected to form two conductors. As the size of the condenser increases rapidly with a low frequency

INDUCTION MOTORS. 87

and voltage, it is best adapted for circuits of over 100 cycles, and when motors are used for not less than 500 volt circuits.

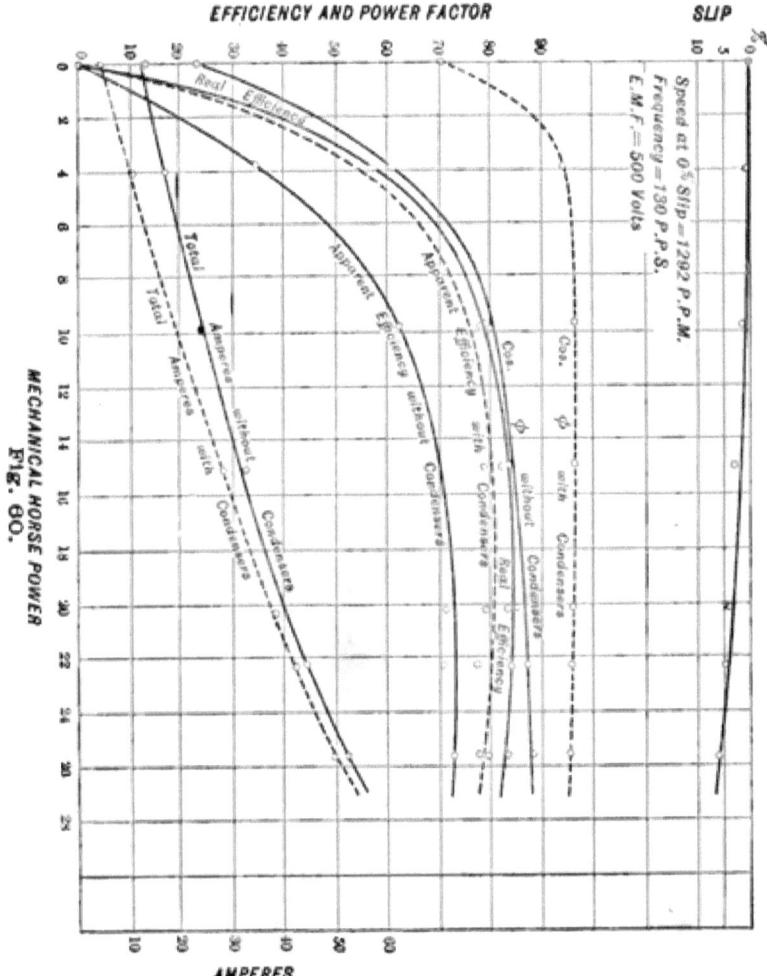

Fig. 80.

Single-Phase Motors. — Single-phase induction motors have only recently been commercially introduced on a large scale. They have the characteristic form of poly-

88   POLYPHASE APPARATUS AND SYSTEMS.

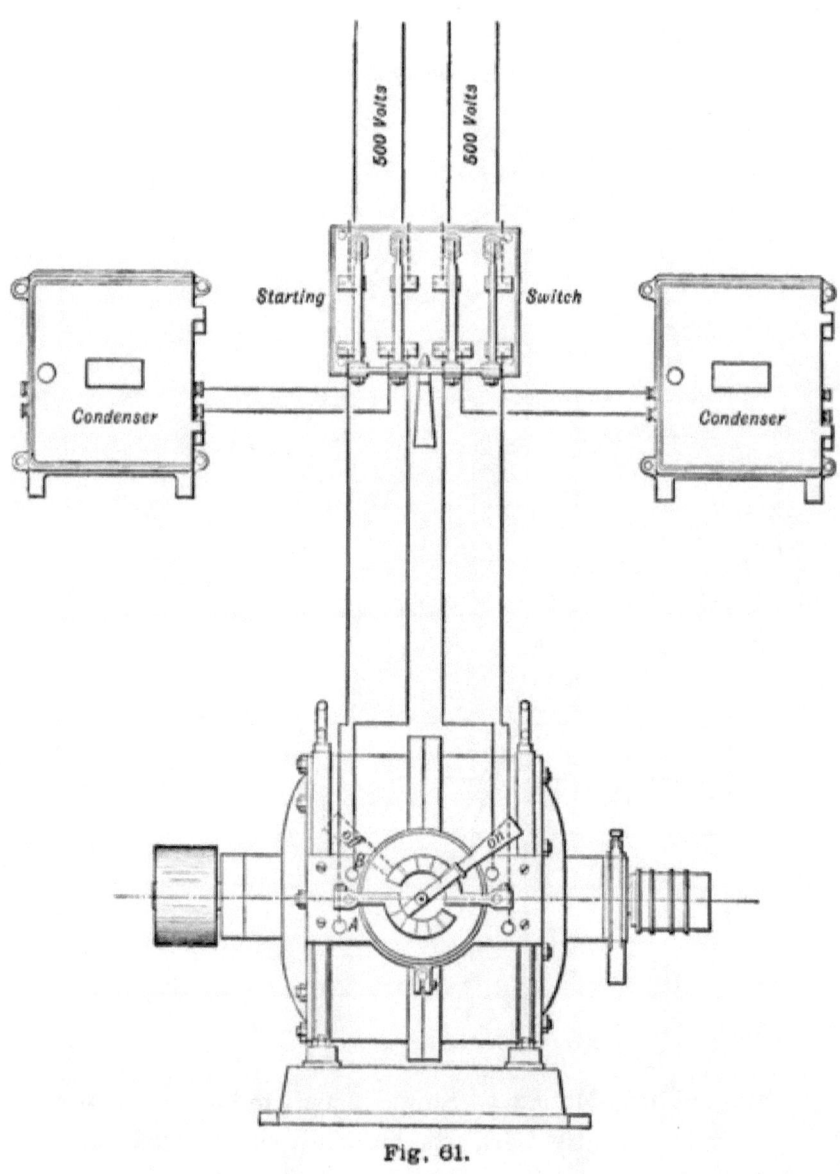

Fig. 61.

INDUCTION MOTORS. 89

phase motors. As the flow of energy in the single-phase system is not continuous, as in a polyphase system, their capacity is less than a polyphase motor of same dimensions. In respect to torque, power factor and efficiency, even the best commercial motors are not so good as polyphase motors. An external starting arrangement, sometimes called a "phase-splitter," is sometimes used with these motors, for artificially producing a torque sufficient to enable them to start from rest under a partial load.

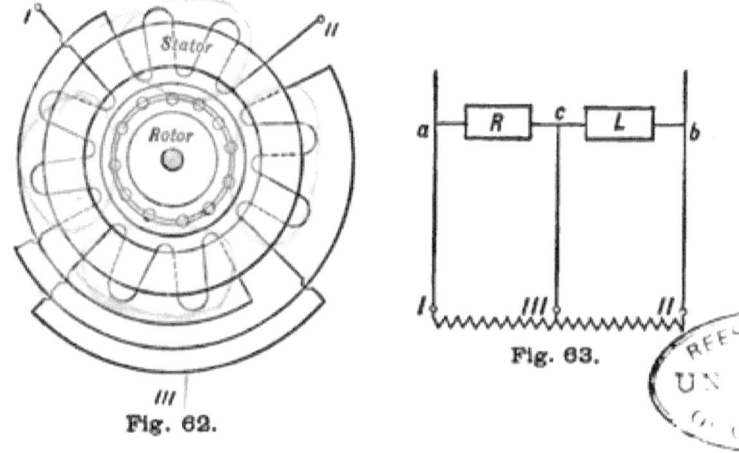

Fig. 62.

Fig. 63.

The winding of a two-pole, single-phase motor is shown in Fig. 62. It has a two-phase, interlinked winding, the common terminals being at III. If two currents, having a difference in phase, are introduced, the dead point common to all single-phase motors will be overcome, and the armature will revolve. The displaced phase is produced by a combined resistance and impedance coil, the outline connections of which are shown in Fig. 63. a and b are the main leads; c is a lead to the common terminal of the motor two-phase winding. R is a resistance and L a choking coil. The current passing through R will differ in phase from that flowing through L, and the motor will start, when the switch is thrown, with a torque dependent upon the phase difference. The maximum torque will be developed when the currents are 90° apart. This, of course, cannot be obtained with this device. By replacing the resistance by a condenser, a phase difference of 90° or over can be obtained, with a correspondingly increased torque, and a decreased starting current. When the motor reaches speed, the starting coils are cut out, and it then runs as a single-phase motor.

The usual form of motor is provided with a starting device that gives half-load torque at about 150 per cent of full-load current. Full load torque may be obtained at somewhat over twice full-load current, by a special starting device. The advantage of the single-phase induction motor over the single-phase synchronous motor lies principally in the fact that the latter motor is liable to be thrown out of step by any fluctuation in the generator speed. The synchronous motor is fairly efficient, and has a power factor of nearly unity, but the current at starting is quite out of proportion to the torque.

A three-phase induction motor will give about 40 per cent of its output when used single-phase. A two-phase motor will give 50 per cent of its two-phase rating under the same conditions. The same motors can be rewound as single-phase motors, and will then have an output of over 75 per cent of their former rating. The unaltered two-phase and three-phase motors can, however, be made to yield, on a single-phase circuit, about 75 per cent of their rating by increasing the voltage 30 per cent above that for which they are wound.

In Fig. 64 is shown the connections of a Wagner

INDUCTION MOTORS. 91

Electric Company's self-starting, single-phase motor. In starting, the armature and field are connected in series. On attaining full speed, this connection is automatically broken by a governing device within the armature. Simultaneously, the armature is short-circuited on itself, and the

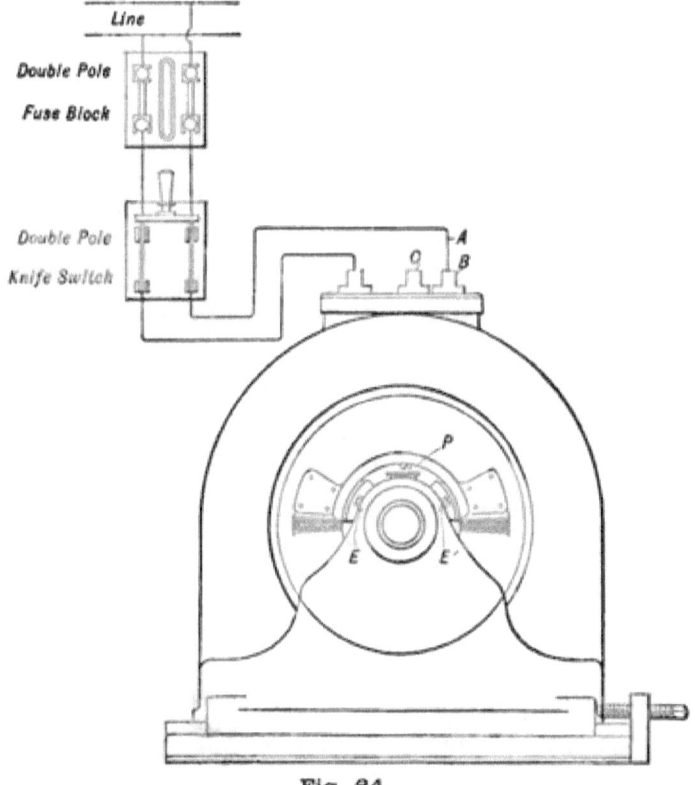

Fig. 64.

field remains connected across the line. The motor then operates as a simple induction motor.

As seen in the diagram, no external starting device is required, there being only two wires from the mains to the motor. The third binding post, C, is for use in case the voltage of the supplying circuit is low, a third connection and a double throw switch being required.

CHAPTER V.

SYNCHRONOUS MOTORS.

General.—Any alternating-current generator, with little or no change, can be used as a synchronous motor. Electrically and mechanically the motor resembles the corresponding generator, and must be provided with the same station equipment, including some source of exciting current. The synchronous motor, especially in units of large output, possesses a number of features which makes its use at times preferable to that of the induction motor. Besides the advantage of an unvarying speed at all loads, the power factor can be altered at will by changing the exciting current and made equal to unity at any load. The current can even be made leading, to offset a lagging current in other parts of the system. The synchronous motor, especially at low speeds, is cheaper to build than the induction motor, and its efficiency, as a rule, will be found to be higher.

As a partial offset to these advantages, the synchronous motor is not adapted for use where a large starting torque or frequent starting of the load is necessary. It does not admit of independent speed regulation. It also has the disadvantage of requiring certain station appliances and an exciting current, which is usually obtained from some source other than the motor.

Speed.—The speed of the synchronous motor is not

necessarily the generator speed, but a speed which, multiplied by the number of poles, gives a product equal to the generator alternations. A motor, having twice the number of poles that the generator has, will have half the speed, or *vice versa*. As load is thrown on the synchronous motor, there is a lag in the relative positions of armature winding and pole face, or retardation of the armature. The effective counter $E.M.F.$ is thereby reduced, which gives rise to a larger flow of current.

The motor speed is independent of the voltage and cannot be altered except by changing the generator speed. It is important therefore that the regulation of the prime mover be as perfect as possible, both in the number of revolutions per minute and in the angular speed; otherwise, as the fly-wheel capacity of the motor armature is sufficient to absorb considerable energy without changing its speed, fluctuating currents will pass between generator and motor, reducing the motor capacity, and producing bad regulation.

Torque and Output.—A synchronous motor at starting acts somewhat as an induction motor. Consequently any variation of its proportions, such as the shape of the pole pieces, armature reaction, and nature of the winding,—i. e., distributed or unitooth,—affects its starting torque. The starting torque may vary from nothing to 20 or 30 per cent of full-load running torque, depending upon the motor design. When once in motion, the motor will rapidly attain synchronous speed. Polyphase motors, as usually constructed, will carry four to five times full load. If further loaded, they fall out of synchronism, and can be brought up to speed by being relieved of the load. Single-phase synchronous motors have dead points, and will not start from rest; monocyclic generators used as motors develop too feeble a torque to start, and may be regarded as single-phase motors in their action at starting, and when running under load. It is necessary to use some extraneous source of power to start single-phase motors, and bring them up to speed. This is usually effected by an alternating-current motor. In some cases where a direct-current source of power is available, the exciter may be used as a starting motor.

The limit to the torque and output of a synchronous motor is dependent mainly upon the terminal voltage. Under rated voltage the margin of most motors, before the break-down point is reached, is sufficient to enable them to stand a heavy overload. Variation of the speed of the prime mover will reduce the maximum output.

Voltage.—The relation of impressed volts to the maximum output is the same in synchronous as in induction motors, the output and the starting torque varying within certain limits as the square of the volts. It is essential, therefore, that the pressure be kept at the rated voltage of the motor; otherwise the motor may not start at all, particularly if it consumes an excessive starting current.

Synchronous motors can be wound for the same voltage as the corresponding generators. Standard motors of 100 H.P. and over, of the revolving armature type, are wound for potentials up to three 3,400 volts. Motors of the stationary armature type can be safely wound for potentials as high as 7,000 volts, in sizes from 100 to 500 K.W.; motors of larger capacity can be wound for 12,000 volts. Motors of the revolving field type, as ordinarily proportioned, have a somewhat greater starting torque than those of the revolving armature type, on account of the greater arc covered by the pole face.

SYNCHRONOUS MOTORS. 95

Methods of Starting.—When a large torque is required to turn over the load, as in the case of mill machinery or long lines of shafting and belting, a friction clutch must be used. This permits the load to be gradually thrown on the motor after it reaches synchronism. The clutch may be mounted on the motor base extended, an extra standard being required for this purpose; or the motor may be belted to a line shaft on which there is a coupling. This is the cheaper and more usual method. Fig. 65 shows a 500 H.P. motor, built with extended base, carrying a clutch and driving pulley. In selecting a coupling for this class of work, one of ample proportions should be used, as it must start the load gradually, without exceeding the breakdown point of the motor, and without overheating.

The operations in starting a synchronous motor are about as follows: First, the main switch is closed and the motor with its fields unexcited will start with a small torque due to the induced currents in the pole pieces, and soon speed up to almost synchronism. The current from the exciter, which is either belted to or mounted on the motor shaft, can now be switched into the fields, and the motor will be brought up to synchronism. The full load can then safely be thrown on the motor by the friction clutch, if one is used.

The current taken at starting may be anything from 150 per cent of full-load current to several times normal current, being limited by the resistance and self-induction of the armature windings, i. e., its impedance. This excessive starting current, as it is of an inductive character, may cause a large drop in the line.

If the motor takes a large proportion of the generator output, or is used in connection with lights, and started and

96   POLYPHASE APPARATUS AND SYSTEMS.

SYNCHRONOUS MOTORS. 97

stopped at frequent intervals, some other means should be employed to reduce the current. This can be done, as in the case of the induction motor, by the use of a resistance, a reactance, or a compensator in the main circuit. A compensator starter, like that shown in Fig. 66, is sometimes used. This particular starting device closely resembles the compensator starter for three-phase induction motors, shown in Fig. 50. It is provided with three taps, giving voltages 40 per cent, 50 per cent, and 60 per cent of running full-load voltage. With 50 per cent of the impressed volts, the synchronous motor, when properly proportioned, will take, at starting, a current equal to about full-load current, and start with a torque about 15 per cent of the full-load running torque. The operation of this starting device is plainly indicated. The triple pole switch is down at the moment of starting, and, when nearly synchronous speed is reached, is thrown up to the running side.

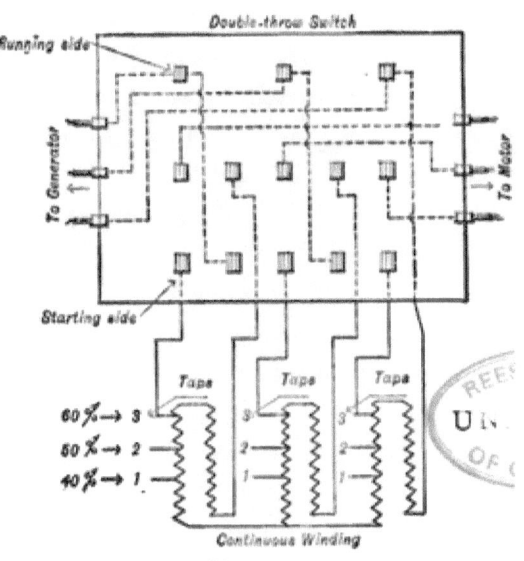

Fig. 66.

The current may also be reduced by means of a starting motor, usually of the induction type, either single-phase or polyphase. The current taken by this motor is too small to seriously affect the voltage of the circuit. This method should be employed when the motor is started frequently, or when a low starting current is essential to preserve good regulation. A starting motor, one-tenth the capacity of the synchronous motor, will be found of sufficient size to meet all average conditions. When an auxiliary motor is used, the synchronous motor must both be brought up to slightly above synchronous speed, and the speed of the motor $E.M.F.$ brought into opposition with the generator $E.M.F.$

Many forms of self-starting synchronous motors have been devised for use on single-phase circuits. Most of these are provided with a commutator for self-excitation, and a starting device. A commutator, in series with the field winding, rectifies the current at the instant the main armature current is in phase for producing a slight torque. When the motor reaches speed, the commutator is cut out. One of these types is the single-phase motor made by the Fort Wayne Company, which embodies a modification of this construction. The main current is first thrown on a continuous current winding connected to a commutator, and laid over the alternating-current winding on the armature, which is connected to collector rings. When the motor reaches synchronism, the main current is switched into the alternating-current winding, and the field circuit closed on the starting winding through the commutator.

In starting a synchronous motor, difficulty is sometimes encountered in the high voltage induced in the fields by the armature current. This is overcome in the revolving field type of motor by using an exciting current of low potential, — sometimes as low as 50 volts, and in the re-

SYNCHRONOUS MOTORS.   99

volving armature type by breaking up the fields into a number of parts, or by open-circuiting each field spool, as shown in Fig. 67. Leads from each spool are brought out to convenient switches on the motor frame. The motor is started with these open. When synchronism is reached the switches are closed, thus putting the field coils in series, and throwing them in circuit with the exciter.

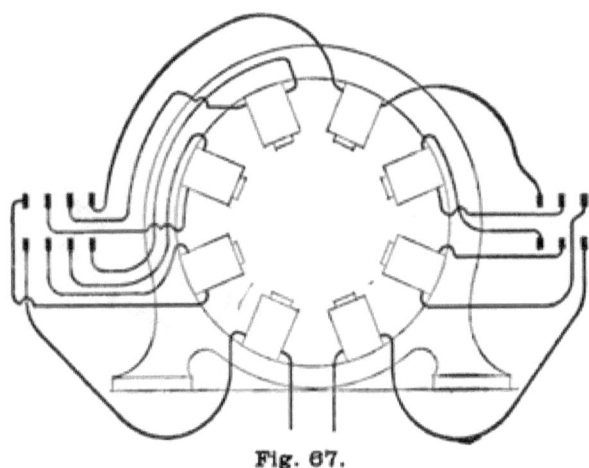

Fig. 67.

Field Excitation.—An increase of the field excitation of the synchronous motor will cause a corresponding increase in the $E.M.F.$ generated in the motor. By properly proportioning the field excitation, this $E.M.F.$ of the motor can be made considerably greater than the impressed volts at the motor terminals. It will be seen that an opposite condition exists from that when the induced $E.M.F.$ is small, due to a small exciting current. In the first case, the phase of the current will be found to be in advance of the impressed volts, and in the second case, to be lagging behind. It follows, then, that for any condition of load of the synchronous motor, by simply changing the strength of the exciting current, the armature current can be made lagging, in phase with, or in advance of, the impressed E.M.F. In other words, the amount of current consumed by the motor depends upon the field excitation.

The effect upon the armature current, produced by varying the field excitation, is shown by the curves in Fig. 68. Up to a certain point, as the excitation is increased, the armature current is lagging, and decreases. Further increase of the exciting current causes the armature to consume more

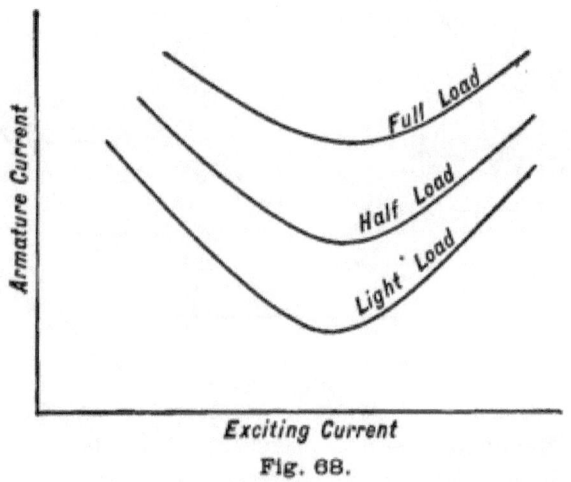

Fig. 68.

current, which is now leading. There is one value of the exciting current for which the armature current is a minimum. In motors of good regulation this value varies but slightly with different loads.

The result obtained from this property of the synchronous motor, of producing at will any displacement of phase between current and E.M.F., is the possibility of annulling the reactance due to the inductance of the line, and at the same time compensating for a certain amount of lagging current due to inductive loads in other parts of the circuit.

SYNCHRONOUS MOTORS.

When over-excited, the synchronous motor acts like a great condenser. It will take care of a total current made up of energy and wattless components, to an extent equal to its rated ampere output.

Synchronous motors of the polyphase type are separately excited. No series winding or automatic compounding is required.

Exciting Current and Exciters for Standard Polyphase Generators and Synchronous Motors.

Generator or Motor. Rating K.W.	25-60 Cycles.		Exciter Capacity.
	Separate Exciting Current.	Voltage.	
50 – Generator	6	125	1½ K.W.
50 – Motor	10	125	2 K.W. to 2½ K.W.
75 – Generator	8	125	2 K.W. to 2½ K.W.
75 – Motor	13	125	2½ K.W.
100 – Generator	10	125	2½ K.W.
100 – Motor	15	125	2½ K.W.
150 – Generator	12	125	2½ K.W.
150 – Motor	20	125	3½ K.W. to 4½ K.W.
250 – Generator	19	125	4½ K.W.
250 – Motor	32	125	7½ K.W.

When generators provided with automatic compounding are converted into synchronous motors, it will be found that increased separate excitation is required; since the series fields are necessarily omitted in the motor. The standard exciters usually furnished with generators under 250 K.W. capacity must, as a rule, be replaced by the next larger sizes. The preceding table gives the average separate exciting current required by standard polyphase generators and motors of moderate output, power factor being taken as unity. The exciter capacities given are sufficient to take care of inductive conditions. The exciters should have more capacity than is actually required, as they are the weaker part of the system, and should not be taxed to their full capacity. In a station where several synchronous motors or generators are used, it is customary to install two exciting dynamos, each one of which has capacity to furnish sufficient excitation for all machines.

Power Factor. — The maximum efficiency of the motor and circuit exists when the current and $E.M.F.$ supplied to the motor are in phase, — i.e., when the power factor is unity. This is also a condition of minimum current, and the drop in the line is that due to ohmic resistance only. When the current is in advance of, or lagging behind the impressed volts, the power factor is less than unity. It is possible, as we have seen, to suitably proportion the exciting current of a synchronous motor, so that its power factor may be unity at any load. In this way a low power factor of the supplying circuit, due to induction motors, may be raised any amount.

On account of armature reaction, a motor, which has its excitation adjusted to give a power factor of unity at full load, will take a leading current, and have a power factor less than 100 per cent at all points below full load. For the average case, it will be found most desirable to so excite the motor fields that the minimum current and highest power factor are reached at about average load. The power factor will be leading at lighter, and lagging at greater, loads. Except in the case of synchronous motors of abnormally bad design, the power factor, with properly excited fields, will have a high value over a wide range of load. Even motors with considerable armature reaction will have only a slightly drooping curve of power factor.

SYNCHRONOUS MOTORS.   103

Motors which, as generators, would have excellent inherent regulation, — i.e., small armature reaction and self-induction, — can be made to have, with one adjustment of the field, practically 100 per cent power factor at all but light loads. The advantage of a more uniform power factor in such motors is offset by their instability during voltage fluctuations. Some self-induction is desirable in order to prevent exchange of current between motor and lines when the impressed volts vary, as often happens in power transmissions. In selecting a synchronous motor, therefore, preference should be given to that one which, as a generator, would not have very close inherent regulation. Machines, of not such good regulation, have, as a rule, a higher efficiency, and take less starting current.

To predetermine the proper field strength which will give the maximum condition of efficiency, it is necessary to know the conditions of the system, — the reactance of the generator and line, the average load and its power factor, and the characteristics of the motor. Each case is a problem by itself, and must be judged by the special conditions affecting it.

A synchronous motor will take no more than its rated amperes without overheating, whatever the phase relation of current and $E.M.F.$ may be. If the inductive load at the receiving end is large, as compared with the motor load, the synchronous motor may prove inadequate to carry its own load, and appreciably annul the inductive effects.

It will be found that, for every load and every power factor, there is a synchronous motor capacity which will make the efficiency of the system a maximum. Mr. E. J. Berg has calculated the influence of synchronous motors upon the efficiency of alternating systems. Fig. 69 shows the different efficiencies of a transmission of a constant current of 200 amperes when a synchronous motor of 50, 100, or 150 K.W. is running as a compensator at the receiving end, which is assumed to have varying power

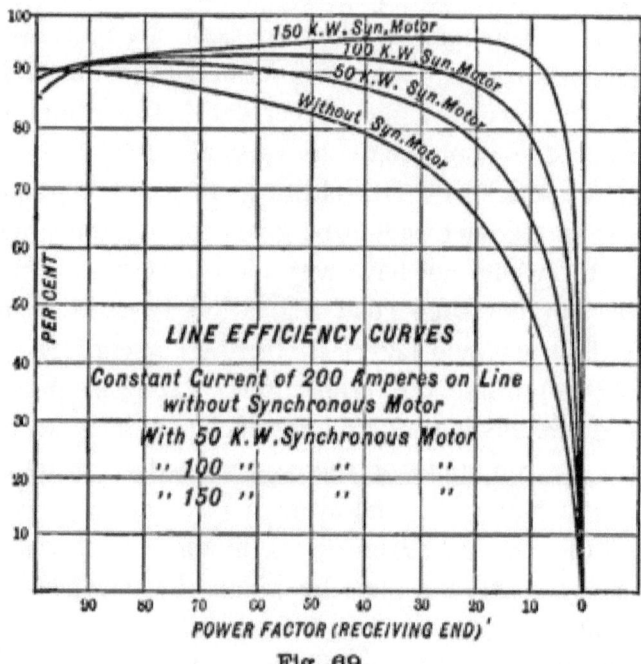

Fig. 69.

factors. The circuit is supposed to have the following constants: —

Current	= 200 amperes.
Resistance	= .52 ohms.
Reactance	= 1.45 ohms.
Voltage at motor	= 1000.

It will be noticed that, as the power factor diminishes at the receiving end, the line efficiency is increased by using the larger synchronous motors — i.e., will transmit a great amount of energy for the same loss. The line efficiency is greatest when using the 150 K.W. motor at all power factors below 87. The line efficiency is improved by entirely dispensing with the motors when the power factor is greater than 95. The leading current of the motors is then in excess of the lagging current of the receiving circuit, thereby increasing the total current, or when maintaining a constant current, as in the present case, decreasing the energy current — i.e., the amount of power that can be transmitted over the lines with the conditions as given.

CHAPTER VI.

ROTARY CONVERTERS.

General. — Any direct-current generator can be used as a rotary converter by tapping the armature windings at particular points and connecting the leads to collector rings. Direct current can be taken from the brushes of the machine at the commutator end, if an alternating current is supplied to the collector, or *vice versa*. If connections are made with the armature at points differing from each other by 180 electrical degrees, the machine becomes a single-phase rotary converter; while connections at points 90° apart will give a two-phase relationship. Connections made at points 120 electrical degrees apart permit the use of the machine on three-phase circuits.

The output of such a machine is increased when used as a rotary converter. This is partly due to the absence of armature reaction. The direct current flowing out may be said to neutralize the armature reaction of the alternating current flowing in. Again, at certain positions of the armature, the current flows through the shortest possible path from collector to commutator. When used as a motor, taking current from either the direct or alternating current end, a rotary will heat more for the same current input than when used solely for the conversion of the current.

While a direct-current generator may be made into a rotary converter in the manner described, it is not desirable to do so, on account of the low frequency which such a machine will have. It does not follow, moreover, that the direct-current generator will fulfil the conditions of successful commercial operation. On the contrary, it is probable that, without some change in the proportioning of parts and windings, such a rotary converter would be a failure.

As usually designed, rotary converters vary but little in mechanical construction and in general appearance from direct-current generators. Fig. 70 illustrates a 400 K.W. Westinghouse converter. This machine as shown is provided with an induction-starting motor, which is used when the converter is started from the alternating-current end, and, like the similar motor in a synchronous motor, reduces the starting current. No pulley is provided, unless it is intended to operate the rotary as a double-end generator or as a motor. The armature is usually of large diameter, to give efficient ventilation. That of a 600 K.W. rotary, recently built, has the high peripheral speed of 7,500 feet per minute.

Connections. — A number of connections of the alternating end of rotary converters are diagramatically shown in Figs. 71 to 75. Fig. 71 is a single-phase arrangement. The armature windings are tapped at two opposite points, and leads are brought out to two collector rings. The connections for three-phase rotary converters are shown in Fig. 72. The three collector rings are connected to three points in the armature, 120° apart. Fig. 73 illustrates the usual method of making connections for a two-phase rotary converter. These are the simple connections of bipolar machines. In multipolar rotary converters, the collector rings are connected to as many points of the armature as

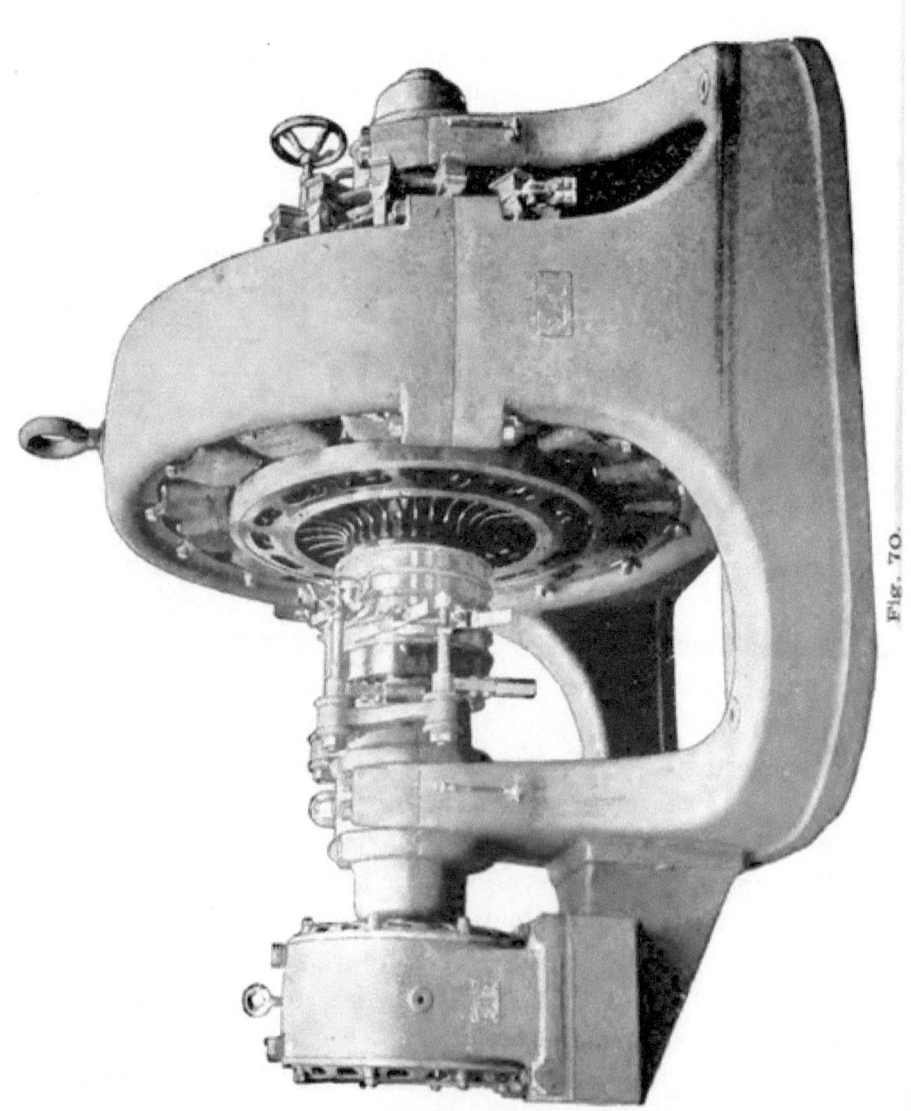

Fig. 70.

ROTARY CONVERTERS.

there are pairs of poles, — i.e., the connections must be duplicated for each 360 electrical degrees of the machine. Fig. 74 shows the connections of a four-pole single-phase rotary. The two pairs of leads run from points of the armature winding, 180 electrical degrees apart.

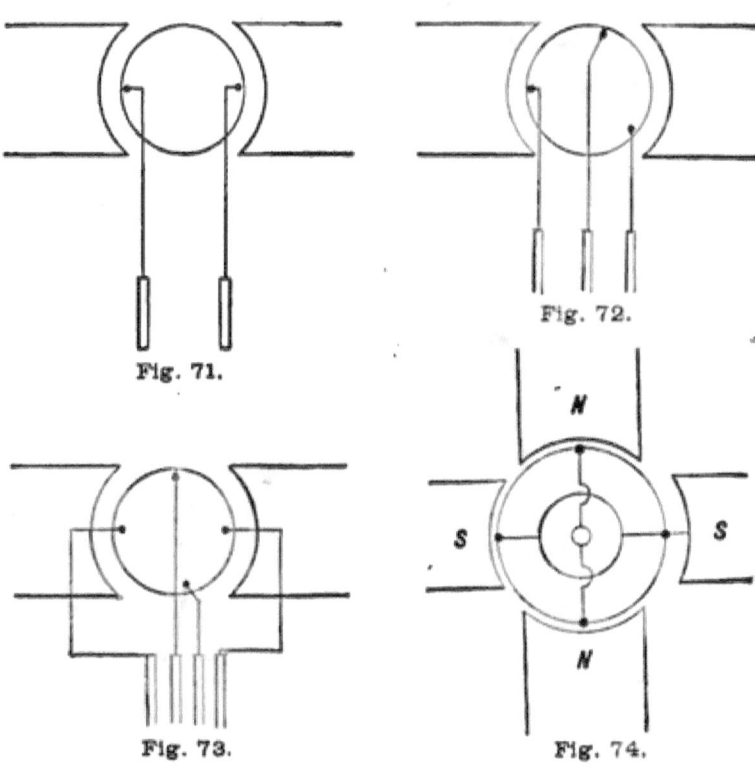

Fig. 71.

Fig. 72.

Fig. 73.

Fig. 74.

It has been noticed that the increased output of a machine, when used as a rotary converter, is partly due to some of the current passing directly from collectors to commutator. The output can be made still greater by increasing the number of collector rings and connections. For instance, a three-phase arrangement can be made with six collector rings, as in Fig. 75, and a two-phase, with eight collector rings. In the three-phase arrangement, the phases are not interlinked at the collector rings.

Ratio of Alternating to Direct-Current Voltage.—The voltage of the alternating current of a rotary converter is always less than that of the direct-current end, the value of which is equal to the crest of the $E.M.F.$ wave, while the alternating pressure is rated by the mean effective value. The ratio of voltage for any particular converter cannot be appreciably varied. In fact, it is practically unalterable, except by a change in the wave shape of the $E.M.F.$ The natural $E.M.F.$ of a direct-current generator is alternating in character, and is rectified by the commutator when the impulses are at their maximum. The measured or effective value of this unrectified $E.M.F.$ is $\frac{1}{\sqrt{2}} = .707$ of the $E.M.F.$, at the commutator brushes. This is the relation between the alternating and direct volts of a single-phase and of a two-phase rotary converter. From the nature of the three-phase system of electro-motive forces, the ratio of voltages in a three-phase rotary converter is $\frac{\sqrt{3}}{2\sqrt{2}} = .613$ of the direct current $E.M.F.$ Accordingly, to obtain a direct current from a converter of 600 volts, alternating currents of 375 to 420 volts must be supplied to it. Step-down transformers are consequently used in all cases where the primary current is not of the proper voltage.

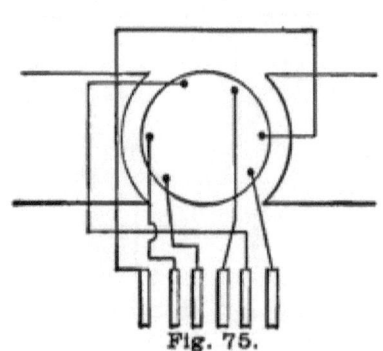

Fig. 75.

ROTARY CONVERTERS.

The theoretical ratios are not always found in practice, due mainly to the departure of the generator voltage from a true sine-wave, affecting the mean value of the alternating E.M.F., and to the drop in the machine, which may be 1 or 2 per cent.

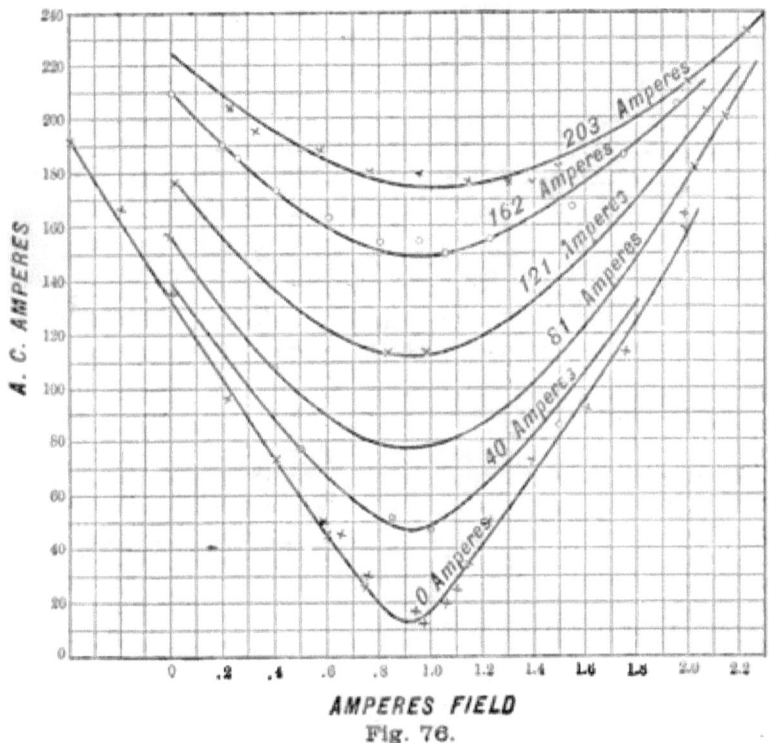

Fig. 76.

The divergence from the theoretical ratio in rotary converters is rarely more than 6 or 7 per cent.

Types of Converters determined by Field Excitation.—Rotary converters may be either separately excited or have both series and separate field excitation,—i.e., be shunt or compound wound. A third type is sometimes constructed, which has neither separately nor series excited

112   POLYPHASE APPARATUS AND SYSTEMS.

fields, but in which the magnetic field is induced by the armature current. This type is known as the "Induction" converter, and has the characteristic of an induction motor, of a lagging current at all loads. It runs, however, at a synchronous speed.

The current for the separately excited fields is usually supplied from the direct-current end, so no exciter is required. The shunt-wound rotary can be made to give

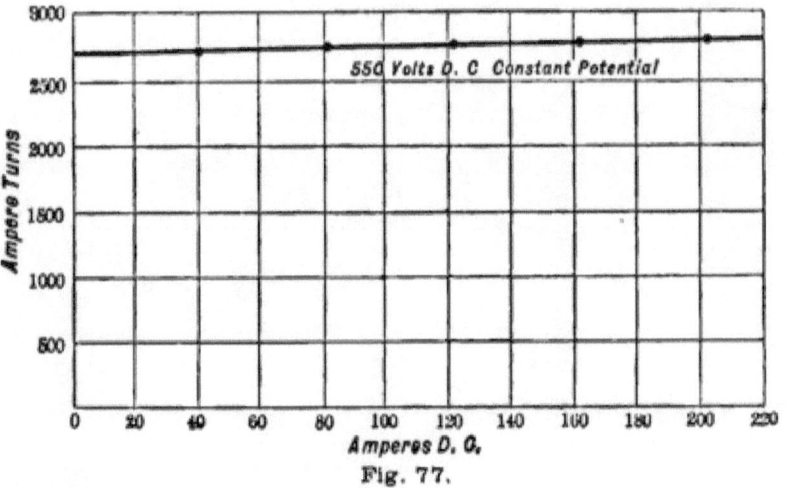

Fig. 77.

any power factor, either leading or lagging, by either over or under exciting the fields. The power factor will remain practically constant for all loads. This property is graphically shown in Fig. 76. Each curve represents the variation in the current input at the alternating end, for varying field strengths at different loads, of a 100 K.W. rotary converter. The field strength for minimum current, or 100 per cent power factor, is 9.2 amperes at no load, and 9.55 amperes at full load of 182 amperes, proving that the armature reaction is very slight.

Fig. 77 shows, in another way, the insignificance of the armature reaction. The ampere turns at no load are 2,700, and at full load 2,790, an increase of about 3 per cent.

The shunt-wound converter is particularly adapted for lighting and other steady loads, where good regulation and constant power factor are of importance.

Compound-wound converters are used to advantage, as will be shown, for supplying current to fluctuating circuits, as in railway service, and in cases where it is necessary to maintain constant or increasing voltage with increasing load. Various combinations of field excitations are possible, and more or less prominence can be given the shunt or series windings, as may be required.

Limit of Frequency. — While 60 cycle rotary converters of a capacity as great as 500 K.W. have been built, the greatest success, up to the present time, has undoubtedly been obtained by using a frequency of approximately 40 cycles and under. The limit of frequency of a rotary converter is due solely to mechanical reasons. In designing a machine for a given number of alternations, the problem is to keep the peripheral speed of the commutator within practical limits. Too high a peripheral speed will cause the commutator segments to buckle, through the action of centrifugal force. A reduction in the diameter of the commutator, on the other hand, may reduce the width of the segments below the lowest limit fixed by experience with commutator construction and operation. The voltage and output will determine the general dimensions of the commutator. Take the case of a 600 K.W., 550 volt, 60 cycle rotary converter, the speed of which, on account of its size, is limited to, say, 600 $R.P.M.$ The number of poles would be twelve. The peripheral speed of the commutator being limited, the circumference is at once fixed. The average volts per bar being also limited, the total number of segments is determined. In a 40 cycle rotary recently constructed, the average voltage between segments was limited to $13\frac{1}{4}$ volts, and the commutator speed to 4,500 feet per minute. If we apply this data to the 60 cycle rotary, we have the following :

Number of segments between poles $= 550 \div 13\frac{1}{4} = 41$
Total number of segments $= 12$ (number of poles) $\times 41 = 492$

That circumference of the commutator which will keep the peripheral speed within the limits set—i.e., 4,500 feet per minute—is $90''$, thus allowing only $.18''$, for the width of each segment. For mechanical reasons this width is less than can be used. It will be seen that, unless the speed of the rotary can be increased, thus permitting a lesser number of poles, or the peripheral speed of the commutator can be increased, permitting a larger circumference, and consequently wider segments, the difficulty can only be overcome by using a double commutator. This, however, involves a complication of collector rings and connections, and the current must be commuted twice and the commutator losses doubled. This rotary could be built with one commutator, if wound for 110 volts or thereabouts. The general statement may be made that, for frequencies over 35 to 40 cycles, it is more difficult to build rotaries for high voltage than for low voltage,—i.e. for, say, 555 volts,—than for 100 to 200 volts, but not such a difficult problem to wind a converter of under 35 cycles for the higher voltage.

Regulation of Voltage by Field Excitation.—Like the synchronous motor, the rotary converter can be used to

ROTARY CONVERTERS. 115

annul self-induction of the line and the results of poor power factors of other parts of the system. For purposes of automatic compounding, the shunt-wound rotary converter is useless on account of its constant power factor. The compound rotary, however, fulfils the exact conditions required for overcoming the drop in line, and thereby maintaining constant voltage at the direct-current end, or for raising the alternating voltage with increasing load, and, thereby, the direct-current voltage. This regulation can be effected without any change in the generator excitation simply by varying the phase relationship of current and volts.

As an illustration of the use of this valuable feature of a rotary converter, let us take the case of a generator, with constant field excitation, supplying current to a converter for street railway service, over transmission lines having a reactance and resistance. The voltage drop is still further increased at full load by the reactance of generator and converter.

The compound field of the rotary is proportioned so that at no load it is underexcited. The $E.M.F.$ of the rotary is then considerably less than the impressed $E.M.F.$, and current in the line is made lagging. The $E.M.F.$ of self-induction is thereby increased so that the voltage of the system is cut down, giving a voltage at the collector rings corresponding to the 500 volts direct current.

As the load increases, the excitation is increased by the series fields, thereby increasing the rotary $E.M.F.$, and at some intermediate point bringing current and $E.M.F.$ in phase. The drop of voltage is then due to resistance only. At full load the converter is overexcited, and the rotary $E.M.F.$ is greater than the impressed. The current is then leading, and the voltage is actually higher at the converter than at the generator. In this way the pressure at the commutator of the rotary is made 550 volts.

The excitation can be adjusted so as to maintain constant voltage at the commutator brushes, the automatic regulation taking care of line and converter drop only.

For any particular over-compounding or compensation of voltage drop, a certain amount of self-induction must be present in the system. The best results in compounding are obtained when the rotary is operated from its own independent circuit, and when generator, line, and converter are carefully adjusted for the compounding required. This adjustment not infrequently includes an artificial reactance such as a choking coil.

A graphical demonstration of the variation of voltage due to power factors, both lagging and leading, is given in Chapter I.

Power Factor. — The power factor of the compound-wound rotary converter excited for unit power factor at full load is not so good at light loads. The power factor of the shunt-wound converter we have seen is the same at all loads. The induction type has a variable power factor which is not so good as that of the compound rotary.

A variation of the reactance in the supplying circuit will change the curve of power factor for various loads. This is due to the fact that the field excitation must be increased, or reduced, as the case may be, in order to maintain a 100 per cent power factor at any predetermined percentage of load. To obtain 10 per cent over-compounding, the fields of the compound rotary converter are excited to give a power factor of unity at usually ¾ load; and when it is desired to maintain a constant voltage at the commutator, the fields are ordinarily adjusted to give this power factor at full load. Mr. E. J. Berg, who has given much study to the practical application of these principles, has calculated some power-factor curves which illustrate the amount of reactance necessary to effect a compounding of the direct current in a rotary converter to which current is supplied by its own transmission line. In Fig. 78, curve 2 is the curve of power factor of a series-wound rotary when excited to have a power factor of unity

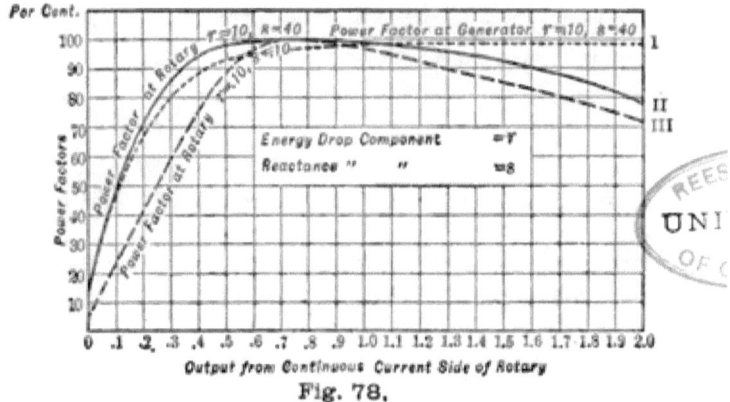

Fig. 78.

at $\tfrac{3}{4}$ load. The reactance of the generator, line, and converter is assumed as 40 per cent; the resistance as 10 per cent; the generator excitation is also assumed as constant under these conditions. The power factor at full load is $98\tfrac{1}{2}$ per cent; at $\tfrac{3}{4}$ load, 100 per cent; $\tfrac{1}{2}$ load, $97\tfrac{1}{2}$ per cent; $\tfrac{1}{4}$ load, 79 per cent; and at $\tfrac{1}{10}$ load, 47 per cent. Mr. Berg then assumes that, instead of constant field excitation of the generator, the terminal voltage is kept constant. This would correspond to a case where the rotary transmission lines were fed from the station bus-bars. The total reactance of the system is then reduced by that of the generator, becoming 10 per cent. Curve 3 shows the power factor at all loads for these conditions. It is necessary to reduce the excitation in order to maintain the power factor unity at $\frac{3}{4}$ load. The power factor is much lower at other loads, and the condition of operation is by no means as satisfactory as before. The plant can be made so by introducing in the line an external reactance equal to the generator reactance. This may be any form of a choking coil. The power-factor curves at the generator terminals, with the former constants, are plotted in the figure as curve 1.

The power factors of an induction converter of 600 K.W. capacity are as follows:

$$\begin{array}{lll} \text{Full load} & \ldots\ldots\ldots & 91 \text{ per cent} \\ \tfrac{3}{4} \text{ load} & \ldots\ldots\ldots & 87 \text{ per cent} \\ \tfrac{1}{2} \text{ load} & \ldots\ldots\ldots & 77 \text{ per cent} \end{array}$$

Starting of Rotary Converters. — Self-starting rotary converters are set in operation by introducing either alternating current to the collector rings, or direct current to the commutator. When starting from the alternating-current end, the fields should not be excited. The starting current in a well-designed rotary is rarely more than 50 per cent greater than normal full-load current. This can of course be reduced by the same means employed in the starting of synchronous motors. The rotary converter is started from the direct-current end in the same way as a shunt-wound direct-current motor. The fields should be fully excited, and there should be a resistance in series with the armature when the motor switch is closed. Failure to excite the field may cause the rotary to race like any shunt motor. Converters are also frequently started by auxiliary motors.

ROTARY CONVERTERS. 119

Rotary converters can be run in parallel either on the direct-current or the alternating-current ends. When two or more rotaries are to be run together, they can be brought into synchronism by the same method as in the practice with alternating-current generators. After the main switch is closed, the field switch is then closed, if the rotary has been started from the alternating-current end. When started from the direct-current end the machine is synchronized; then the field switch, which supplied excitation for starting, is opened, and finally the switch, supplying its own field, is closed.

In starting a self-exciting or shunt-wound rotary from the alternating side, there is no way of telling whether the polarity will be positive or negative. This difficulty may be overcome by separately exciting the machines.

Equalizers must always be used with compound type of rotary converters. The equalizing switch should be closed before the machines are thrown together, as then the rotary will always maintain the same polarity at the commutator brushes; otherwise, if the series field predominates, the current may be so far in advance as to reverse the polarity.

CHAPTER VII.

STATIC TRANSFORMERS.

Polyphase Transformers. — Transformers for use on polyphase circuits may be either of a compound type, wound polyphase, or plain single-phase. Many European firms manufacture two and three-phase transformers, but this practice has been seldom followed in this country. Polyphase transformers usually have as many magnetic circuits as there are phases, the flux in which follows the same course as the flow of current in the corresponding conductor mesh. The iron, therefore, is used to better advantage than in separate single-phase transformers, and less is required for the same output. The two-phase transformer is sometimes made with three magnetic circuits and connected on the three-wire, two-phase system. Fig. 79 shows a three-phase transformer, with its case removed, made by the Siemens-Halske Company.

American engineers use an appropriate combination of single-phase transformers for all the commercial polyphase systems. Aside from the simpler construction and greater flexibility of the single-phase type, this arrangement has the advantage of not being rendered entirely inoperative by damage to one transformer. The remaining uninjured transformer or transformers can frequently maintain continuous, though possibly crippled, service.

The growing application of electricity to the transmis-

STATIC TRANSFORMERS.   121

sion of power over long distances, and the increasing size of electrical units, has necessitated a change in transformer construction. The radiating surface of a transformer increases as the square of its linear dimensions, while its mass varies as the cube of the dimensions. For this reason transformers of a certain type of moderate sizes easily remain cool by self-radiation, but, if made of greater capacities, would burn out unless cooled by some artificial means.

The ordinary lighting transformer is cooled by being immersed in oil. The heat generated in the coils and the iron easily finds its way to the iron casing, and is thence dissipated by radiation. Transformers of this type are rarely built of larger size than 50 to 75 K.W. Transformers of greater capacity must have some special means

Fig. 79.

of getting rid of the heat generated within them. A number of methods are employed for cooling transformers, but all may be classed under the headings of self-cooled and of artificially cooled transformers. It will be more satisfactory, however, to describe the various types under their trade, and at the same time descriptive, names.

Self-Cooled Oil Transformers. — The ordinary lighting transformer is of the self-cooling type. The magnetic cir-

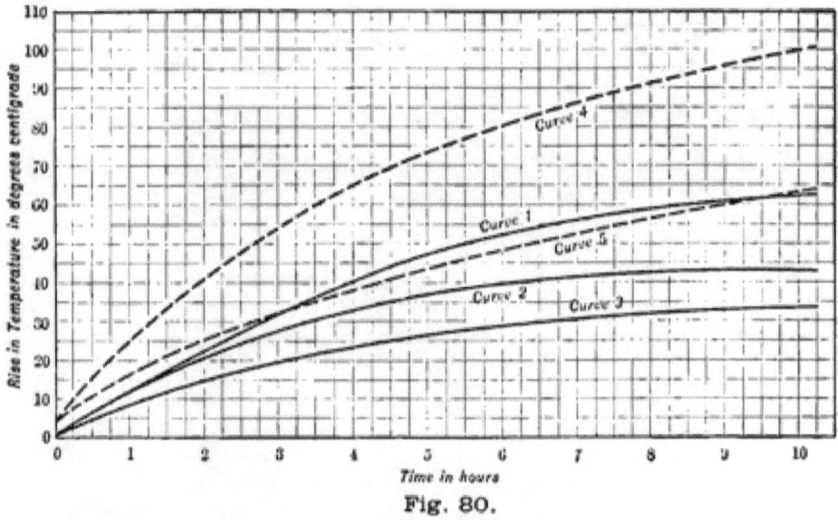

Fig. 80.

cuit is usually a plain rectangle of interlaced strips of iron, permitting a simple form of winding. The insulation between primary and secondary is tested to 10,000 volts alternating. A twofold advantage is gained by immersing these transformers in oil: First, the temperature is reduced by offering a ready means of escape for the heat; second, punctures in insulation are immediately repaired by the inflow of the oil.

The reduction of temperature by the use of oil is shown in Fig. 80. Curve 1 gives the rise in temperature of a

STATIC TRANSFORMERS. 123

Fig. 81.

transformer not submerged in oil, as determined by the increase of resistance method. Curve 2 shows the temperature of the transformer immersed in oil. Curve 3 is the temperature of the oil. Curve 4 is the temperature of the windings of another transformer of poorer design. Curve 5 shows the temperature of the same as determined by thermometer. This last curve does not give the true heating, for the thermometer cannot reach the inaccessible portions of the transformer. These transformers cannot be wound for higher potentials than 3,000 volts, without a serious loss in capacity, as the copper must be sacrificed for the increased thickness of insulating material required.

Transformers of the self-cooling oil type for high voltages and for power service are modified, to facilitate the dissipation of the heat which, in the larger sizes, could not be radiated without some special arrangement.

Fig. 81 illustrates a number of this type, as made by the Westinghouse Electric Company, with the cases removed. The windings are divided into a number of coils which, as will be seen, are spread apart at the ends, thus presenting a large surface to the oil. The heat generated in the iron and in the coils, is readily communicated to the oil. The heated fluid rises, flows to the top, and down the sides of the case, which is deeply ribbed, thus presenting a large surface to the air. In this way the internal heat of the transformer finds its way to the external surface, and is thence radiated into space.

A 300 K.W. transformer of this type, manufactured by the Wagner Electric Company, is shown in Fig. 82. This transformer is unusually interesting, from the fact that it is wound for 40,000 volts, and is one of a number in daily use in the power-house, and the substation of the

Telluride Transmission Company. The transmission is from Provo to Mercur, Utah, the distance being nearly

Fig. 82.

forty miles. The generator current of 700 volts is raised to 40,000 volts, and reduced, at the receiving end, to a suitable voltage for supplying motors and lights, principally

126 POLYPHASE APPARATUS AND SYSTEMS.

Fig. 83.

for mining operations. The essential features of the self-cooled oil transformers, when designed for power service, are a liberal proportioning of the mechanical parts, and a corrugated sheet-iron case. The first feature produces a rapid convection of the internal heat, and facilitates a rapid

Fig. 84.

oil circulation. By means of the latter feature, the external radiating surface is two or three times greater than that which a plain case would have.

Water-Cooled Oil Transformers. — When provided with some artificial method of cooling the oil, these transformers are smaller and cheaper to build than those dependent for cooling upon natural radiation. There are a number of methods of cooling such transformers; one of these is by circulating cold water in a worm or system of pipes surrounding the transformer (Fig. 83); another method of cooling is by drawing off the oil, cooling it, and pumping it back, the operation being continuous. A 1,000 H.P. oil-cooled transformer is in daily use by the Carbide Manufacturing Company, Niagara Falls. A motor, pump, and system of oil-tanks for circulating and cooling the oil are used to control the temperature of the transformer. The oil is forced upward through spaces left around and between the coils, overflows at the top, and passes down over the outside of the iron laminations.

Fig. 85.

In still another transformer the windings are cooled by the circulation of water in flat, thin ducts, interposed between the windings (Fig. 84). One form of this transformer of low secondary voltage has flat copper tubes for the secondary winding, through which cold water is circulated. The primary windings are placed between the secondaries, so that the water circulation in the latter keeps both windings at a low temperature.

The transformer is incased in a circular iron tank, with solid base, and filled with oil. The province of the oil is to cool the iron laminations, and also to prevent the condensation of moisture from the air on the cold windings.

Another form of oil transformer is cooled by means of a water jacket, surrounding the case containing the trans-

Fig. 86.

former proper. Fig. 85 shows a Wagner transformer of this type. The case is completely channelled by water passages. A low water pressure of 10 or 15 pounds is sufficient for all ordinary requirements of service.

Some outside source of power is required to operate the cooling devices, which slightly reduces the total efficiency of the transformation. The water coil may be conveniently supplied by water mains, or, in the case of a water-power transmission, by the water under head.

130   POLYPHASE APPARATUS AND SYSTEMS.

Air-Blast Transformers. — In this transformer the cooling is effected by means of a forced current of air circulating through the windings and core.

The primary and secondary coils are separately wound on formers and insulated, and then assembled in groups (Fig. 86), the coils being intermingled. The groups are

Fig. 87.

assembled in the form of a case, being separated from one another by vertical air spaces. The iron case is then built up around the windings (Fig. 87), the laminations being horizontally spaced at frequent intervals.

It is evident that this construction permits the most complete ventilation, as the very heart of the transformer

STATIC TRANSFORMERS. 131

is reached by the blast of air. The flow of air is controlled by means of two dampers, one of which is located at the top of the transformer, regulating the air between the windings; the other is on the side of the frame, and controls the flow of air through the core. Fig. 88 shows the arrangement of iron and copper parts and ventilating ducts; and Fig. 89 a completed transformer in its frame.

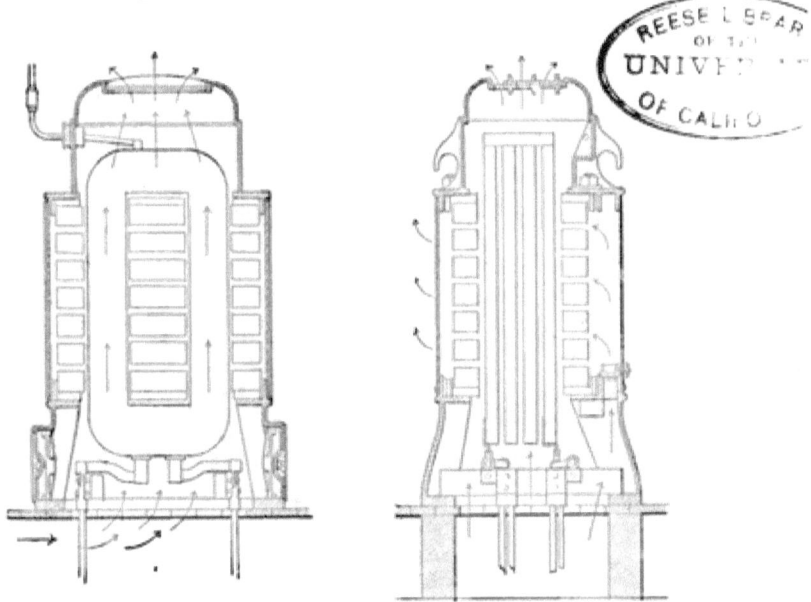

Fig. 88.

The apparatus for funishing the air blast consists of a blower, and is usually operated by a motor, the air being delivered to the transformer by means of a flue. The volume of air required for cooling purposes varies with the number, size, and efficiency of the transformers.

The following table gives the volume and pressure of air required for transformers of various sizes, of the average efficiency.

Total K.W. of Transformers.	K.W. Size of Transformer Units.	Size of Blower.	Speed of Blower.	Output Blower Cu. Ft. Per Min.	Ounce Pressure Per Sq. In.	Cu. Ft. Air Required Per Transformer.	H. P. to Drive Blower.
300	50	40″	375	1,800	.30	250	.25
900	100	50″	350	3,200	.40	350	.60
1,800	200	60″	325	5,900	.50	600	1.10
2,700	300	70″	310	8,800	.60	850	2.25
4,500	500	80″	310	13,000	.80	1,300	4.25
6,750	750	90″	295	17,600	.90	1,800	6.75
7,500	1,250	100″	280	23,600	1.	3,000	12.

From the table it will be seen that the power consumed in cooling the transformers is less than .1 of 1 per cent of the output of the transformers. If the transformers have an efficiency of 97.5 per cent at full load, the total efficiency of transformation is reduced to 97.4 per cent by the use of the air blast — a perfectly negligible quantity.

In case of damage to the cooling arrangement, the transformers can operate for a few hours without the air blast. It is desirable, however, to always provide this apparatus in duplicate.

The material protecting the primary and second coils and the windings from the case, has for the same thickness a considerably greater insulating property than oil or air.

Operation of Air-Blast Transformers. — When transformers of this type are run in groups or "banked" together, care should be take that the air enters each transformer at the same pressure, otherwise the transformers will heat unequally. This can be accomplished by having the flue from the blower to the transformer of such area that the velocity of the air will not exceed 200 feet per minute.

STATIC TRANSFORMERS. 133

The most desirable installation of the transformer is over a closed chamber of sufficient size to admit inspection of the windings. Unequal pressure in different transformers

Fig. 89.

may be compensated for by means of the two dampers with which each transformer is provided. The temperature of the outgoing air affords a ready means of determining the proper amount of air to be admitted to each transformer. The air supply is sufficient, if, at full load, it does not heat more than 20° Centigrade above the surrounding atmosphere.

Transformers of different capacities, or even of the same capacity, should not be operated in parallel unless they have the same electrical constants; otherwise, the load will be unequally divided. Parallel connections should

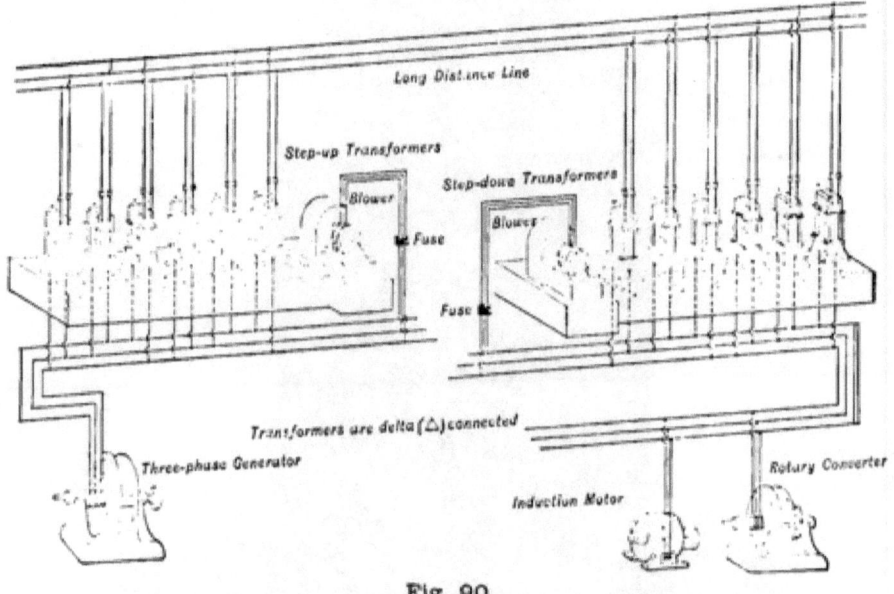

Fig. 90.

have the least possible resistance for the same reason. Fig. 90 shows the installation and connections of air-blast transformers in a long-distance power transmission.

Natural-Draft Transformers. — Transformers of this type are self-cooled by a natural circulation of air. Fig. 91 shows a transformer without its case. They are designed to have very large radiating surfaces, compared with their capacity. As usually constructed, the windings are on the

STATIC TRANSFORMERS. 135

outside of the core, instead of being surrounded by it. Every facility is, therefore, present for the radiation of heat from the coils. The transformer is mounted upon a solid foundation, and then covered with a corrugated sheet-iron cylinder, provided with bottom openings and a ventilating roof. This construction allows a free and natural circulation of air through the casing and around the transformer.

These transformers are built for 10,000 volts or 15,000 volts, and of capacities from 5 to 50 K.W. They are, as might be expected, more expensive than either oil or air-blast transformers. They have the compensating advantages of not requiring any artificial cooling device.

Efficiency and Losses.—The characteristic efficiency curve of a well-designed transformer shows a high efficiency at all but very light loads. In Fig. 92 the efficiency of a 250 K. W., 60 cycle transformer does not fall below 90 per cent from $\frac{1}{4}$ load to about $\frac{1}{10}$ load. Good efficiency, at light loads, is a valuable feature,

Fig. 91.

epecially in motor and lighting transformers, where the average load rarely makes a demand of more than one-half of the transformer capacity. The efficiencies of the 250 K.W., taken from the curve, are as follows:

$\frac{1}{10}$ load	87	per cent
$\frac{1}{4}$ load	94.6	per cent
$\frac{1}{2}$ load	97	per cent
$\frac{3}{4}$ load	97.7	per cent
full load	98	per cent
$1\frac{1}{4}$ load	98.1	per cent

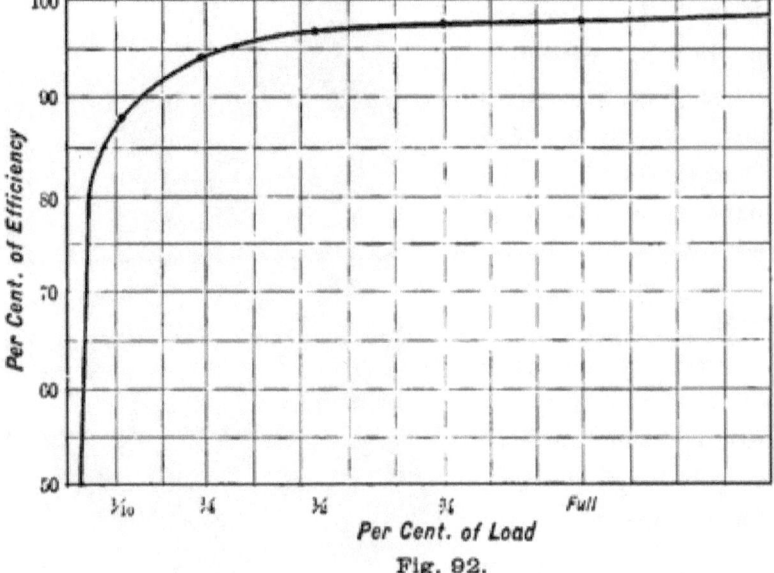

Fig. 92.

The losses in a transformer consist only of copper and iron losses. The former vary with the load, while the iron or core losses remain about the same for all loads. It is necessary, therefore, in order to obtain good efficiency at light loads, to reduce the core losses to a minimum. Judging from the shape of the curve in Fig. 92, the core

STATIC TRANSFORMERS. 137

loss must be small. This is shown to be the case in Fig. 93, which gives the watts lost in the iron of the same transformer, and also the corresponding exciting current. At full voltage, the exciting current is 2.3 amperes, and the core loss 3,380 watts, or 1¼ per cent of the full-load input of the transformer. The exciting current being a lagging current does not, of course, represent a corresponding waste of energy. The loss in the copper conductors is only ¾ of 1 per cent. By reducing the amount of copper in both primary and secondary coil, say, one-half, we obtain a proportionately increased loss in the copper, or a reduction in the efficiency of transformer from 98 per cent to approximately 97.5 per cent. But the total cost of the transformer is thereby decreased from 10 to 20 per cent.

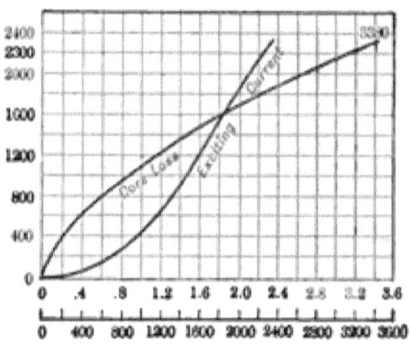

Fig. 93.

It is not always wise to select the more efficient transformer, especially in water-power transmissions, where the chief item in the cost of delivered power is the interest on the plant, nor in plants where there is not a demand for every horse-power developed. As an illustration, take the case of a power transmission of 1,000 H.P. using the cheaper transformer, which has an efficiency of 97.5 per cent. The power delivered is about 1 per cent, or 10 H.P., less than with the more efficient step-up and -down transformers. If a market were found for every horse-power transmitted at, say $30 per H.P. per year, the loss in revenue to the power company would be $300 a year. As a partial offset, there would be the interest on the difference in the first cost of the transformers. Few water-power transmissions, however, are run at their full capacity. When such is the case, the power company is usually warranted in buying the expensive transformer. In the transmission of steam-generated power, fuel is generally the most important single factor in the make-up of the total

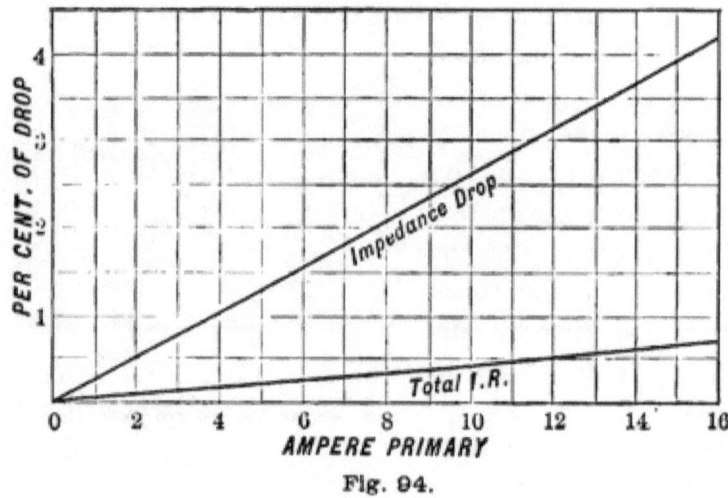

Fig. 94.

cost of power, and, as a rule, the most efficient transforming devices should be used.

Regulation. — Regulation in a transformer is the percentage drop of secondary voltage from no load to full load, the primary voltage remaining constant. Good regulation is more desirable in a transformer than in a generator, as there is no means in the former apparatus of compounding for the voltage drop. On a non-inductive load, the regulation is equal to the $I.R.$ drop of the secondary. On an inductive load, the regulation is the drop due to the resultant of the ohmic and inductive components of resistance. The regulation in this case is the same as the impedance. Fig. 94 shows the $I.R.$ and the impedance drop of a 250 K.W., 60-cycle transformer. The impedance curve is obtained by short-circuiting the secondary, which gives the most inductive condition of operation, and measuring the voltage drop from no load to full load. The non-inductive regulation is seen to be .7 of 1 per cent, and regulation on full inductive load 4.29 per cent.

CHAPTER VIII.

STATION EQUIPMENT AND GENERAL APPARATUS.

Switchboard for Generating Apparatus. — The station equipment of a polyphase plant is practically the same as that of a simple single-phase installation. The chief difference lies in the new features necessitated by the use of large generating units.

In a power plant, consisting of a number of generators, the modern practice is to instal one panel for each generator and one panel for the exciter dynamos. The generator panel will contain the generator switches, current and potential measuring instruments, fuses, field switch, and rheostats. The exciter panel usually has mounted on it the exciter switches, main line switches, and measuring and controlling instruments for the total output of the generators.

Marble is the material on which the instruments are mounted. Slate is not suitable for pressures greater than 600 volts, on account of its liability to current leakage, due to the presence of metallic veins. The instruments are mounted on the face of the panel, the electrical connections for the appliances being made behind the panel. Separate panels are connected electrically by copper tie-bars, uniting the bus-bars at the back. They are connected mechanically by bolts through the angle-iron frame behind the board.

Panels for single units are sometimes made up to suit requirements by uniting, piecemeal, smaller marble panels containing the various appliances. The angle-iron framework, used to support the panels, is arranged to form part of each individual panel. Fig. 95 shows one of the standard forms of three-phase generator panels, composed of two pieces only. These panels usually consist of a slab of marble about 62″ × 30″ × 2″, with a sub-base 28″ × 30″ × 2″, supported by a metal frame. The panel will ordinarily contain the following instruments:

    3 fuse-holders, or 6 for two circuits,
    2 pilot lamps, one for generator and one for exciter,
    1 current indicator, or ammeter, for generator,
    1 potential indicator, or voltmeter, for generator,
    1 ground detector, plug, and receptacle,
    1 main three-pole switch for three-phase generator,
    1 double-pole switch and fuse-holder, for exciter,
    1 rheostat for generator field,
    1 rheostat for exciter field,
        And behind the panel,
    3 lightning arresters,
    1 station transformer,
    1 ground detector.

Fig. 96 indicates diagrammatically the apparatus and connections of the panel just described.

In the selection of instruments for a switchboard, a liberal excess allowance should be made. For instance, the range of the ammeters should exceed the nominal rating of the generators at least 25 per cent. The voltmeters should have the same conservative rating. All switches, connections, bus-bars, and terminals should be designed to carry full-load current continuously, without appreciable heating.

For the measurement, regulation, and control of the output of generators on a large scale, as at Niagara, ordinary methods and experience do not apply. The maximum current in any part of the bus-bars in the plant at Niagara is about 3,000 amperes. The difficulties met with here were the necessity of insulating the bus-bars, thus compelling the use of round bars; the virtual resistance or skin effect, which reduced the effective copper area, and the small radiating surface of round bars, as compared with flat strips. These difficulties were overcome by the use of hollow copper rods.

The design of the switches for the same installation, capable of opening, without damage, circuits conveying 5,000 H. P. at 2,000 volts, was a difficult problem. The main switches used for this purpose are pneumatically operated. The increasing use of initial high-voltage generators has

Fig. 95.

STATION EQUIPMENT AND APPARATUS. 143

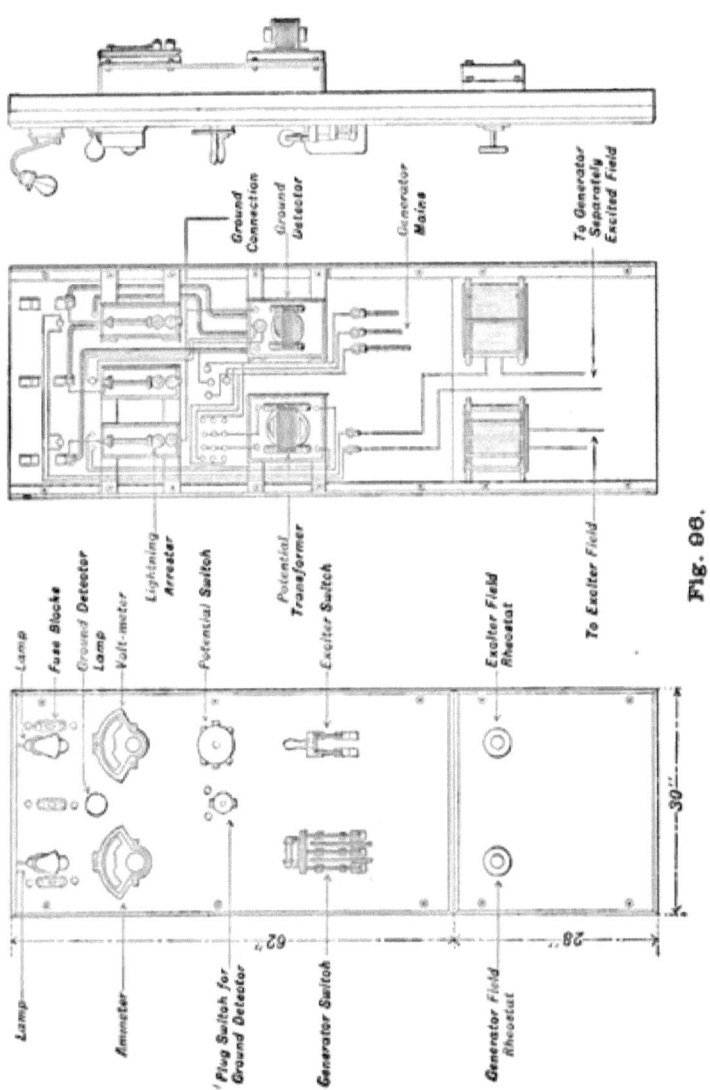

Fig. 96.

necessitated the development of special switches. While other and slower methods of opening a high-voltage circuit of great current volume are in daily use, the necessity may arise for suddenly interrupting the main circuit, and the proper appliances should be found in every installation of this character.

Switchboards for Power-Transmission Apparatus. — The switchboard equipment of the power house of a transmission plant includes panels for the step-up transformers, when such apparatus is used, and a high potential panel board, which serves as a connecting link between the transmission lines and the station wiring.

Fig. 97 shows the connections, in the generating station of a large power transmission plant, consisting of four 1,000 H.P. generator units, one of which is held as a spare. The three-phase machines are wound for 800 volts, and are each connected to the generator panels by cables of 550,000 circular mils. Behind the panels are two sets of bus-bars, which are connected to the measuring and controlling instrument on the central or exciter panel. From the exciter panel the total output of the generator is led by two circuits of 6 wires, each conductor consisting of two 800,000 $C.M.$ cables, to the step-up transformer board, where any combination of generators and transformers can be made by means of the double-throw switches. The high potential board contains the switches for making any desired connection of lines and step-up transformers. The transmission system is seen to consist of two pole lines, each composed of two circuits of three wires. By means of the distributing board, the total output of the station can be transmitted over either pole line, or, in parallel, over both lines. The output can also be divided among

STATION EQUIPMENT AND APPARATUS. 145

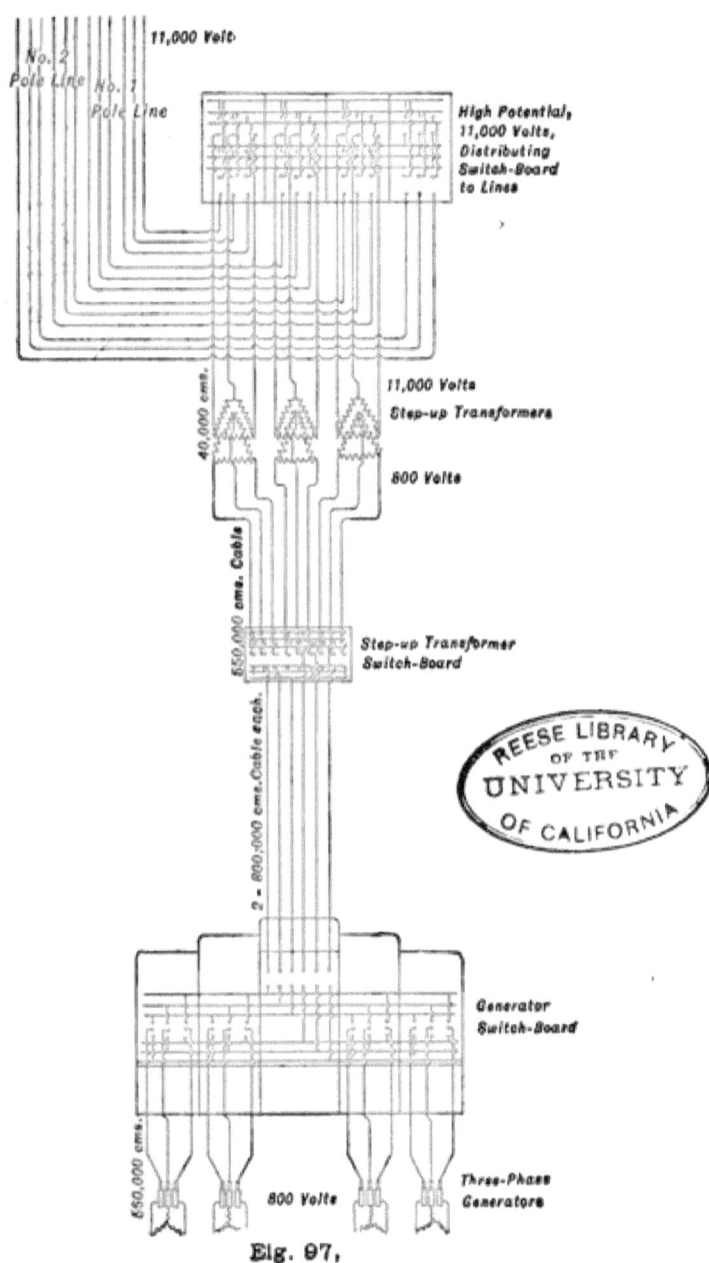

Fig. 97.

the two transmission lines. One of the generators can deliver power to one of the pole lines, and the remaining two active generators run in parallel over the other pole line, or, singly, over separate transmission lines.

A simple arrangement of transformer panels for smaller plants is illustrated in Fig. 98. The generating plant is composed of two units. The lower row of double-throw switches connects the low-tension primaries of the transformers to either set of bus-bars on the generator board. The upper row of switches is used for connecting the high-tension leads from the transformer secondaries to either one or both of the transmission lines. The small panel on the right contains the switch for connecting the transmission lines in parallel.

The connections and instruments, in the generating station and substation, of a two-unit transmission plant, are diagrammatically shown in Fig. 99. The switchboard equipment in the power station is composed of two generator panels, one exciter panel, and two transformer panels. The generator panels are provided with but one set of bus-bars. At the substation are shown two step-down transformer panels. The additional panels to be installed will be determined by the extent and character of the current-consuming appliances. Provision for an increase in the plant can be made without disturbing the general arrangement here shown, by simply adding the necessary generator and transformer panels.

Lightning Protection. — There is no problem with which the electrical engineer has to deal, that presents greater difficulties in the way of a positive solution, than that of lightning protection. The uncertainty among the highest authorities as to the exact nature of lightning phenomena

STATION EQUIPMENT AND APPARATUS. 147

is largely accountable for this state of affairs. The oscillatory character of a direct lightning stroke has been estab-

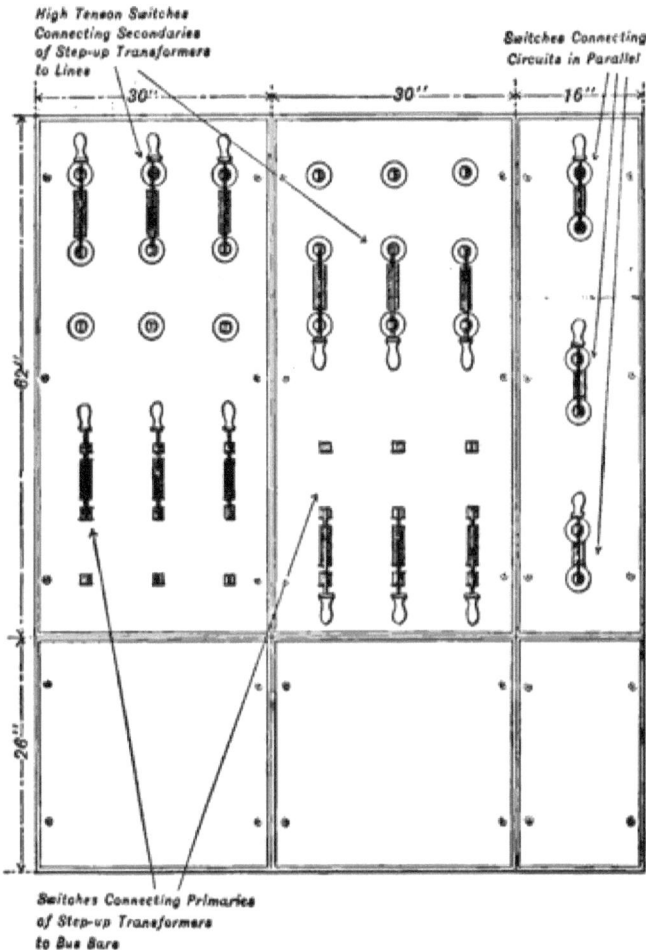

Fig. 98.

lished beyond a doubt, but experience with lightning effects would indicate that some of the disruptive discharges act mainly in one direction. For this reason no one single

148 POLYPHASE APPARATUS AND SYSTEMS.

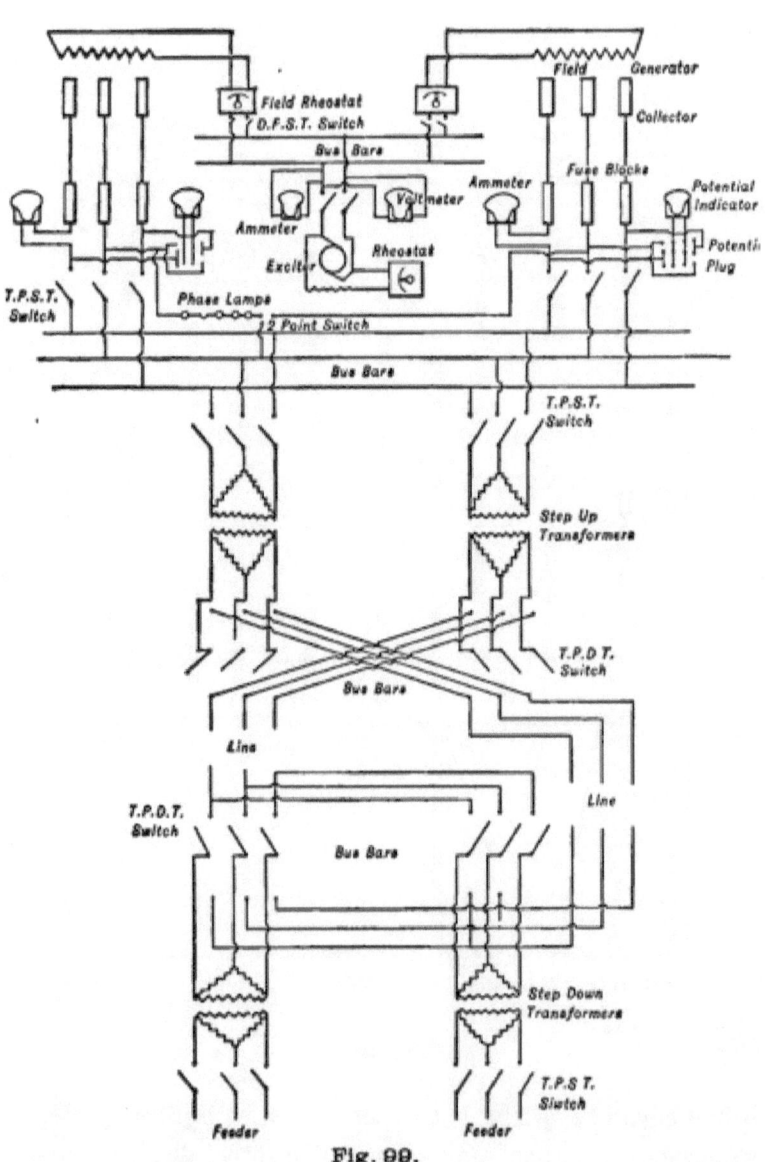

Fig. 99.

device can be depended on to protect electrical apparatus from all kinds of lightning phenomena. In other words, there is not, and cannot be, a universal lightning arrester. The discharge current from any system of conductors, produced by the various phenomena, can be described under three general headings:

1st. — The direct discharge due to the transmission lines being in the direct path of the lightning stroke.

2d. — The cumulative discharge, due to a gradual and sometimes enormous rise of potential from a changing electrostatic condition of the atmosphere.

3d. — The secondary discharge due to secondary currents induced in the lines by parallel lightning strokes.

There are other kinds of lightning discharges from transmission lines, which partake, more or less, of the character of the above, but do not differ greatly in their effects.

Provision for the protection of the station apparatus should be made, not only in the station itself, but along the transmission lines as well. The means usually employed for protecting the lines, consist of guard wires outside of the conductors, or even of one guard wire strung at the top of the pole. It is better to ground this wire at every fourth or fifth pole. In long-distance transmissions, it is also well to install, every ten miles or so, line arresters, similar to those used in the station. The guard wires protect the conductors from the direct lightning stroke, by discharge to the ground. They also have a dampening effect on the secondary induced currents, and those due to a change of the electrostatic equilibrium.

Commercial Lightning Arresters. — From the foregoing, it will be understood that there is a good deal yet to be learned about the most suitable form of lightning protection for alternating current apparatus. Nevertheless, experience has narrowed down the many ancient devices to one type of arrester, i.e., an arrester composed of a number of metal balls or cylinders, separated by short air gaps. Fig. 100 shows one of this class, devised by Mr. Wurts of

Fig. 100.

the Westinghouse Company. It is seen to consist of seven cylinders, each one inch in diameter and three inches long, and separated by spaces $\frac{1}{4}$ of an inch. The particular arrester shown is of the double-pole type, and designed for alternating circuits of 1,000 volts. When the discharge takes place simultaneously from two separate conductors, a short circuit would follow, if the arc were not immediately interrupted. It is found, with the arrester described, that the flash is instantaneous, and is not followed by an arc. The passage of the static discharge through the arrester is evidenced by burns or pit-marks on the cylinder surfaces.

These can be rotated on their axes, in order to bring fresh surfaces opposite each other.

Another form of this lightning arrester is shown in Fig 101. This device, made by the General Electric Company, consists of a combination of short metal cylinders and a graphite resistance. The single-pole arrester for 1,000 volts has one spark gap of $\frac{1}{32}$ of an inch, separating two metal cylinders two inches in diameter and two inches long.

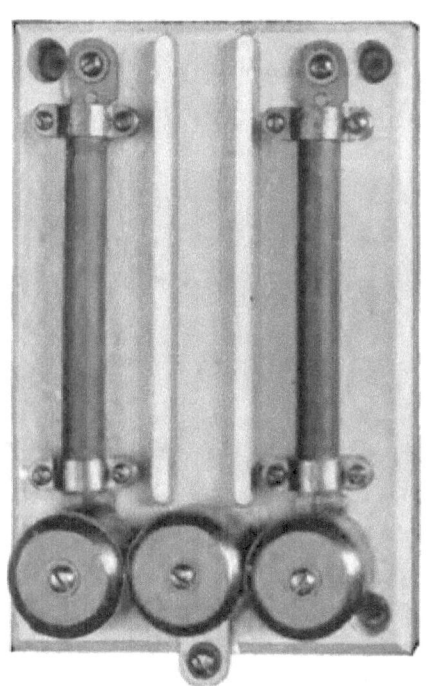

Fig. 101.

A non-inductive graphite resistance is placed in series with the ground wire. The 2,000 volt single-pole arrester has three cylinders and two air gaps of approximately $\frac{1}{32}$ of an inch each, and a graphite resistance.

The arrester first described is made of an alloy of zinc and antimony, and will operate with better results than when the cylinders are made of copper. The last-described arresters have bronze cylinders. The arc-extinguishing action of these arresters is dependent mainly upon the cooling effect of large metal masses, and not materially upon the kind of metal. This cooling effect is increased by the introduction of the non-inductive resistance, which, even in the event of the formation of an arc of short circuit, would materially limit the volume of current. The reversal of the alternating current itself extinguishes the arc, in the absence of vapor, which cannot arise from the chilled metal surfaces. This is proved by the fact that a lightning arrester, which will not short-circuit on 2,400 volts alternating, will hold an arc on 500 volts direct-current.

Installing Lightning Arresters.—The principle on which a lightning arrester is selected for any particular voltage is, that it must be the weakest spot in the line. The voltage required to jump all the air spaces should be less than that which will puncture the insulation of the apparatus to be protected. The proper number of gaps for different voltages can be determined by experiment with plants in actual operation It has been ascertained by tests at Niagara that, for 11,000 volts, 14 air gaps of $\frac{1}{32}$ inch in connection with carbon resistances, afford full protection with a margin of safety. Circuits above 2,000 volts are protected by standard 2,000 volt arresters placed in series.

Fig. 102 shows the connections and method of installing the $G.E.$ arrester for 10,000 volt circuits.

The oscillatory character of the lightning discharge gives rise to great self-induction in the circuit. It would seem as if a choking coil placed between the arrester and the electrical apparatus would offer such resistance to the discharge as to force it, under all conditions, through the

STATION EQUIPMENT AND APPARATUS. 153

arrester, and thence to the ground. In actual service it has been found that the choking coil does not always offer this resistance, and for this reason its usefulness has been questioned.

The uncertainty of action of one choking coil in the circuit is no proof of its inefficiency. There is good reason

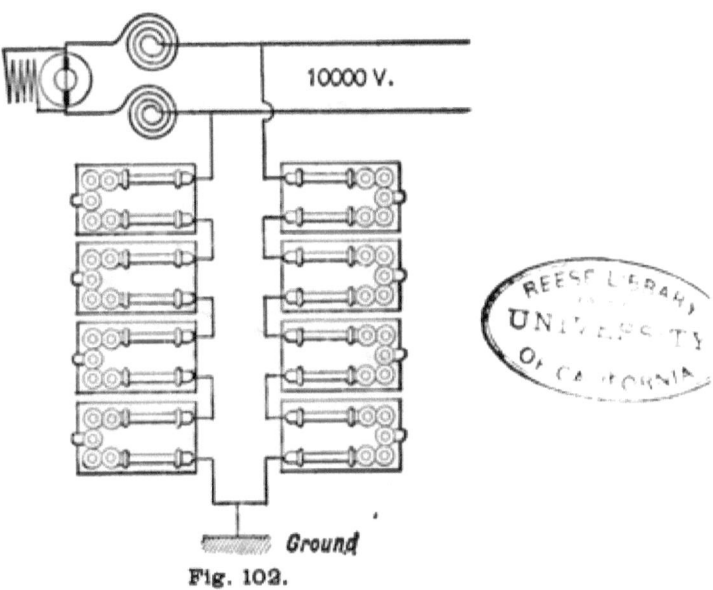

Fig. 102.

to believe that this oscillatory discharge has a wave-like motion, with maxima and minima points. If the arrester happens to be placed at a point of interference,—a nodal point—the coil cannot force the discharge through the arrester. This difficulty may be overcome by the use of a series of coils and arresters, arranged as illustrated in Fig. 103. This shows one end of a 2,000 volt, three-phase system of conductors. The choking coil may be made by winding 150 feet of the line wire into a coil, the inside diameter of which is not less than 15 inches.

The grounding of lightning arresters must be most carefully made, as upon attention to this depends the reliability of the working of the arresters. The connections to ground and line should be made by short straight wires, of not less than No. 4 size. A metal plate, or long pipe,

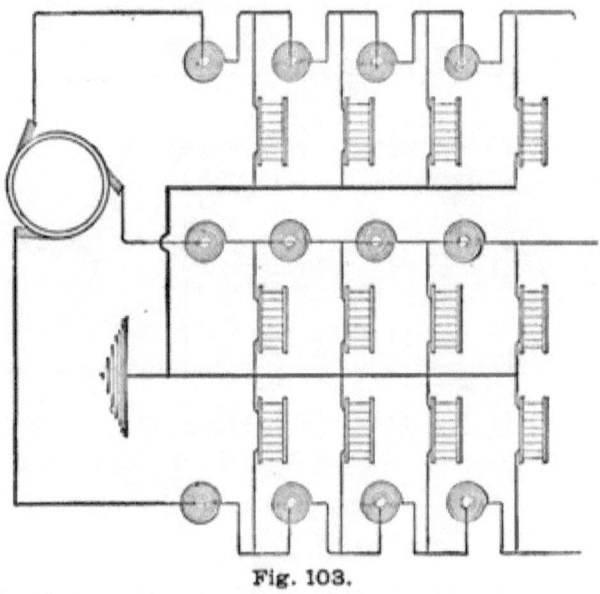

Fig. 103.

should serve as the ground terminal, embedded in coke or sunk in damp ground if possible. Fig. 104 illustrates a very effective method of grounding a line arrester. It is better to use a ground plate with station arresters.

Synchronizing Devices. — The ordinary method of determining whether two alternating generators are in parallel, is by the use of two transformers and lamps, as described in Chapter III. This is an excellent and effective method,

STATION EQUIPMENT AND APPARATUS. 155

and is reliable under almost all conditions. A special device, called the acoustic synchronizer, is sometimes used.

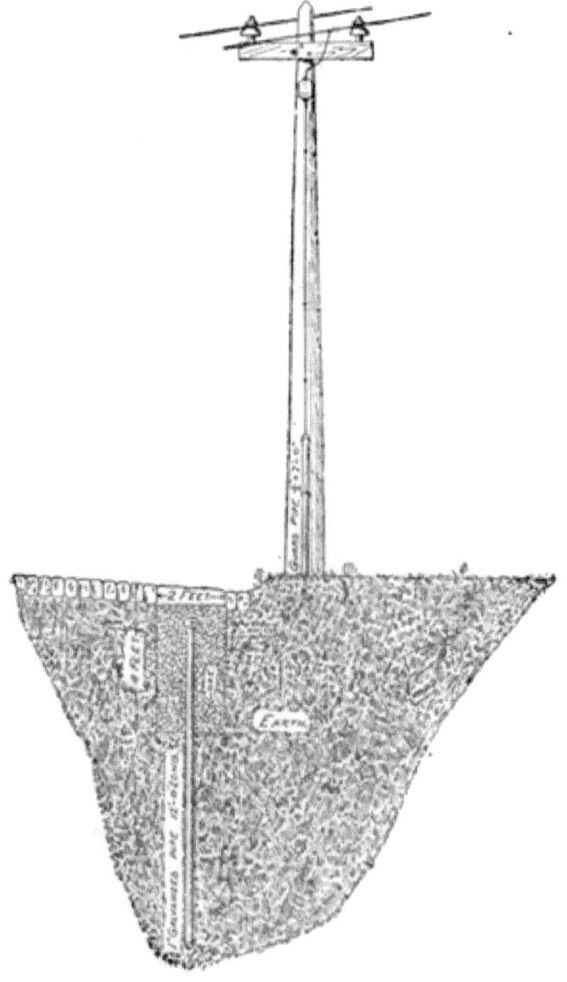

Fig. 104.

This consists of two electro-magnets, actuating two enclosed diaphragms by currents from the machines to be synchronized. When the generators are out of phase, the instrument gives out a loud pulsating note, which grows feebler as synchronism is approached. The acoustic synchronizer, while accurate, is not vigorous in its action, especially in noisy stations and on circuits of low frequency. An instrument called the synchronoscope has been developed for low-frequency circuits, by the Westinghouse Company. This apparatus is similar in appearance to a round-dial voltmeter or ammeter. When no current flows between the machines, the needle stands at zero. When there is a phase difference, a slight current flows around a magnet, which deflects the needle.

Insulators. — On transmission lines, conveying currents at potentials of 10,000 volts, or thereabouts, and over, it is common practice to employ porcelain insulators. Glass is generally used, and has been found most satisfactory as an insulating line material for potentials lower than 10,000 volts.

Line insulators for heavy service, such as high-tension transmission of power, should, in an eminent degree, possess two qualities:

1st. — Thorough insulation under all conditions of operation.
2d. — Great mechanical strength.

When formed into large masses, porcelain is supposed to be superior to glass in both these respects. Glass is an almost absolute non-conductor of electricity, but is said to be hygroscopic, i. e., condenses water on its surface from the atmosphere, and thus allows a leakage of the current. When massive, glass is somewhat difficult to anneal, and hence is not always as strong mechanically as desirable.

STATION EQUIPMENT AND APPARATUS. 157

Porcelain for insulators should be thoroughly vitrified and homogeneous. The material should be absolutely non-absorbent of moisture, and sufficient to insulate the line even without the surface glazing. Poor porcelain can easily be detected by the appearance of the fracture, and its porous quality by soaking in red ink. Well-vitrified porcelain will show no signs of ink when washed; the poor material will readily absorb it. An inch thickness of porous porcelain will be punctured by 10,000 volts, while the same thickness of vitrified material has failed to break down under a pressure of over 100,000 volts. Only the general character of porcelain insulators can be determined in this rough manner. To determine the actual insulating

Fig. 105.

strength, each insulator should be submitted to a high potential test.

This test is best made by placing a number of insulators inverted in a metal pan, filled with a brine solution to the depth of two inches. The brine also fills the pin holes. In each pin hole is placed a metal rod. All the rods are connected to one terminal of a high-potential circuit, and the pan to the other. The testing pressure used is generally about 40,000 volts for 25,000 volts service. When the circuit is closed, the defective insulators are punctured, and are manifested by a shower of bright sparks. Fig. 105 shows a group of high-tension porcelain insulators.

While porcelain is a superior material for insulators, its much greater cost than glass is a serious drawback. Experience in their manufacture has largely overcome the difficulty of properly annealing large glass insulators. In dry climates, the hygroscopic property of glass is practically *nil*.

Under such conditions it would seem as if glass insulators would be entirely satisfactory, even for the highest voltages that may be commercially employed. It is not at all improbable that, with the experience to be obtained as their use increases, glass insulators will replace porcelain insulators. They have been already successfully used for very high voltages,—notably in the Provo transmission, which employs 40,000 volts, this being the highest voltage yet attempted in practice. The insulator known as the Provo type is illustrated in Fig. 106. It is a triple petticoat insulator, having a diameter of 7 inches and a height of 6 inches. It weighs 4 lbs. 7 oz.

A novel insulator, embodying the insulating properties of glass and the non-hygroscopic property of porcelain, has

STATION EQUIPMENT AND APPARATUS. 159

Fig. 106.

recently been brought out. This insulator consists of a porcelain body and an inner glass sheath, containing the screw pin hole.

Pressure Regulators.—One form of regulator, for varying the pressure of an alternating-current circuit, may be likened to an induction motor with its armature blocked so as to remain stationary, but which at the same time is capable of being placed in various positions, thereby changing the mutual induction of the coils. As ordinarily constructed, the regulator consists of what corresponds to the field and to the armature of an induction motor. A hollow cylindrical structure built of laminated iron is provided, on its interior surface, with four slots, in which are placed two coils at right angles to each other. Inside of these coils a movable laminated core is placed, in such a manner that its position can be changed with respect to the field. The winding of the primary or field is connected across the lines. While in the induction motor, the armature, or secondary winding, is short-circuited upon itself, in the regulator the armature or secondary winding is connected in series with the circuit so as to add its voltage to, or subtract it from, that of the line, according to its relative position in regard to the primary winding. Since the regulator has some self-induction, and requires magnetizing current, the maximum possible boosting obtainable is about 10 per cent less than the minimum reducing effect. The arrangement and the connections of this regulator can be seen in diagram Fig. 107.

Another type of regulator, built on the same lines, is sometimes constructed to take care of all the branches of a two- or three-phase circuit. The regulator described enables the voltage of a circuit to be raised and lowered

STATION EQUIPMENT AND APPARATUS. 161

without change of connections, and adjustments of pressure are obtained by imperceptible degrees.

The Stillwell regulator is another form of apparatus for raising or lowering the pressure in feeder wires. It is a transformer, the primary of which is connected across the

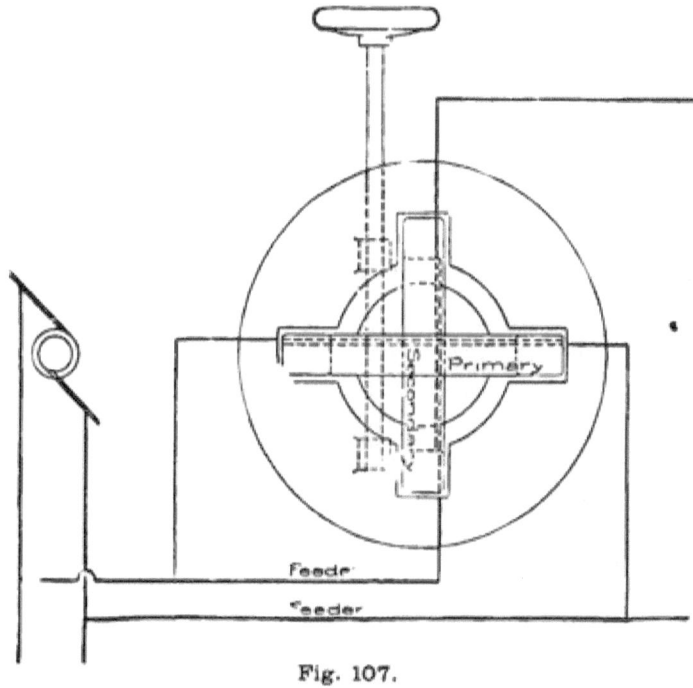

Fig. 107.

circuit and the secondary of which is in series with the feeder whose voltage is to be regulated. The cut (Fig. 108) shows the general appearance of this regulator. The secondary is divided into a number of coils which can be inserted or removed from the circuit, according to the amount of variation of voltage desired. A reversing switch is provided, so that the $E.M.F.$ generated in the regulator can be either added to or subtracted from the pressure of the feeder.

Some of the important uses to which pressure regulators can be put are the following: For regulating the voltage of alternating-current feeders; for equalizing voltage on unbalanced polyphase circuits; as dimmers for theatres; as regulators for series-alternating circuits, either for arc or incandescent lights.

The rating in watts is the product of the secondary current in amperes, by the boosting capacity in volts.

Rectifiers.—A rectifier is a device for changing an alternating current into a direct current, and is intended mainly for the operation of series arc lamps. The apparatus usually consists of a constant-current transformer, giving constant alternating current at all loads, and a rectifying device which runs in synchronism with the alternating, and converts the constant

Fig. 108.

alternating current into a direct current, but more or less pulsating.

At light loads the rectifier has an idle current of nearly 100 per cent of full-load current, and at full load a low power-factor. For polyphase circuits, therefore, to avoid unbalancing of the phases, the rectifier should preferably be of polyphase design.

Frequency Changer. — In alternating-current plants, employing a low frequency, there is sometimes a need for a limited amount of current of a higher frequency. For instance, in 25 and 40 cycle installations, incandescent and arc lighting may be required. To meet such cases a frequency of 60 cycles, or any other number of cycles suitable for lighting, may be obtained most economically and cheaply by means of a frequency changer. This is essentially an induction motor, the armature of which is rotated by a synchronous motor in a direction usually opposite to its natural rotation. The lower frequency current is fed to the primary or field, and the current at the higher frequency is taken out of the secondary or armature by means of collector rings. The frequency and voltage of the output will depend on the speed of the secondary, and will be the algebraic sum of the current pulsations in both members. If the secondary is run at rated speed, but in opposition to its natural rotation, the frequency will be twice that of the normal current, or if run at one-half speed in its natural direction, the frequency will be one-half the normal. To change a frequency of 40 cycles to 60 cycles, the secondary would be run at one-half speed in an opposite direction, while to obtain 60 cycles from a 25 cycle current, the secondary would run nearly two and one-half times the rated speed in an opposite direction.

164 POLYPHASE APPARATUS AND SYSTEMS.

The capacity of the driving-motor end of the frequency changer bears the same proportion to the total output that the increase in frequency bears to the final frequency. The secondary of the frequency changer proper must equal the output. The capacity of the primary has the same proportion to the total output that the initial frequency has to the final frequency. As an illustration,— a 100 K.W.

Fig. 109.

frequency changer, primary 40 cycles, secondary 60 cycles, would be composed as follows: A 40 cycle synchronous motor, capacity 33 K.W., speed 600 R.P.M., direct-connected to the secondary, capacity 100 K.W. Primary capacity would be 66 K.W. The primary would be four polar. The natural speed of the secondary would be 1,200 R.P.M. By driving it at a speed of 600 R.P.M. in the opposite direction to its natural rotation, the number of reversals will be that due to an equivalent speed of 1,800 $R.P.M.$, or 60 cycles. For the sake of illustration, the capacities as given above are on the assumption of a 100 per cent efficiency, which, of course, is an impossibility. Fig. 109 depicts the general form of this apparatus.

Motor Generators.—A motor generator for alternating-current work consists of an induction or synchronous motor, mounted on the same base and direct connected to a generator. It may perform the functions of a frequency changer, in which case the generator, of course, is of the alternating-current type, or it may be used in place of a rotary converter, the generator then delivering a direct current. Although more expensive and less efficient than a rotary converter, the motor generator has the advantage of not always requiring step-down transformers. It is self-regulating, and is not materially affected by potential fluctuations of the transmission lines.

CHAPTER IX.

TWO-PHASE SYSTEM.

Polyphase Systems and Combinations.— Any arrangement of conductors, carrying two or more single-phase alternating currents, definitely related to one another in point of time, constitutes a polyphase system. The systems commonly employed for the generation and distribution of power by polyphase currents are the two-phase, three-phase, and a third system, which is a combination of a single-phase and polyphase conductor arrangement, called the monocyclic system.

Polyphase currents are usually produced by generators, the armatures of which are so wound that the electromotive forces at the terminals correspond to the number of phases, and arrive at a maximum in a fixed and definite relation to one another.

In the two-phase system the two electro-motive forces and currents are 90°, or one-fourth of a cycle, apart. The relations of the curves to each other, and their instantaneous values, can be seen from the development of the diagram of single harmonic motion (Fig. 110). The maximum of one wave occurs when the value of the other is zero. If the pressure in any one of the coils Oa or Ob is 1, the pressure between the ends ab is $\sqrt{2} = 1.414$.

The windings of a polyphase machine may be combined in a number of ways, each affecting the relation of the

TWO-PHASE SYSTEM. 167

electro-motive forces of the outside conductors, as shown in Figs. 111 to 114. These diagrammatically represent the coils of a two-phase machine, in which the electro-

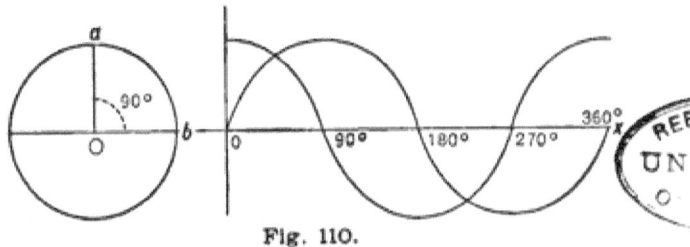

Fig. 110.

motive forces may be considered as being either generated or absorbed. In Fig. 111 all the coils are in series, forming a continuous winding, tapped at four points. This arrangement is known as an interlinked winding. Leads 1 and 2 constitute the circuit of one phase, and 3 and 4 that of the second phase. The $E.M.F.$ between the wires of different phases is 1.4 times that between leads of the same phase. In Fig. 112 the windings of each phase are separate. This arrangement can be made interlinked by joining the two circuits where they cross, thus forming a common centre, as shown in Fig. 113. The relation of $E.M.F.$

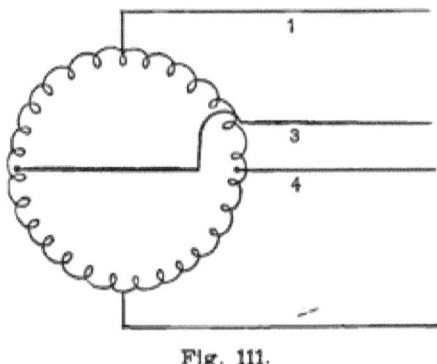

Fig. 111.

is the same as in Fig. 112. The grouping of coils, shown in Fig. 112, may also be made interlinked by joining leads 3 and 4 (Fig. 114), which become a common return for 1

168   POLYPHASE APPARATUS AND SYSTEMS.

and 2. The *E.M.F.* between the two outgoing wires is 1.4 times that between each outgoing wire and the common return.

The windings of interlinked systems are classed according to their connections as "Ring," or "Star." Figs. 111 and 113 respectively, show the ring and star connections of the two-phase system.

In the three-phase system, the ring and star connections

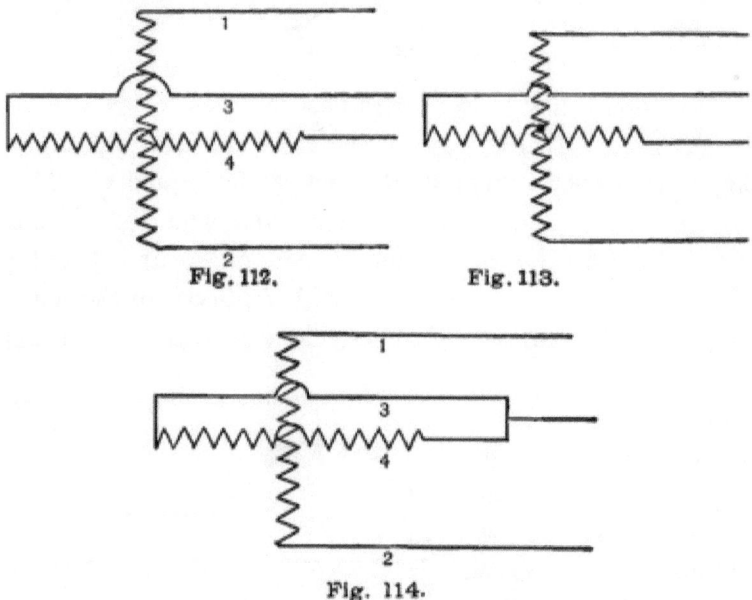

Fig. 112.   Fig. 113.

Fig. 114.

are usually designated as Y and Δ (Delta), from their resemblance to these symbols.

The winding connections of most commercial two-phase machines are interlinked. Fig. 115 shows the connections of a Westinghouse two-phase 2,000 volt generator. Connections are made to the winding at four points.

The current in the circuit 1–3 is 90° apart from, or in

TWO-PHASE SYSTEM. 169

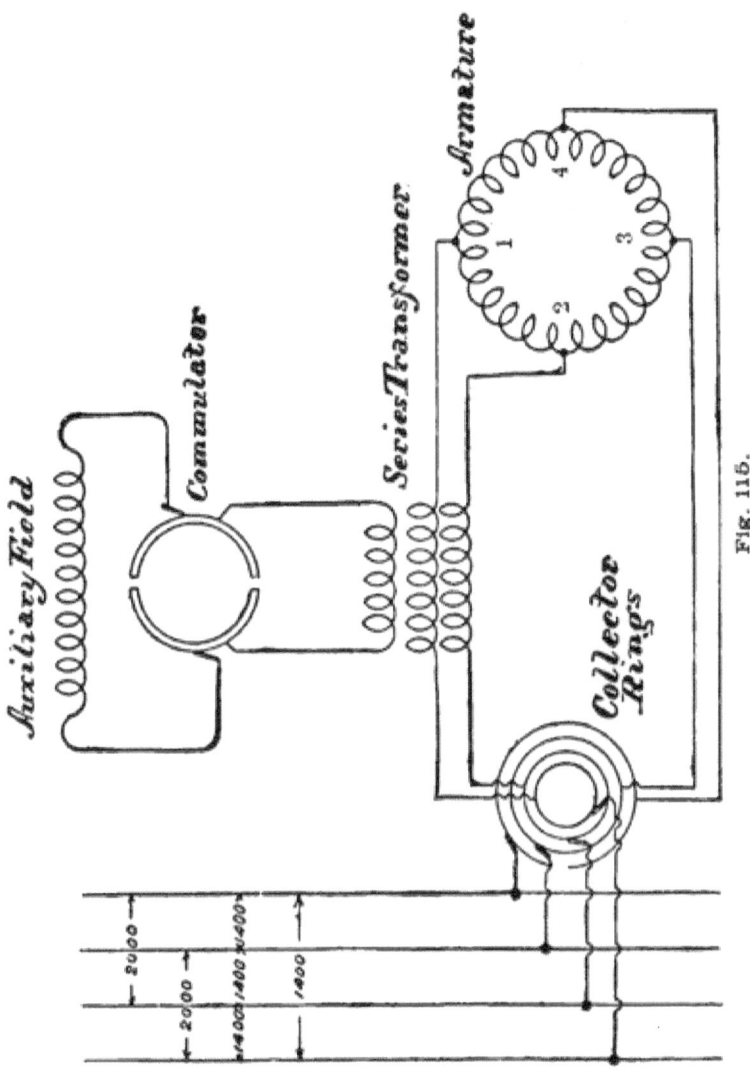

Fig. 116.

quadrature with, the current in the circuit 2–4. The *E.M.F.* existing between any two adjacent terminals is 1,400 volts. If the *E.M.F.* is raised or lowered, the same proportions hold; and for a 1,000 volt machine, the electro-motive forces are respectively 1,000 and 700 volts.

No matter what the arrangement of the winding may be in a polyphase machine, whether the coils are interlinked, or separately grouped, ring or star connected, the principles of action are the same, and the characteristic polyphase results are equally present.

Polyphase systems have two desirable features: First, the supply of power is continuous and uniform, thus increasing the capacity of apparatus, and in some systems,

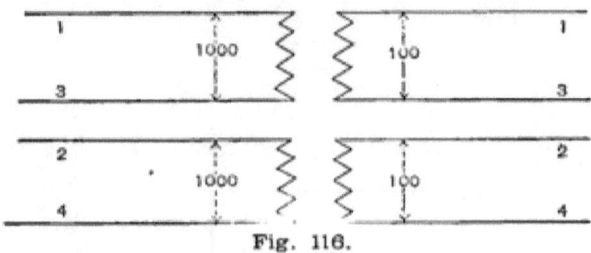

Fig. 116.

that of transmission conductors; and, second, the use of revolving types of induction apparatus is permitted, which do not require any form of moving contacts.

Transformer Connections.—A number of combinations of two-phase circuits can be made by suitably arranging transformers with due regard to the generator windings. Fig. 116 shows the connections commonly used for lighting and transmission of power. The arrangement consists of two single-phase transformers, the phases being separated in both primary and secondary. Two of the secondary leads are sometimes joined (Fig. 117), making a common return for the other wires. The two circuits being 90° apart, the voltage between 1 and 4 is $\sqrt{2}$ times that between the outside wires and the common return. This arrangement is best adapted for supplying current of minimum potential to apparatus in the vicinity of the transformers. It is more frequently used in connection with motors operating from the secondaries of the transformers.

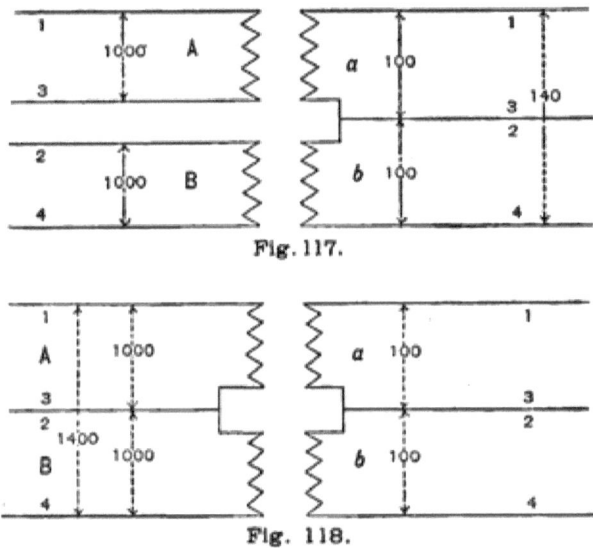

Fig. 117.

Fig. 118.

Fig. 118 shows another arrangement of transformers where the common return is used on both primary and secondary. As will be explained farther on, this connection is permissible only when the power of the two circuits is consumed by one unit, or when both sides of the system are balanced.

Two-Phase to Three-Phase.—It is possible, by a combination of two transformers, to change one polyphase system into any other polyphase system. The transformation from two-phase to three-phase, or *vice versa*, is effected by proportioning the windings, as shown in Fig. 119. One transformer is wound with a ratio of transformation of 1,000 to 100; the other with a ratio of 1,000 to 86.7. The secondary of this transformer is connected to the middle of the secondary winding of the first. In Fig. 120, *AB* represents the secondary volts from *A* to *B* in one transformer. At right angles to *AB* the line *CO* represents, in direction and quantity, the pressure *O* to *C* of the second transformer. From the properties of the triangle it follows that, at the terminals *A*, *B*, *C*, three equal pressures will exist, each differing from the others by 60°, and giving rise to a three-phase current.

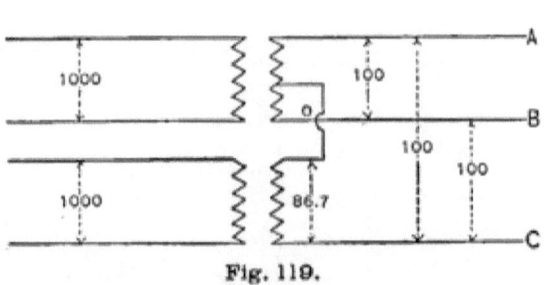

Fig. 119.

For this transformation on a small scale, it is customary to use standard transformers, the main transformer having a ratio of 10 to 1, and the teaser a ratio of 9 to 1.

The current in the winding *OC*, being a resultant of the other two phases, is greater than if the change to three-phase were not made; and, consequently, for the same heating,

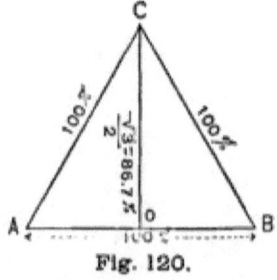

Fig. 120.

necessitates more transformer capacity. Only one transformer, the teaser, need be of greater output. The increase is in the secondary, being 15 per cent, or about 4 per cent of the total transformer capacity. If the transformers are interchangeable, the excess capacity required in the two transformers is over 12 per cent. The secondary of each interchangeable transformer has two taps, giving 50 per cent and 86.7 per cent of the full voltage, so that either transformer can serve as the teaser, or supplementary one, by using the proper terminals.

In the long-distance transmission of power the generators are sometimes wound two-phase, and the secondary

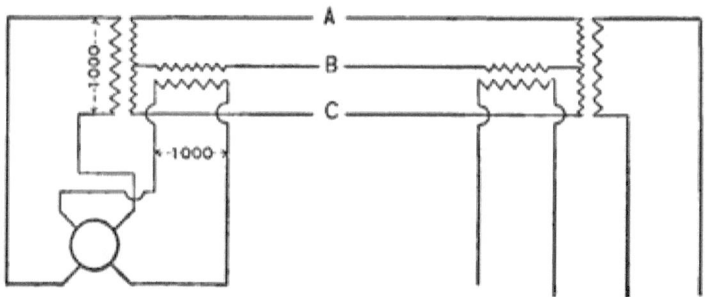

Fig. 121.

distribution at the receiving end is likewise by the two-phase system, while on account of the saving in copper the transmission is by the three-phase system. Such is the arrangement of the apparatus at the generating end of the Niagara-Buffalo plant. The distribution in Buffalo, however, is mainly by the three-phase system. Fig. 121 shows the transformer connections for changing two-phase to three-phase and back again.

Two-Phase Four-Wire System. — This system consists of two separate circuits, derived from two independent armature windings in quadrature with each other, or from a continuous armature winding tapped at four equidistant points. The practical application of this system is illustrated in Fig. 122. Each of the two generators A and B delivers two-phase currents of low potential to the step-up transformers RT, RT', RT'', RT''', through the switchboard D. The transmission lines L, L', L'', L''', receive and transmit current, at a high pressure, to a substation conveniently located with reference to the districts where lights and motors are to be supplied. The high-potential current is here reduced by the transformers LT, LT', LT'', LT''', to a commercial pressure suitable for local distribution, through the switchboard F. Beginning at the right of the figure, the first four-wire system is used to supply alternating current to the rotary converter, which, in turn, delivers direct current at 500 volts to a trolley line operating the street-car systems K. The second circuit supplies the motors M, M', M'', M''', either of the synchronous or induction type. The next four-wire system is divided into two distinct circuits, supplying current to incandescent lamps through the transformers b, b', B'', B'''. The next circuit supplies current for arc lighting through a rotary converter. Another rotary converter is operated from the last circuit, and delivers low-voltage current for electrolytic purposes. The rotary converters in practice are supplied with transformers, not shown in the diagram, which deliver, at the rotary terminals, an alternating current of the proper voltage.

The two single circuits must be balanced as nearly as possible, and for this purpose the four wires must be carried through the same district to be supplied with power or light. In order to obtain economy in copper in a secondary system of distribution, it is desirable to use three-wire mains. In the two-phase four-wire system, where

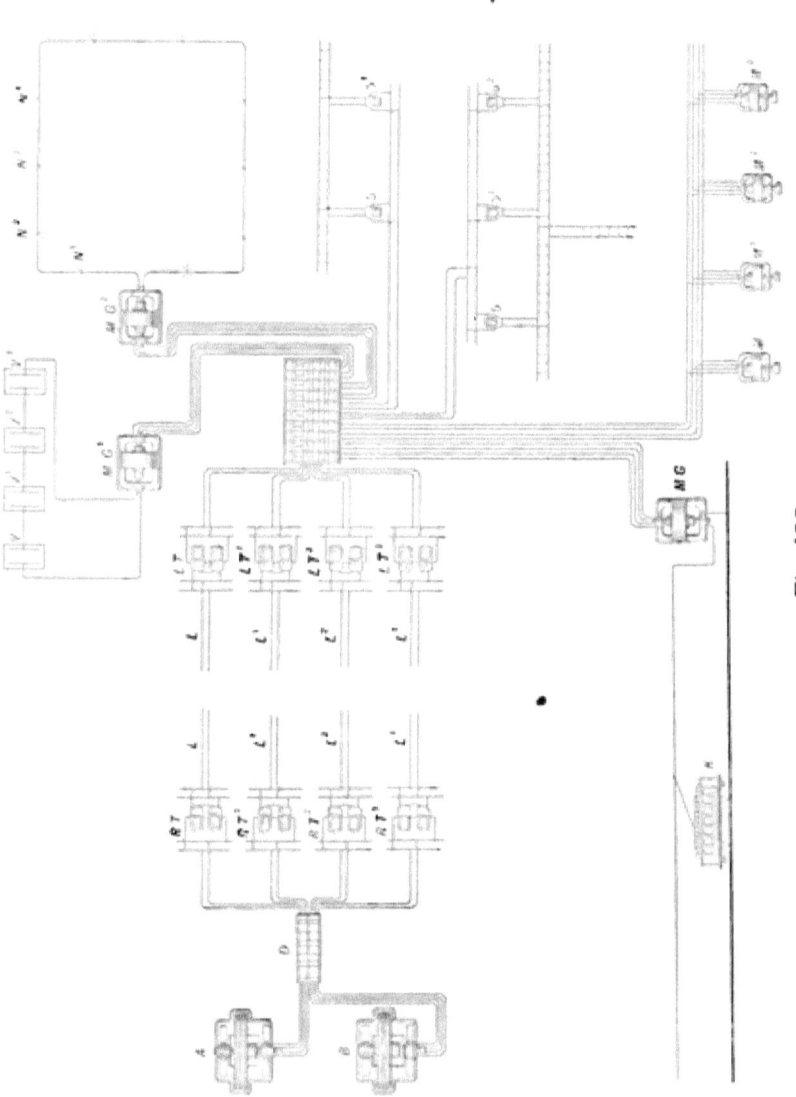

Fig. 122.

motors are to be supplied, the two independent three-wire circuits must be brought together, making six wires in all.

The measurement of power by this system is obtained by the use of a wattmeter inserted in each circuit, as in a single-phase system. The sum of the two readings gives

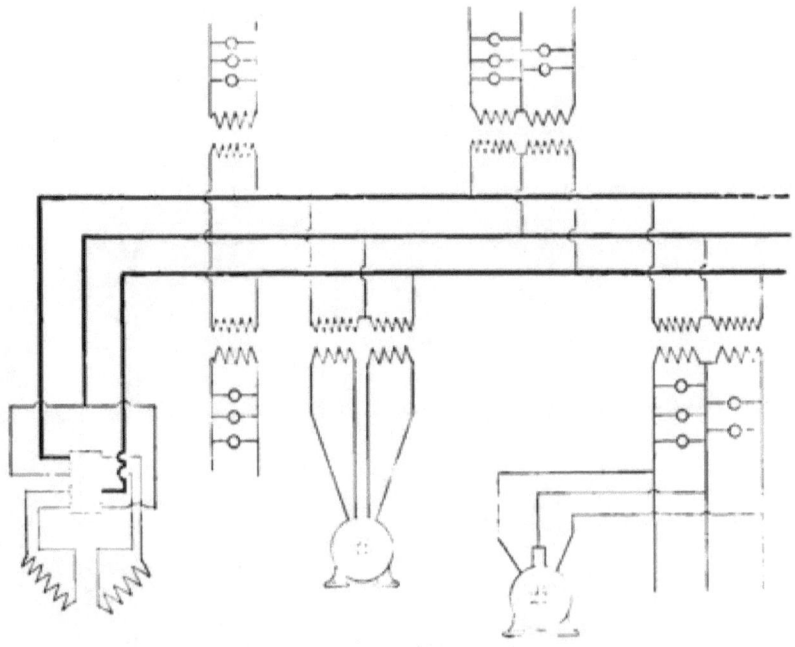

Fig. 123.

the total power supplied. In a balanced system, twice the reading of one wattmeter will give the power.

Two-Phase Three-Wire System. — By joining any two conductors in the four-wire system, a common return is made for the two circuits. This arrangement of circuits is called the two-phase three-wire system. As previously shown, the pressure between the common conductor and the others is 42 per cent higher than that which existed before. With a given load and insulation strain, the common conductor must be made larger in proportion, in order to keep the loss the same.

The general application of this system is shown in Fig. 123. Two terminals of the generator coils are united; and the three leads, forming an interconnected two-phase system, are run to wherever motors and lights are to be supplied. When motors are used, connection is made directly with the main leads, or, if the motors are wound for low voltage, connection is made through two transformers. The motors, which are of the ordinary two-phase type, may have their terminals connected either on the three-wire or four-wire system.

Where lights are supplied, the transformers may be connected singly to only one circuit, or in pairs on two circuits, with a common return. In practice, it is essential that both phases be equally loaded.

In this arrangement of conductors there is an unbalancing of both sides of the system on an inductive load, which exists, even though the energy load is equally divided. This unbalancing is due to the fact that the $E.M.F.$ of self-induction in one side of the system is in phase with the effective $E.M.F.$ in the other side, thus distorting the uniform current-distribution in both circuits.

The distribution of currents and electromotive forces in the three conductors in the single-phase three-wire, the three-phase and the two-phase three-wire system, is shown in the following table. The figures are the results of experiments to determine the self-induction of underground tubes.

175 Feet 250,000 C.M. Edison 3 Conductors. Main Tube.	Amperes in Conductors.			Volts Between Conductors.						At End of Line.			Watts Lost in Line (Governing Capacity of Tube.
				At Feeding Point.			60 Cycles			125 Cycles.			
	a	b	c	a & b	b & c	a & c	a & b	b & c	a & c	a & b	b & c	a & c	
Single-Phase 3 Wire	400	0	400	100	100	200	97	97	194	96.6	96.6	193.2	2,400
Three-Phase 3 Wire	462	462	462	100	100	100	94	94	84	93.4	93.4	93.4	4,800
Two-Phase 3 Wire	400	566	400	100	100	142	90	97	134	87.	99.	136.	4,800

TWO-PHASE SYSTEM. 179

The single-phase and the three-phase systems give equal drops, but the induction unbalancing of the two-phase three-wire system is beyond the range of practical operation. These results were obtained with low-tension systems and moderate drops. The unbalancing effect is much greater with higher voltage and drops. The four-wire two-phase system would, of course, show no such unbalancing.

The two-phase system is admirably adapted for lighting distribution when the two circuits are not connected. In places having already single-phase wiring, the change to polyphase would often require considerable and expensive alterations with any system but the two-phase.

CHAPTER X.

THREE-PHASE SYSTEM.

Curves of E.M.F. — The *E.M.F.* impulses in a three-phase system follow one another at intervals of 60°. The instantaneous values and the relation of phases, developed from the diagram of simple harmonic motions, are shown in Fig. 124. The curves Oa, Ob, Oc, represent the electromotive forces produced by three sets of generator coils. If the distance from O to a, b, and c, be taken equal to 1, it

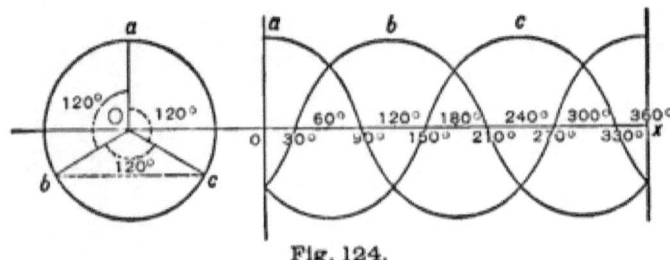

Fig. 124.

follows from the diagram that the lines joining a, b, and c are equal to $\sqrt{3} = 1.732$. That is, the pressure between the ends of any two of the generator coils in a three-phase system is 1.732 times that between the common juncture O and the terminals of the coils.

It will be seen from the diagram that each one of the coils successively serves as a return for the other two, and that the algebraic sum of the currents in the system is zero. The three-phase system may be resolved into three single circuits, with a common or grounded return. The sum of the currents being zero, no current will flow in the return conductor, and it may be dispensed with. The system then becomes the ordinary Y-connected arrangement.

Transformer Combinations. — The ring and the star connections of three-phase windings, — whether of armature in

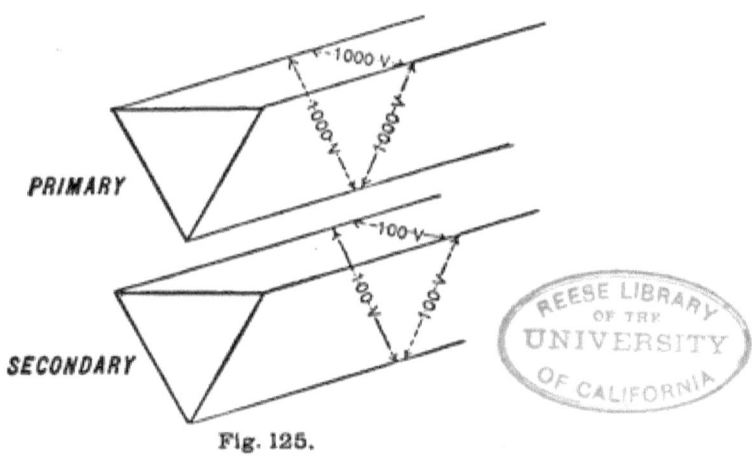

Fig. 125.

which the electromotive forces are induced, or transformer, or motor in which the electromotive forces are absorbed, — are designated by the symbols Δ and Y respectively. Figs. 125 to 129 illustrate the various three-phase combinations of single-phase transformers in practical operation. Fig. 125 shows Δ connection of both primary and secondary terminals of transformers, having a ratio of 10 to 1. Fig. 126 shows three transformers, Y connected in both windings. The ratio of pressures between any two corresponding terminals in primary and secondary are the same as in the Δ arrangement. The individual transformers

182   POLYPHASE APPARATUS AND SYSTEMS.

thus connected have fewer turns for the same voltage than when Δ connected, and thus this arrangement is suitable for very high line-pressures. Fig. 127 shows a combination of Δ and Y connection, the primaries of the transformers being

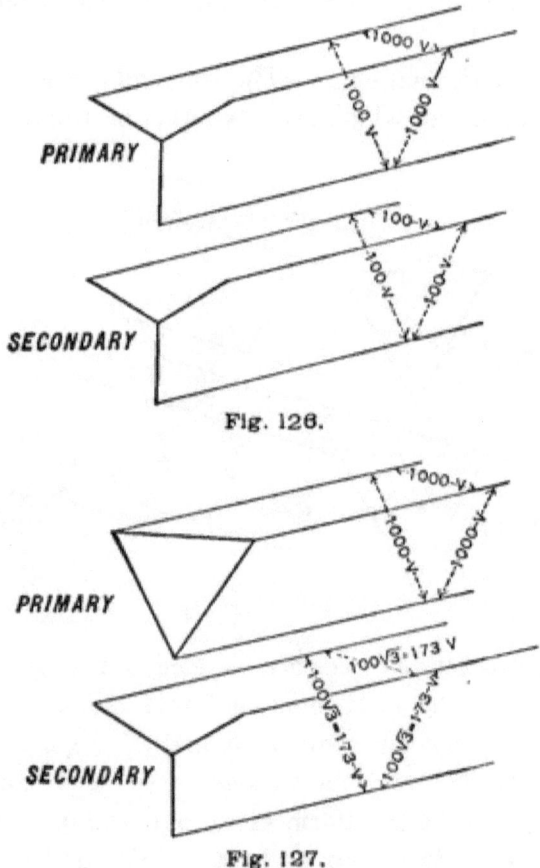

Fig. 126.

Fig. 127.

connected Δ, while the secondaries are connected Y. A fourth wire may be led from the common centre of the three secondaries. The pressure between this neutral and any one of the outside wires is $\dfrac{1}{\sqrt{3}}$ of the pressure between the outside wires. This arrangement is known as the "three-phase four-wire system," and is especially convenient and economical in secondary distributing systems. In

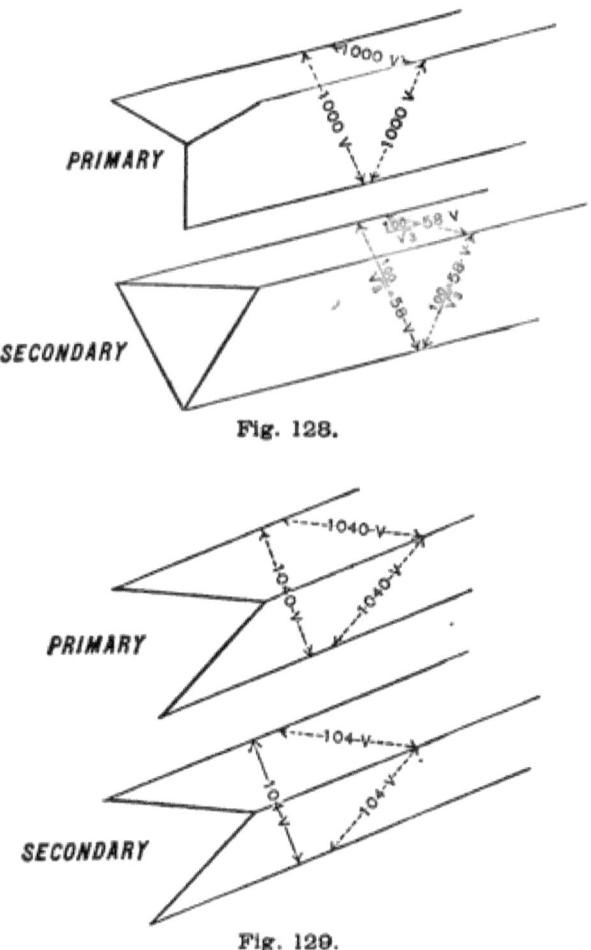

Fig. 128.

Fig. 129.

Fig. 128, the primaries are connected Y, the secondaries Δ. The Δ connection is sometimes made up of two transformers (Fig. 129), instead of three. The pressures be-

184   POLYPHASE APPARATUS AND SYSTEMS.

tween all three terminals are equal, that from the open side of the triangle being the resultant of the $E.M.F.$ in the existing windings. This arrangement is frequently used with motors, its chief advantages being its simplicity, and permitting the use of available transformers, when the motor cannot be fitted with three transformers of exactly the capacity wanted. Its disadvantage is that the motor will stop in case of accident to one transformer. The combination of three transformers, arranged in Δ, is most convenient and desirable, for the reason that an accident to

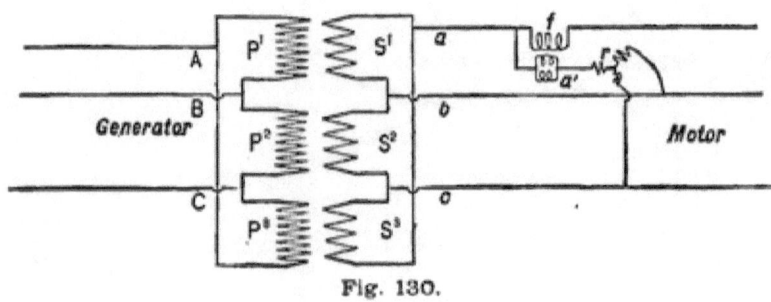

Fig. 130.

one does not interrupt the service; the only requirement being, that the load be reduced one-third, to prevent heating of the transformers. Another disadvantage of the resultant Δ arrangement is the increased transformer capacity required, as, for the same total energy, the flow of current is increased through the two existing secondaries. This disadvantage is not so noticeable in small transformers, but must be allowed for when working with large transformers.

Motor Connections. — Motors are connected to the secondaries of three transformers in a three-phase system, as shown in Fig. 130.

The primaries, p–1, p–2, p–3, of three transformers are connected between the three lines A, B, C, leading from the generator, and three secondaries, S-1, S-2, S-3, are connected in delta to the three lines a, b, c, leading to the motor. A recording wattmeter of the three-phase type, for measuring the power consumed by the motor, is shown connected in the system with the field spools at f, the armature circuit a' and its resistances r, between the three secondary lines.

Induction motors may be supplied from a three-phase generator by means of two reducing transformers in the manner shown in Fig. 131. This arrangement is identical

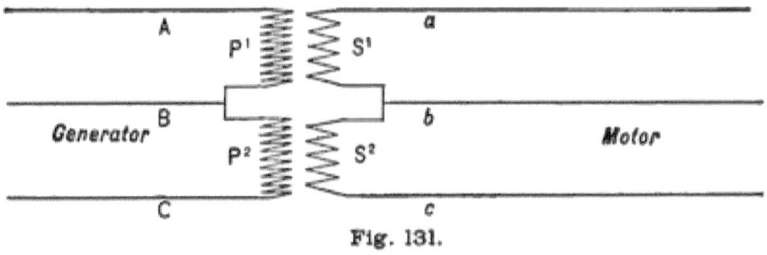

Fig. 131.

with that in Fig. 130, except that one of the transformers, P-3, S-3, is left out, and the two other transformers are made correspondingly larger. The recording wattmeter is connected in the secondary circuit in the same way as in the use of three transformers.

The connections of three transformers for a low-tension distribution system, by the three-phase four-wire system, are shown in Fig. 132. The three transformers have their primaries, P-1, P-2, P-3, joined in delta connection, and their secondaries, S-1, S-2, S-3, in Y connection. Lines a, b, c, are the three main three-phase lines, and d is the common neutral. The difference of potential between a and b, b and c, and a and c is 200 volts, while that between them and d is 115 volts. 200 volt motors are joined to a, b, and c, while 115 volt lamps are connected between a and d, b and d, or c and d. Line d, like the neutral wire in the Edison three-wire system only carries current when the lamp load is unbalanced.

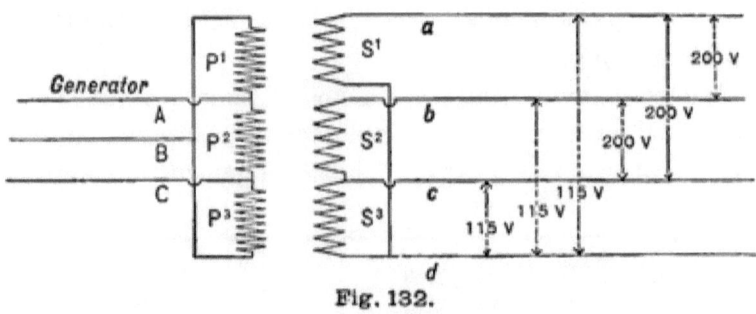

Fig. 132.

Measurement of Power.—In a Y connected generator the $E.M.F.$, induced in each phase, is $\dfrac{E}{\sqrt{3}}$, and the energy in that phase is $I \times \dfrac{E}{\sqrt{3}}$, E being the $E.M.F.$ at the generator terminals. In a Δ connected generator the current in each phase is $\dfrac{I}{\sqrt{3}}$, I being the line current, and the energy is $E \times \dfrac{I}{\sqrt{3}}$. The total energy for the three phases, in the cases both of a Y and a Δ connected generator, is $= \sqrt{3} \times E \times I$. This formula is correct when the generator output is of a non-inductive character. If a phase displacement exists, the expression becomes $\sqrt{3} \times E \times I \times \cos \phi$. These formulas apply equally well for determining the power in a three-phase circuit, irrespective of the method of connections of the supplying source or of the consuming devices.

THREE-PHASE SYSTEM.

As an illustration, — the power in a non-inductive three-phase circuit, in each branch of which 100 amperes is flowing, the voltage between lines being 2,500, is found as follows: the energy in each phase is = 100 amperes × 2,500 volts × $\frac{1}{\sqrt{3}}$ = 145 K.W., and, for the three circuits, is therefore 435 K.W. If the circuit had a power factor of 80 per cent, the energy would then be 435 × .80 = 348 K.W.

The power supplied by three-phase circuits can be measured by the use of three, two, or one wattmeter. Three wattmeters will give the power of a circuit irrespective of the condition of balancing or lag. The sum of the readings of the three instruments is the total power. Each wattmeter must be connected to the common centre or neutral of the system. If the apparatus is connected delta, it is necessary to make an artificial neutral with resistances. Two wattmeters can be connected so that, as long as the power factor is greater than 50 per cent, the sum of the two readings equals the total power. The difference of the two readings will give the power when the power factor is less than 50. As it is not possible to tell when the power factor falls below this point, without reversing the connections, this method is inconvenient and undesirable.

The usual method of measuring power in three-phase circuits is by one wattmeter. Three-phase circuits when interlinked are easily kept in balance in respect to load and power factor. Three times the readings of the single wattmeter will give the total power in the circuits, if they are balanced. Figs. 133 and 134 show the connections of three-phase recording wattmeters for low and for high voltage circuits. The wattmeter is provided with resist-

188   POLYPHASE APPARATUS AND SYSTEMS.

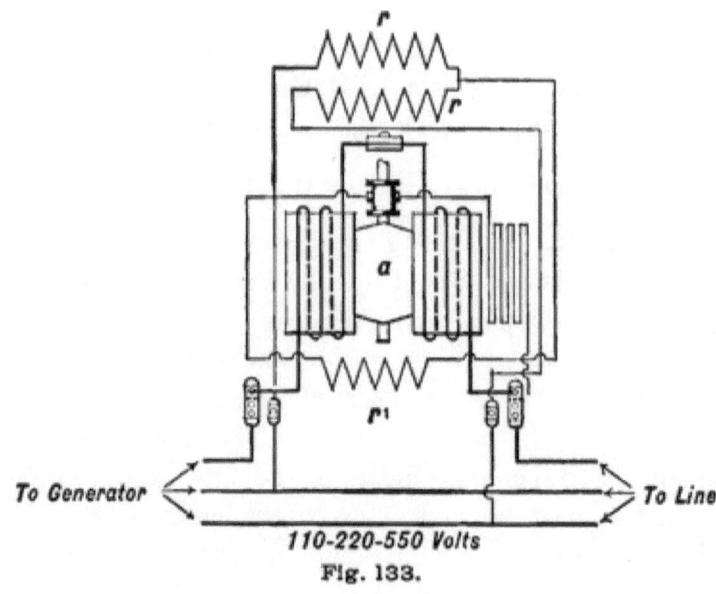

Fig. 133.

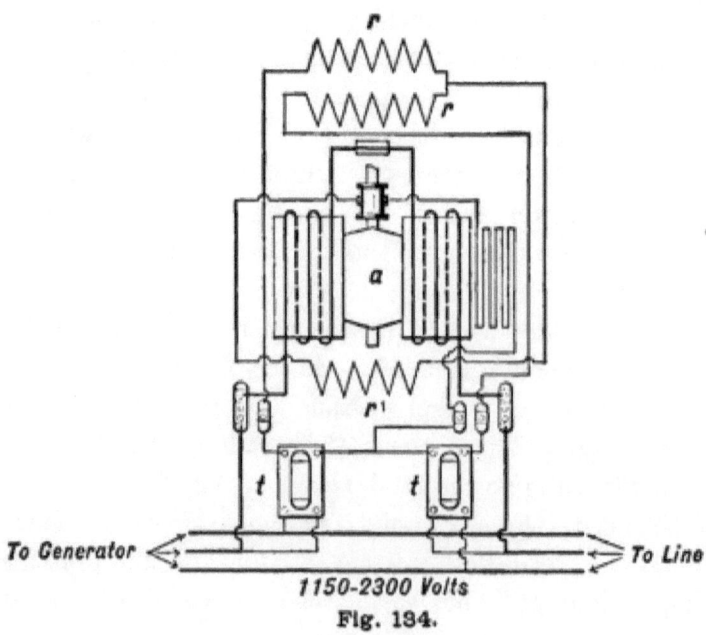

Fig. 134.

THREE-PHASE SYSTEM. 189

ances, rr and r', for creating an artificial neutral. The armature windings are in series with r', so that $r'+a=r$. The wattmeter, diagrammatically illustrated in Fig. 133,

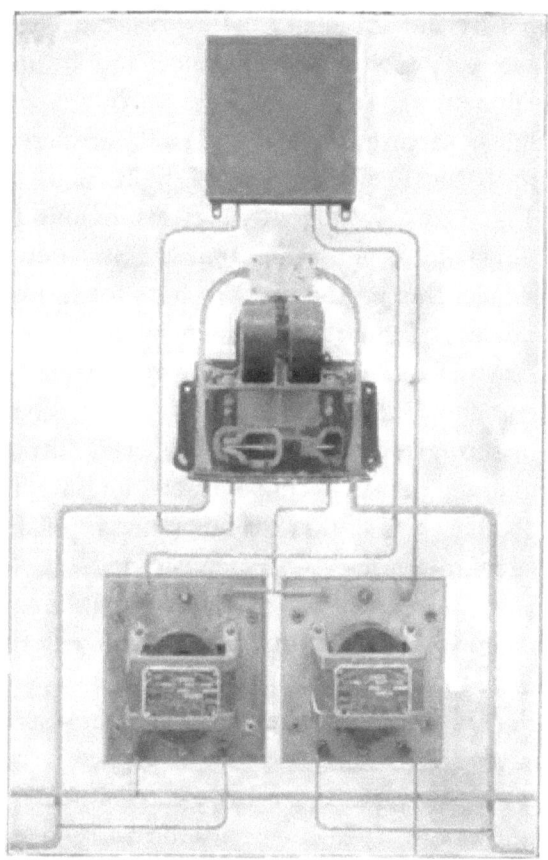

Fig. 135.

is adapted for circuits of 550 volts and less. Fig. 134 shows the connection of a voltmeter for circuits of from 1,000 to 3,000 volts. Station transformers t and t are required to reduce the pressure for the armature windings.

The method of installing, and the connections for this wattmeter transformer, are illustrated by Fig. 135.

The connections for an indicating wattmeter are the same as those for a recording wattmeter. The main current is taken by the stationary or low-resistance coil, while the pressure coil is of high resistance, and connected to the artificial neutral.

Three-Phase Circuits.—The general arrangement of circuits for a local distribution of light and power is shown in Fig. 136. The generators are wound for 2,000 volts, feeding direct into the mains. Step-down transformers reduce the power to 100 volts for light and 200 volts for motors. In one arrangement alternating enclosed arc lights are shown, operated from a transformer. A 200 volt motor is supplied by three transformers, constituting a system of secondary mains. In the second arrangement a motor running from two transformers, and a general distributing system, are shown. The general practice is to wind the generators for 1,040 or 2,080 volts, no load, and use transformers reducing to 115 volts for lights and small motors. Where secondary mains are employed the motor pressure is 200, 220, 440, or 550 volts.

Where lights and motors are located a considerable distance from the generators, the cost of copper is reduced by employing transformers to raise the current pressure. An arrangement of three-phase circuits for transmitting power over long distances is shown in Fig. 137. The generator, direct-connected to the source of power, a water-wheel, is shown at A. B is a bank of step-up transformers, raising the voltage to, say, 20,000. As this voltage is higher than can be used with any apparatus for direct utilization of the current, step-down transformers, C_1, C_2, and C_3, are required.

THREE-PHASE SYSTEM. 191

The main substation contains the transformers, C_1 and C_2. This is a true central or distributing station. From this point the distributing feeders are taken out at, say, 2,080 volts, for the commercial primary circuits and through the bank C_2 at 115 volts, to feed a low-tension network. Through the transformer C_1, a current of 2080 volts is fed direct into a synchronous motor, and into transformers

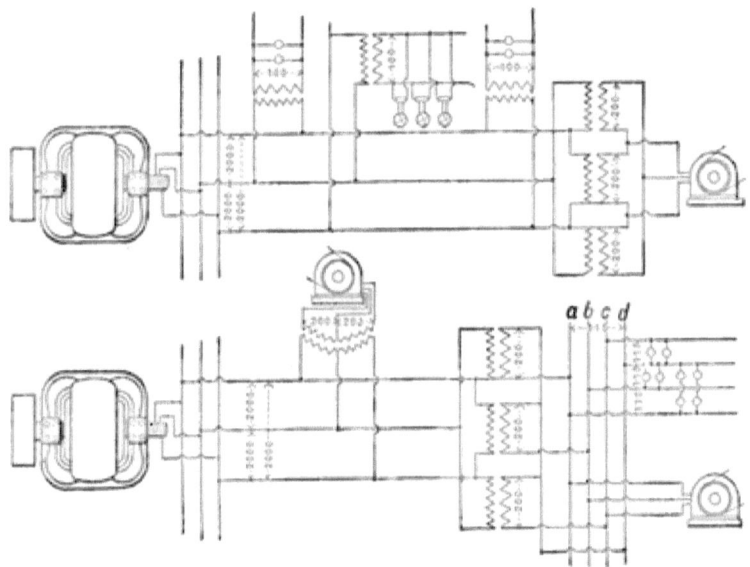

Fig. 136.

reducing to 115 volts for supplying motors and lights. The substation transformers C_2, furnish current for a general lighting and motor service at I, J, and H. The voltage for this distributing system is controlled by the regulators G.

At C_3 another bank of step-down transformers is located. An alternating current of suitable voltage is delivered to the rotary converter D, which supplies continuous current to the electrolytic vats or storage battery E. A rotary might also furnish direct current for electric railway service.

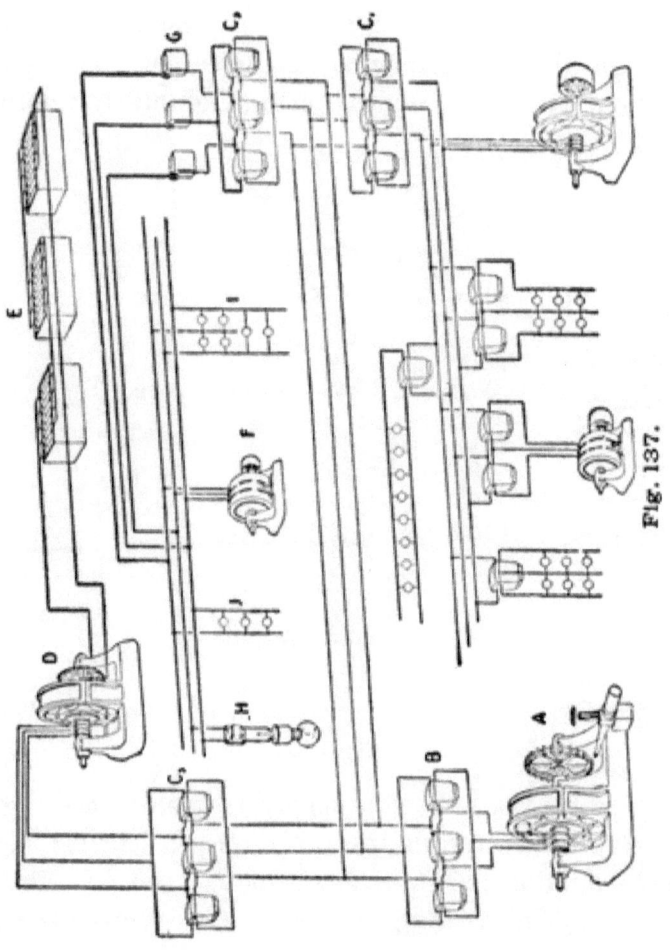

Fig. 137.

A modified three-phase system, in which the lighting service is supplied from one branch of the system, has been used by Mr. Steinmetz, and designated as the poly-

THREE-PHASE SYSTEM.

cyclic system (Fig. 138). It is practically a single-phase system for lighting service and three-phase for motor work.

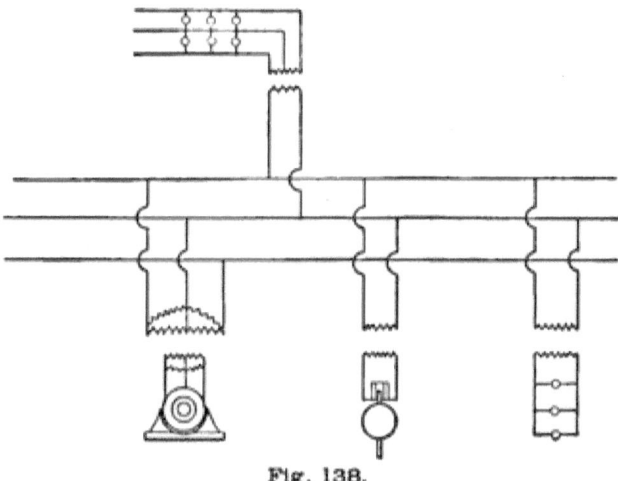

Fig. 138.

This system may be used when the lighting load is not over 25 or 30 per cent of the total load. The lighting circuit is perfectly balanced for all loads.

CHAPTER XI.

MONOCYCLIC SYSTEM.

General. — The two-phase and three-phase systems have made possible the transmission of power over long distances. These systems also possess notable advantages in the local distribution of power involving large units, and in many special applications. For general central station work, such as the distribution of alternating currents for lighting, with incidental power, the monocyclic system designed by Mr. C. P. Steinmetz is especially suited.

The monocyclic system is essentially a single-phase system, consisting of two wires in combination with a third auxiliary, or teaser wire; the main lines being used for supplying lights, while the third wire, which carries an intermediate, or displaced, current, is used, together with the main lines, for supplying power to polyphase motors. The teaser wire need only be run to the motors. Indeed, the teaser wire need not start from the generator, but may start from any motor, or multiple-circuit apparatus, of the system. The motors operate practically the same as polyphase motors. As the lights are connected to the single-phase circuit, there is no possibility of unbalancing. The monocyclic generator can be loaded to its fullest extent with either lights or motors, or partly with lights and partly with motors, in any proportion.

It has been noted that the regulation of polyphase generators varies with the inductive character of the load. The monocyclic generator, when designed with shunt and series excitation, possesses the superior advantage of automatically compounding for all kinds of load. The power

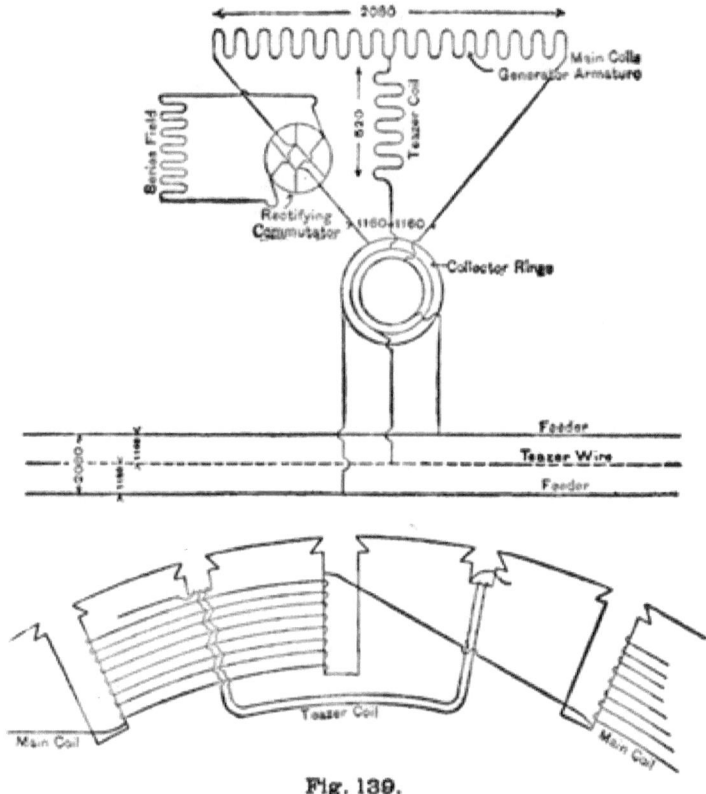

Fig. 139.

wire of the monocyclic system supplies the magnetizing current to the motors, which current is returned over the main wires, adding to the magnitude of the current in one lead, and reducing it in the other. The commutating device is placed in the main carrying the largest current. As the increase over the normal depends on the motors, —

the inductive load, — the greater the inductive character of the load, the larger will be the series-exciting current. In this way the monocyclic machine can be made to give perfect compounding, on either inductive or non-inductive loads.

Generator Armature Connections. — The connections and detail of the monocyclic generator armature are shown in Fig. 139. The armature coils are made up of a single-phase main winding, similar to the ordinary armature winding of a single-phase alternator. Midway between the main slots of the armature is a set of smaller slots, containing the auxiliary winding of the same cross-section as the main winding, but of only one quarter the number of turns. One end of the teaser coil is connected to the middle of the main coil, and the other to a third collector ring. In this teaser coil, an $E.M.F.$, in quadrature with that of the main coil, is established, which is made use of for supplying magnetizing current for the operation of alternating-current motors.

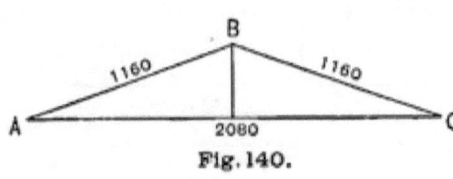

Fig. 140.

When the generator is wound for 2,080 volts, the teaser coil has one-quarter the number of turns, and gives an $E.M.F.$ of 520 volts. The $E.M.F.$ between the terminals of the main coil and the free end of the teaser, is the resultant of the $E.M.F.$ in the two coils, and is shown in magnitude and direction by Fig. 140. The teaser may be wound to have 86 per cent of the main turns, instead of 25 per cent; in which case the electromotive forces of the three terminals are equal, and we have a three-phase relationship.

When the single-phase circuit is loaded, the potential be-

MONOCYCLIC SYSTEM. 197

tween the mains does not bear the same phase relationship to the teaser terminal that it did on open circuit. The current lags behind the impressed volts, due to the self-induction. The triangle of the terminal electromotive forces is distorted, so that, if the main potential is 2,080 volts, that between the teaser and one main may be 1,320 volts, and the other 800 volts (Fig. 141). Loading, now, the teaser wire, produces a current lag, and shifts its potential so that

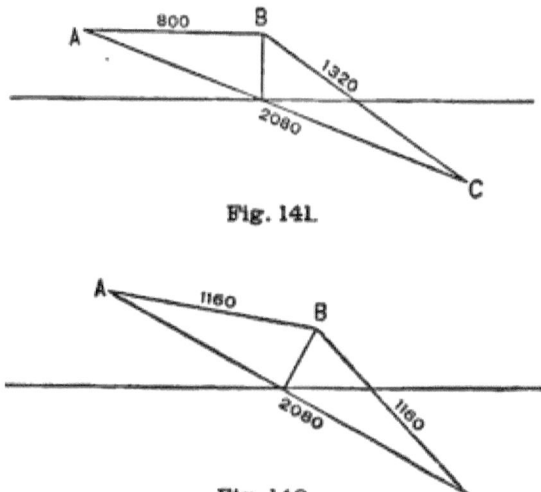

Fig. 141.

Fig. 142.

the triangle of $E.M.F.$ regains its normal shape, and the electromotive forces their magnitude and normal relationship (Fig. 142).

The wiring for monocyclic circuits, when lights only are supplied, is the same as for single-phase circuits.

Systems of Distribution. — In Fig. 143 is shown a diagram of a monocyclic system of light and power distribution.

The generator, A, sends power over the main wires, a

and b, to transformer, T, operating lights and a small single-phase fan motor from its secondaries.

From the same generator issues the teaser, or power wire, of small cross-section, shown in dotted lines, c, which is carried to the pairs of transformers, D and E, supplying motors.

In D is shown the arrangement of transformers suitable

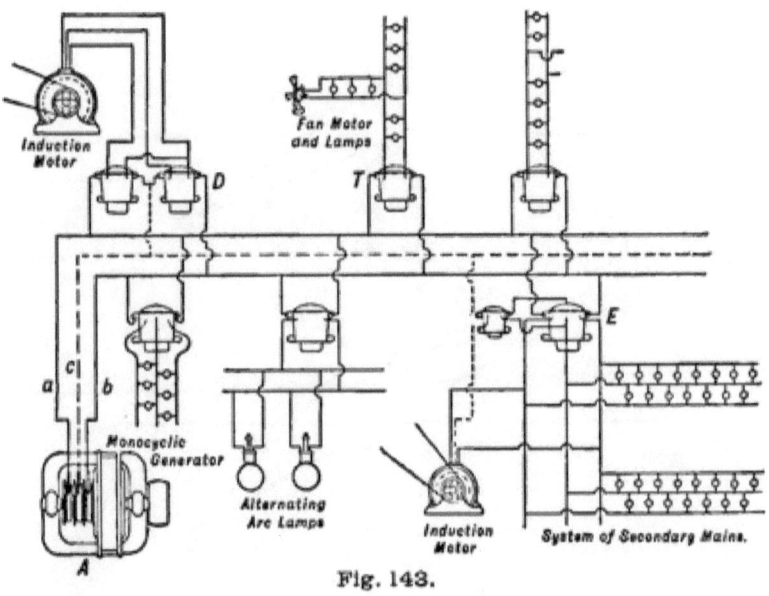

Fig. 143.

for the operation of standard alternating-current induction motors from their secondaries. The two transformers are of equal size and of one-half the main-line voltages, and are connected with their primaries between teaser and main wires, while one of their secondaries is reversed with regard to the primary, and thereby establishes, in the secondary circuit, a relation of electromotive forces suitable for the operation of the motor.

In *E* an arrangement is shown, whereby lights and motors, or, in short, a whole three-wire network, is operated from the transformer secondaries.

The large or main transformer is connected between the main lines, *a* and *b*, and is of a size sufficient to supply the total capacity of the secondary network. An additional or teaser transformer, of one-quarter the primary main voltage, and of very small size only, is connected by one terminal to the centre of the main transformer coils, while the other terminal connects with the teaser wire, *c*, in the primary, and the motor wire in the secondary. This transformer connection is analogous to the connection of main and teaser coil in the generator.

Supplied in this way, a secondary network on the monocyclic system consists of four conductors, — two main conductors, the lightning neutral, and the power neutral or balance wire.

Such a secondary network can be operated in the same way as a continuous-current three-wire system, and offers the essential advantage of saving the excessive amount of copper in the long feeders, by being applied from high-potential lines through transformers. An unbalancing due to the motors is not possible, and motors operated on this system do not affect the lights, except in so far as the ohmic drop in the mains is concerned.

Arc lights can be operated very satisfactorily from the monocyclic system, and are supplied either by compensators from the secondary circuits, or from the primary circuits by transformers, as shown.

Series incandescent lights can be used for street lighting, and are directly supplied from the primary main lines. Where a district has to be supplied, which is too far distant to be reached directly by the primary or generator voltage, step-up and step-down transformers may be used.

Transformer Connections.—The various methods of connecting transformers to monocyclic circuits, and the result-

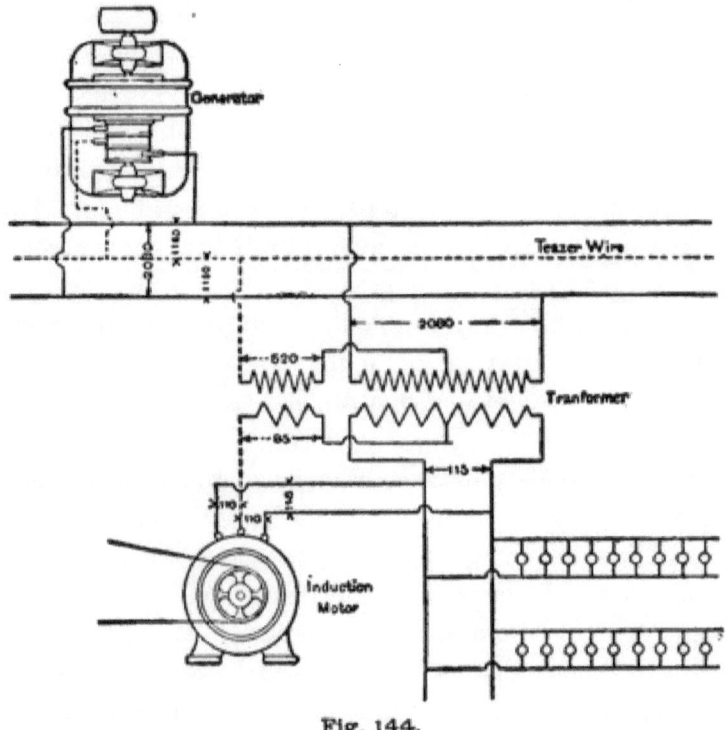

Fig. 144.

ant voltages, are shown in detail in Figs. 144 to 146. It will be noticed the teaser wire is necessary only where motors are used, the lights being connected on the single-phase system. Fig. 144 shows the detailed connections and standard voltages in a system for operating lights and motors from the same transformers.

The three-phase relationship for operating power apparatus may be obtained by the transformer connection, as shown. The primaries of the transformers, which are of different capacities, are connected and wound to produce the exact *E.M.F.* relationship of the generators. The large transformer is connected across the main circuit, while the supplementary transformer is connected to the middle of the large transformer and to the teaser wire. The ratio of transformation of each transformer is selected

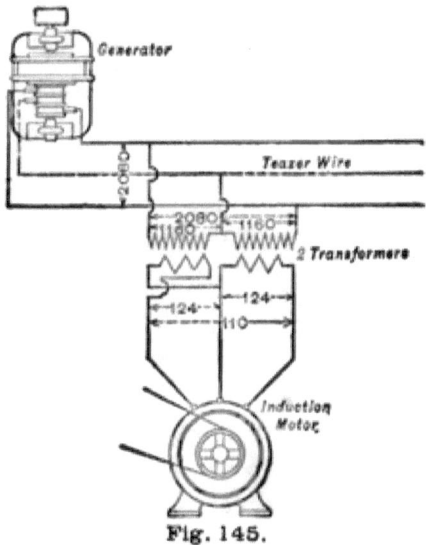

Fig. 145.

so that the secondary *E.M.F.* of the smaller transformer is about 82 per cent of that of the larger. This gives a slightly lop-sided three-phase relationship, from which motors of 110 volts and lights of 115 volts can be operated. Of course an exact three-phase relationship can be obtained by raising the *E.M.F.* of the smaller transformer to 86 per cent. The smaller transformer should be about one-third the capacity of the motor, or, if a number of the motors be used, about one-fourth the aggregate capacity.

A beautiful illustration of the resultant three-phase relationship is the use of two transformers with a monocyclic generator, the secondary of one being reversed (Fig. 145). The diagram of $E.M.F.$ (Fig. 146) shows the effect of

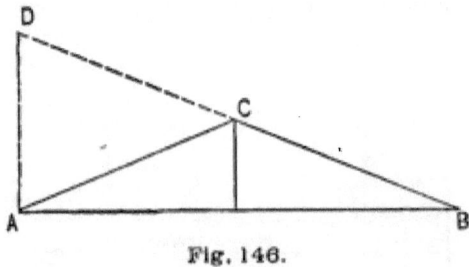

Fig. 146.

reversing the secondary. The three motor wires are connected to A, C, D; the difference in phase being nearly, though not quite, 60°. The secondary circuits, from such an arrangement, may be considered as practically the same, and have all the advantages of a straight three-phase system.

A third method of obtaining the proper phase relationship for motor work is shown in diagram (Fig. 147). In this arrangement only one transformer is required, having half the capacity required for the other methods of operating motors. The primary is connected between one of the mains and the teaser wire. The secondary coil is in series with the primary, and has the same number of turns; the ratio of transformation being, therefore, 1 to 1. As the primary current of a transformer differs from the secondary current 180° in phase, one leg of the circuit is naturally inverted, changing the relation of the phases from monocyclic to three-phase.

MONOCYCLIC SYSTEM. 203

This arrangement is especially suited for the operation of large motors, as the cost of transformers is reduced one-half. The voltage of the motors is fixed at approximately one-half the generator voltage.

The most common and convenient connection of transformers, when motors alone are to be operated from a monocyclic circuit, is that shown in Fig. 145. The ratio of transformation of the transformer here shown is about

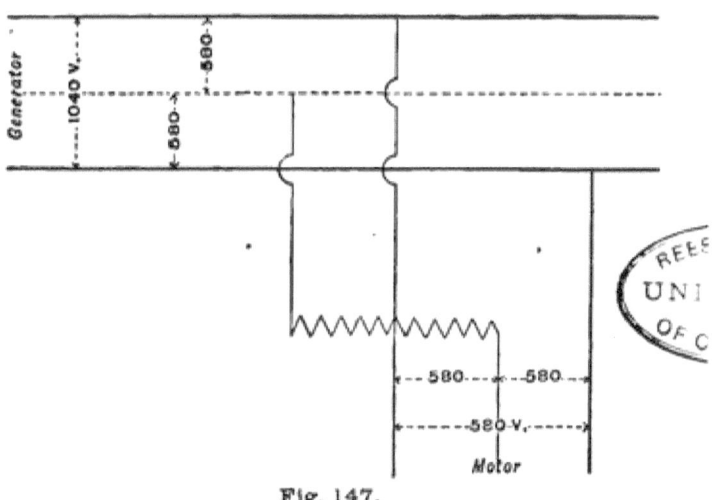

Fig. 147.

9 to 1. In the operation of motors from 1,040 volt monocyclic circuits, transformers of the ratio of $4\frac{1}{2}$ to 1 must be used.

Monocyclic Motors.— The three-phase induction motor is the most suitable for use on monocyclic circuits. The two-phase motor can be used with an increase in the number of turns of the teaser winding, but at the expense of the output of the generator, considered solely as a single-phase machine. The performance of the three-phase motor, connected in a monocyclic system, in regard to efficiency, torque, and power factor, is essentially the same as on a straight three-phase system. The flow of current is different in the three conductors, the teaser wire carrying mainly the magnetizing current. A monocyclic motor of the induction type can be used, the windings of which are exact reproductions of the generator windings,—i.e., are two in number; one having 25 per cent the turns of the other, and connected to the middle of the large coil. Such a motor can be run from two transformers; or, if of a size permitting it to be wound for the high voltage of the main circuits, direct from the mains. While the monocyclic generator can be fully loaded with induction motors, which interchange the magnetizing current by means of the teaser, it is not advisable to run one large induction motor of a size approximating that of the generator. In special cases, where the motor need not have a large starting torque, this arrangement is permissible.

Synchronous motors on a monocyclic system need not be operated from reversed transformers, but can be run direct from the generators, provided they are identical with them. They have little starting-torque, and require an extraneous source of power to bring them to synchronism.

Measurement of Power. — The power supplied to lights and other single-phase current-consuming devices, is measured by the standard forms of wattmeters. On account of the uncertain flow of current in the motor connections, special connections are necessary. Fig. 148 shows a recording wattmeter connected to measure the power delivered to motors. One of the field coils, D, is connected in the common return B; the other coil, E, in the main A, or perhaps in the main C. If the motor is loaded and the meter speeds up, the connections, as shown, are right. If the meter speed diminishes with increasing motor load, the field coil E should be connected in the main C. This meter will be found to give fairly accurate results. At high loads the reading will be found slightly high, but not sufficiently to be commercially objectionable.

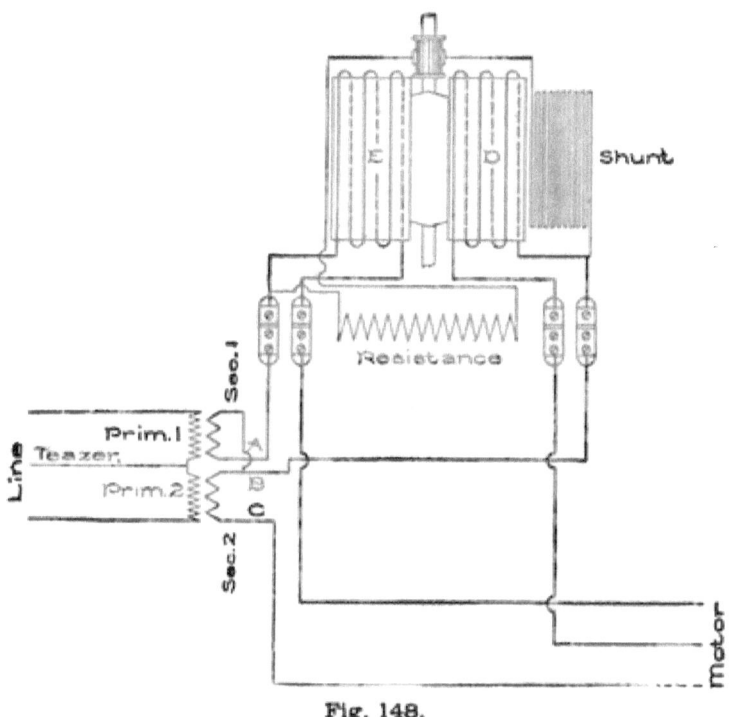

Fig. 148.

In cases where great accuracy is required, two meters can be used, measuring individually the output of the two transformers. Fig. 149 shows the method of measuring the entire output of a monocyclic generator. Each of the field coils, a and b, of wattmeter A, are connected in each of the mains. The other pair of coils, c and d, of wattmeter

B, are in series, and connected in the teaser wire. To obtain a safe voltage, two transformers are needed, connected so as to reproduce the phase relationship of the

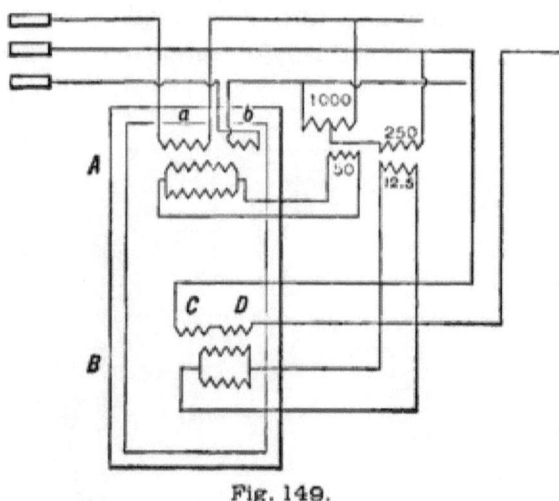

Fig. 149.

generator windings. Both armatures are connected to a single shaft, rotation being due to the resultant action of the two fields.

CHAPTER XII.

CHOICE OF FREQUENCY.

High Frequencies. — In designing a plant for the distribution of light and power by polyphase currents, one of the first considerations that presents itself, is whether the apparatus shall be of high or low frequency. By high frequency is generally understood to mean one of over 60 cycles per second, or 7,200 alternations per minute. Sixty cycles and less are considered low frequencies. Until quite recently, the frequencies generally employed in the United States were 125 and 133 cycles, or 15,000 and 16,000 alternations. Abroad, the commercial frequencies were somewhat lower, varying from 80 to 100 cycles. The adherence to a high frequency in this country for over ten years has resulted in an investment of millions of dollars in this particular type of apparatus, and has made the introduction of new types of lower frequency into old and existing central stations extremely difficult, even when evident economy and advantage have been shown to follow upon such introduction.

The tendency of modern alternating-current practice is in the direction of low frequencies, and in the organization of a new plant, the problem, in nine cases out of ten, is confined to the selection of a frequency of 60 cycles or under.

There are frequently strong reasons for retaining or

adopting 125 or 133 cycles. One of these has been mentioned above. The change from 125 cycles to a lower frequency necessitates a complete revamping of the installation, and, with the exception of the small sizes, the transformers must be replaced. Again, when a low first-cost of a plant is considered of more importance than a possible ultimate saving of operating expenses, and a more satisfactory service, a high frequency will be used. The generators are cheaper, as they run at a higher speed. The transformers are also smaller and cheaper.

One of the drawbacks to the use of high frequencies, especially in the transmission of power over lines of considerable length, is the drop of voltage due to the reactance of the line, which increases with the frequency. For illustration: the reactance of 1,000 feet of No. 1 wire, at 25 cycles, is .0486 ohms, and at 125 cycles, .243 ohms.*

By reducing the frequency from 125 cycles to 25 cycles, in the above case, the voltage drop, due to the reactance and resistance, is reduced almost one-half. With heavier conductors and higher frequencies, the difference is still more noticeable. The effect of frequency on the voltage drop in transmission lines is treated at further length in Chapter XIV. In lighting plants employing large conductors, on account of the varying power-factors due to changing character of load, the irregularity in voltages at high frequencies may become quite marked. As we have seen, this voltage drop is not all energy loss, this loss being only proportional to the energy component of the total drop.

Other disadvantages in the use of high frequencies are the speed at which both generators and motors must run

* See Table of Line Constants for Power Transmission, page 224.

in order not to unduly increase the number of poles, and the difficulty in connection with engine regulation, when a number of generators are direct driven, and operated in parallel. High-frequency as well as low-frequency induction motors operate better at high speeds, but these are undesirable from both mechanical and commercial standpoints. On the other hand, high-frequency induction motors of reduced speeds have, as a rule, low power-factors. The high-frequency induction motor was introduced to meet the demand for motors of small power on high frequency circuits. With the system on which it is at present operated, it may in time become a thing of the past.

To sum up: High frequencies permit the use of cheap generators and transformers, and, in addition, the simple and satisfactory operation of incandescent and arc lamps and synchronous motors. They have the disadvantage of increasing the voltage drop and idle currents of circuits, with consequent bad regulation and heating of the generator at light loads, of not permitting the parallel operation of direct-connected machines of low speed, and the further disadvantage, that induction motors must either run at excessive speeds, or with poor power-factors. Synchronous motors will not start with the same vigor as on lower frequencies.

Low Frequencies. — Up to the present time no arc lamp has been made that will operate satisfactorily on frequencies lower than 40 cycles. At this frequency the interruptions of the arc are plainly visible to the eye. Incandescent lamps cannot be used to advantage on frequencies less than 30 cycles. Low-voltage incandescent lamps show no flicker; but the effect of fatiguing the eye is quite noticeable at 25 cycles, and perceptible after a while at 30 cycles. The current reversals are easily distinguished in high voltage lamps at 25 cycles and under.

Transformers are somewhat bulkier, more expensive, and slightly less efficient at low frequencies. Induction motors, while likewise larger and more expensive, as a rule can be built with equal, if not better, power factors, and at convenient and commercial speeds. Rotary converters can be successfully designed for 60 cycles. The speed is high, however, and the best mechanical and electrical results are obtained at frequencies under 40 cycles. The largest use of miscellaneous power by rotary converters is at Niagara, where a frequency of 25 cycles is employed. The largest use of power for electric railway work by rotary converters is at St. Anthony Falls, Minneapolis; the frequency here being approximately 35 cycles.

The Niagara plant is essentially a power plant. The use of current for both arc and incandescent lighting is of no great importance. The power, electrically generated on a scale never before attempted, is used locally in a great variety of processes, and is delivered in a form most suitable for its diverse uses. Power by the direct-current system, while convenient for some particular operations, would not answer equally well all requirements at Niagara, and would be unsuitable for long-distance transmission. A high-frequency system would restrict the use of motors and rotary converters, and the transmission of power over very long distances. Sixty and 40 cycles, however, permitting the general use of lighting apparatus, do not give the best results with rotary converters of large output. The operation of 25 cycle rotary converters, on the scale employed at Niagara, shows that, for the purely power conditions there existing, this frequency was wisely chosen.

A frequency of 25 cycles is also used by the Brooklyn Edison Illuminating Company in the recent extension of their plant. Four thousand H.P. are transmitted within an area covering 75 miles, to various substations, where 25 cycle rotary converters are stationed. These deliver 115 volt direct-current into Edison three-wire mains. The Chicago Edison Company use a somewhat similar system of distribution and the same frequency.

For the general conditions of a power plant, supplying alternating current for induction motors and lighting, and making a specialty of furnishing direct current on a large scale, at some distance from the generating plant, a frequency of 35 to 40 cycles will be found suitable.

The frequency of 60 cycles, or 7,200 alternations per minute, has come into extensive use. It has the advantage of considerably reducing line reactance and the idle currents present in lighting systems of higher frequencies. It is adapted for the most economical results in a general distributing system of lights and motors. On account of the good regulation possible with this frequency, the highest economy lamps can be used. Sixty cycle motors are excellent in respect to efficiency and power factor, and run at commercial speeds. Both motors and transformers are reasonable in cost.

When the generating units are direct-connected to engines of extremely slow speed and operated in parallel, a frequency of 60 cycles will be found to be not desirable. As explained in Chapter III., the permissible variation in rotative speed is not so great as with lower-frequency generating units.

Choice of Frequency. — It is impossible to make general applications of the foregoing remarks. Each particular case must be studied in the light of its special conditions, before an intelligent decision can be made as to the proper frequency to employ. At the risk of repetition, the following general recommendations are suggested as embodying the latest and standard practice:

For local lighting systems with incidental demand for power in small units, where old transformers have to be retained, and where a cheap plant is of first consideration, a high frequency may be used, but should be discouraged as much as possible.

For general transmission and distribution for lighting and power purposes, conditions which accompany the majority of alternating-current propositions, a standard frequency of 60 or 66 cycles should be used.

In power and lighting plants, — where arc lighting is of secondary consideration, — supplying current to induction motors, as in mill work, and to rotary converters, as in long-distance railway-transmission work, where the generators are direct driven by engines, and finally, for very long transmissions of power, a frequency of 40 cycles, or thereabouts, may be used. This is a good, all-round frequency, and is coming into more general use in this country. It is the frequency generally employed abroad.

For exclusively power plants, where lighting is of no importance whatsoever, and where rotary converters and motors of large size or slow speed are to be supplied, a frequency of 25 to 30 cycles may be used.

Notwithstanding the opportunity for the careful exercise of judgment in selecting a proper frequency, almost equally good results can have been obtained with widely different frequencies. As an illustration, the Brooklyn Edison Company have adopted 25 cycles for their power and rotary converter work. The Boston Electric Light Company obtain practically the same results, using a frequency of 60 cycles.

CHAPTER XIII.

RELATIVE WEIGHTS OF COPPER FOR VARIOUS SYSTEMS.

As the transmission and distribution of power often involves a large outlay for copper conductors, it is most important to ascertain what system and what combination of conductors will give the most economical results. In making any comparison between the copper efficiencies of the various systems, the proper basis of comparison is equality of voltage.

The amount of copper required for transmitting a given power at a fixed percentage loss is found by the rule that the weight of copper varies inversely as the square of the voltage.

The voltage of an alternating circuit, as measured by the ordinary commercial instruments, — i.e., the effective voltage, — is about 40 per cent less than the maximum value of the $E.M.F.$ wave. It is this maximum value that must be considered in determining the break-down point of insulation and the highest voltage that can be used commercially, as in the long-distance transmission of power. On the other hand, when the maximum voltage of a circuit is within the limit of safe insulation strain, the effective voltage carries no limitation with it.

The comparison, then, of the various systems, to determine the most economical method of transmission, will be either on the basis of maximum potential, as in the case of long transmission lines, or on the basis of effective or minimum potential, as in the case of low-potential distributions by secondary mains.

Figs. 150 to 156 show the standard systems of alternating-current distribution and the various combinations of conductors in general use. The name of each system is given, and also the relative amount of copper required.

The percentual amount of copper required by the single-phase system, which is here taken as the standard of comparison for the other systems and combinations, is illustrated by diagram (Fig. 150). The single-phase three-wire system is shown in Fig. 151. If the voltage of the two-wire system is e, the potential between the two outside wires is $2e$. Applying the rule that the amount of copper is inversely as the square of the voltage, only $\frac{1}{4}$ the copper would be needed, if the neutral should have no cross-section, or the return conductor be dispensed with, as might be done in the case of a perfect balance. If the neutral is given a cross-section equal to one of the outside wires, the total copper in the three-wire single-phase system is 37.5 per cent that of the two-wire single-phase system. With a neutral $\frac{1}{2}$ and $\frac{1}{3}$ the cross-section of the outside wires, the total copper is 31.25 per cent and 29.15 per cent respectively of our standard system. In a four-wire system the voltage between outside wires is $3e$, and, under perfect balance, $\frac{1}{9}$ the amount of copper would be required. When the neutral and outside wires are of equal size, the copper must be increased to 22.2 per cent. In like manner the copper in the five-wire system, with neutrals of full cross-section, is 15.62 per cent, and the same system, with neutrals of $\frac{1}{2}$ the area of the neutral wires, requiring only 10.93

216 POLYPHASE APPARATUS AND SYSTEMS.

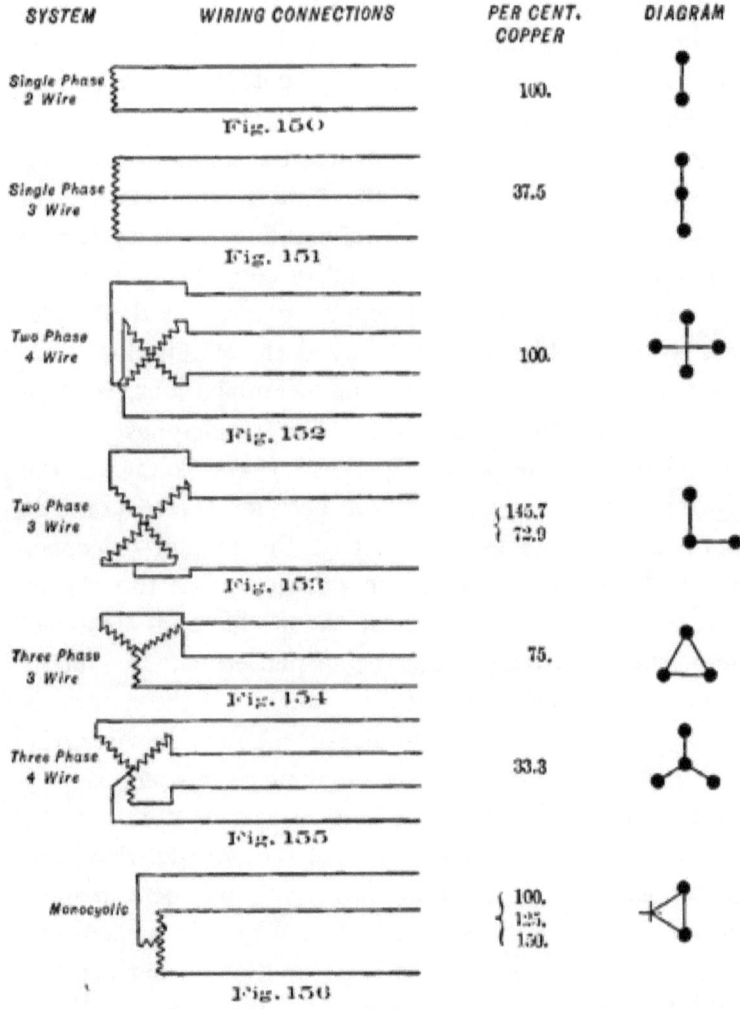

per cent of the copper of the simple alternating circuit. These results are the same whether the comparison is made on the basis of maximum potential, or on the basis of effective or minimum potential

In the three-phase system, the copper required for certain given conditions is 75 per cent of the copper used in the single-phase system. The comparison between polyphase systems can best be made by resolving each into as many single-phase systems as it has phases. The three-phase system consists of three single circuits with a common ground, or, what is the same, with no return; for the total current to and from the centre is zero. If the Δ or line voltage is e (Fig. 154), the pressure or volts between any wire and the juncture is $\frac{e}{\sqrt{3}}$. The two-phase system, having a line voltage e, can also be connected into two single circuits of voltage $\frac{e}{2}$ (Fig. 152). As the weight of copper in each system is inversely as the square of the voltage, we have:

$\left(\frac{2}{e}\right)^2 : \left(\frac{\sqrt{3}}{e}\right)^2 = 4 : 3$ — or the relative amounts of copper, for the two-phase and the three-phase systems, are 100 per cent and 75 per cent.

The two-phase four-wire system, consisting of two single-phase systems, is placed, in respect to the amount of copper required for equal conditions, in the same position as the single-phase system.

Fig. 153 illustrates the two-phase three-wire distribution, two of the wires of the four-wire system being replaced by one of full cross-section. The voltage between the two outside conductors is now raised to $\sqrt{2e} = 1.412\ e$, e being the potential between the conductors of either phase. The amount of copper required, when compared with the single-phase system, will differ considerably according as the comparison is based on the highest voltage permissible for any given distribution, or on the minimum voltage for low-tension service. If e is the maximum voltage, that can be used on account of the insulation strain, or for any other reason, the pressure between the other conductors of the two-phase three-wire system must be reduced to $\dfrac{e}{\sqrt{2}}$. The weight of copper required under this condition is 145.7 per cent of the single-phase copper. If the limiting conditions of voltage do not exist, a comparison of the relative weights of copper can be made with the effective voltage of either phase as a basis, — i.e., on a basis of the minimum voltage. In this case we find a relative saving over the single-phase circuit of about 27 per cent, the actual amount of copper being 72.9 per cent of the single-phase conductors.

Fig. 155 shows the connections of the three-phase four-wire system. When the fourth wire, or neutral, is of full cross-section, the copper required is 33⅓ per cent of the single-phase system. By making the neutral one-half the cross-section of the main conductors, the copper weight is reduced to 29.17 per cent. This arrangement is only used for secondary systems of distribution, as described before. The comparison with any other system is, therefore, made only on a basis of equality between phases of minimum voltage.

The monocyclic system (Fig. 156) is treated as a single-phase system in the calculation of its lighting circuits. When motors are connected to the circuit, the single-phase copper is increased proportionally to the motor load, and by the teaser wire. The rule governing the size of the teaser wire is, that its cross-section should bear the same relation to that of the main wires that the motor load does to the total load.

If the teaser is made of a cross-section equal to one of the main conductors, the total weight of copper is 150 per cent of that in a single-phase circuit of equal voltage and power. If the load is equally divided between motors and lights, the teaser has a cross-section of one-half the main conductors, and the total copper is 125 per cent of the single-phase copper. The main circuit can be connected as a three-, four-, or five-wire system. The amount of copper required is found by adding the proportionate weight of the teaser wire. In this way a three-wire monocyclic circuit, neutral one-half cross-section, loaded one-half with lights, one-half with motors, will require 39 per cent of the copper of the single-phase system.

The following Tables are compiled from data in Mr. Steinmetz's valuable work, "Alternating-Current Phenomena." The first Table gives the relative copper efficiencies of various systems, when the comparison is on the basis of equality of minimum difference of potential. The second gives the relative weights, when the comparison is based on the equality of the maximum potential difference in the system.

Amount of copper required for transmission at a given loss, based on minimum potential.

System.	No. of Wires.	Per Cent Copper.
Single-phase	2	100.
Single-phase	3	37.5
Two-phase, common return	3	72.9
Two-phase	4	100.
Three-phase	3	75.
Three-phase, neutral full section . . .	4	33.3
Three-phase, neutral one-half section .	4	29.17

Amount of copper required for transmission at a given loss, based on maximum difference of potential.

System.	No. of Wires.	Per Cent Copper.
Single-phase	2	100.
Two-phase, with common return	3	145.7
Two-phase	4	100.
Three-phase	3	75.
Direct Current	2	50.

It will be seen that the direct-current system requires only 50 per cent of the copper in the single-phase system when used in long-distance transmission of power. The advantage is not so evident, however; for, as Mr. Steinmetz has pointed out, in addition to the electrostatic stress, an electrolytic effect is set up, which does not exist to the same extent in alternating currents. The difficulties attending the utilization of direct current of high tension, are such that, with the exception of one or two special and isolated cases, its employment in the long distance transmission of power has not been seriously considered.

CHAPTER XIV.

CALCULATION OF TRANSMISSION LINES.

Line Constants.—As explained in Chapter I., the drop of voltage in an alternating-current circuit will vary with the resistance and the reactance of the circuit, and with the character of the load. In the table, "Line Constants for Power Transmission," taken from a publication of the General Electric Company, the relation of reactance to resistance is shown for a number of frequencies, and for the sizes of conductors ordinarily used in power transmissions, and also other constants of transmission circuits, such as capacity inductance and charging current. The following explanations will serve to make the table clear:

The E.M.F. consumed by resistance r, of the line, is $= Ir$, and in phase with the current I.

The E.M.F. consumed by the reactance, S, of the line, is $= IS$, and in quadrature with the current I.

The E.M.F. consumed in the line, is neither Ir nor IS, but depends upon the phase relation of current in the receiving circuit.

The loss of energy in the line is $= I^2r$, hence does not depend upon the reactance, but only upon the resistance.

Two wires in parallel have the same resistance, and about half the reactance (if strung on separate insulators and intermixed) of a single wire of double cross-section. Thus replacing one No. 0000 wire by two No. 0 wires, the resistance, weight of copper, etc., will remain the same, but the reactance will be reduced practically to half, so where lower reactance is desired, the use of several conductors strung on independent insulators and intermixed is advisable.

The values given for L, C, i, and S are calculated for sine-waves of current and $E.M.F.$

This table will be found most convenient for determining the characteristics of transmission circuits when the size of conductor has been fixed.

Let us take, as an example, a case where it is required to deliver, by the three-phase 60 cycle system, 2,000 H.P. at the secondary terminals of the step-down transformers, over a circuit 11 miles in length. It is further assumed that the voltage at the receiving end is 10,000, and the total energy loss in transmission from the generator terminals is not to exceed 15 per cent. The power is to be used for a mixed system of lights and induction motors, the latter forming most of the load. The power factor of the system at the receiving end will be approximately 85 per cent. We can assume that —

The transformers have an efficiency of $97\frac{1}{2}$ per cent.
The copper loss in each being 1 per cent.
The core or hysteresis loss, $1\frac{1}{2}$ per cent.
The reactance can be taken as $3\frac{1}{2}$ per cent.
And the magnetizing current 4 per cent.

The voltage between any branch of the circuit and the common centre of the system is

$$\frac{10,000}{\sqrt{3}} = 5{,}775.$$

The energy delivered by each branch is

$$\frac{1{,}500}{3}\text{ K.W.} = 500\text{ K.W.}$$

The apparent energy delivered by each branch is
$$\frac{500}{.85} = 588 \text{ K.W.}$$

The total current in each branch is $\frac{588,000}{5,775} = 102$ amperes.

The *I.R.* drop in each branch is 10 per cent of $5,775 = 577.5$ volts.

The total resistance $R = \frac{577.5}{102} = 5.66$ ohms.

The resistance of one mile is $\frac{5.66}{11} = .514$ ohms, which is very nearly the resistance of No. 0 wire. Three No. 0 wires, therefore, will carry 2,000 H.P. a distance of 11 miles with a waste of energy of 10 per cent, the pressure at the receiving end being 10,000 volts and power factor 85 per cent.

By referring to the following table the characteristics of this transmission line are readily obtained. The reactance of eleven miles of single conductor is seen to be 6.62 ohms at the frequency employed. The inductance, or what is the same thing, the coefficient of self-induction of the line, is 17.6 Millihenrys. The charging current of each line for the eleven miles, with the given voltage and frequency, is found to be .4 of an ampere.

It is interesting to know what the impressed or generator *E.M.F.* and the distribution of current will be, in this case, when the plant is fully loaded. For this investigation, the entire system may be reduced to a uniform voltage, by multiplying the voltages by the various ratios of transformation, thus bringing both the secondary pressure at the step-down transformers, and the generator pressure, to the line voltage. The current values are, of course, inversely changed. The power factor of the load, having been assumed as .85, the induction factor will be $\sqrt{1 - (.85)^2} = .52$.

224 POLYPHASE APPARATUS AND SYSTEMS.

Line Constants for Power Transmission.

Per 1,000 Feet of Wire B. & S. G.

Size of Wire. No.	Reactance at 25, 40, 60, 125 Cycles, in Ohms.				Charging Current. i_0	Capacity in Microfarads. K	Inductance in Millihenrys. L	Resistance at 75° F. r	Area in Circular Mils. C.M.	Diameter Mils.	Weight Lbs.	Size of Wire. No.
	S_{125}	S_{60}	S_{40}	S_{25}								
0000	.221	.1062	.0708	.0443	.0244	.00388	.282	.049	211,600	460	630	0000
000	.227	.1090	.0727	.0455	.0238	.00378	.290	.062	167,805	410	507	000
00	.232	.1113	.0743	.0465	.0232	.00368	.296	.078	133,079	365	402	00
0	.238	.1141	.0761	.0476	.0226	.00358	.303	.098	105,592	325	319	0
1	.243	.1166	.0775	.0486	.0220	.00351	.310	.124	83,694	289	253	1
2	.249	.1194	.0796	.0498	.0215	.00342	.317	.156	66,373	258	201	2
3	.254	.1220	.0814	.0509	.0210	.00334	.324	.197	52,633	229	159	3
4	.261	.1248	.0832	.0521	.0205	.00326	.332	.249	41,742	204	126	4
5	.266	.1277	.0850	.0532	.0201	.00320	.339	.314	33,102	182	100	5
6	.271	.1301	.0867	.0543	.0197	.00313	.346	.395	26,250	162	79	6
7	.276	.1327	.0885	.0553	.0193	.00306	.352	.499	20,816	144	63	7
8	.283	.1355	.0904	.0565	.0189	.00300	.360	.629	16,509	128	50	8
9	.288	.1380	.0920	.0575	.0185	.00294	.366	.792	13,094	114	40	9
10	.293	.1405	.0936	.0585	.0181	.00288	.373	.999	10,382	102	31	10

Per 1,000 Feet of Wire B. & S. G.

CALCULATION OF TRANSMISSION LINES.

Per Mile of Wire B. & S. G.											
0000	3,376	460	211,600	.26	1.489	.02046	.1286	.234	.374	.561	1.167
000	2,677	410	167,805	.33	1.529	.01993	.1255	.240	.384	.576	1.199
00	2,123	365	133,079	.41	1.562	.01943	.1223	.245	.392	.588	1.225
0	1,685	325	105,529	.52	1.600	.01892	.1191	.251	.402	.602	1.257
1	1,335	289	83,694	.65	1.636	.01854	.1163	.257	.409	.616	1.283
2	1,059	258	66,373	.83	1.674	.01806	.1135	.263	.420	.630	1.314
3	840	229	52,633	1.04	1.711	.01765	.1110	.269	.430	.644	1.343
4	666	204	41,742	1.31	1.750	.01722	.1085	.275	.439	.659	1.379
5	528	182	33,102	1.66	1.788	.01689	.1060	.281	.449	.674	1.403
6	419	162	26,250	2.09	1.826	.01651	.1038	.287	.458	.687	1.431
7	332	144	20,816	2.63	1.860	.01617	.1018	.292	.467	.701	1.459
8	263	128	16,509	3.32	1.901	.01584	.0997	.298	.477	.715	1.492
9	209	114	13,094	4.18	1.934	.01552	.0977	.304	.486	.729	1.519
10	166	102	10,382	5.28	1.968	.01521	.0956	.309	.494	.742	1.544

r = Ohmic resistance.
L = Inductance in millihenrys per 1,000 feet of conductor.
K = Capacity in microfarads per 1,000 feet of conductor.
i_0 = Charging current at 100 cycles and 10,000 volts to neutral, that is, in a 20,000 volt single-phrase, and a 17,300 volt three-phase line.
$i_0 = 2 \times \pi \times \text{frequency} \times K \times E \times 10^{-6}$; where E is the $E.M.F.$ between a line and neutral.
S = reactance = $2 \times \pi \times \text{frequency} \times L \times 10^{-3}$.

226   POLYPHASE APPARATUS AND SYSTEMS.

In Chapter I., it has been shown that the impressed *E.M.F.* is made up of two component parts, one in phase with the current and called the energy component of the *E.M.F.*, the other in quadrature with the current and called the induction component. In symbols:

Impressed *E.M.F.*

$$= \sqrt{\Sigma \text{ (Energy comp.)}^2 + \Sigma \text{ (Ind. comp.)}^2}$$

To obtain the total *E.M.F.*, it is necessary, then, to calculate separately all the energy and induction components of the circuit, and obtain a combined resultant.

With the values already assumed, and consulting the preceding table, we obtain the following results:

CIRCUIT.	VOLTAGE.		CURRENT AMPERES.
	ENERGY COMPONENT.	IND. COMPONENT.	
Secondary Circuit.			
Energy Component, .85 × 5,775,	4,909		
Induction Component, .52 × 5,775,		3,003	
Current,			102
Step-down Transformers.			
Resistance loss = $I.R.$ = 1% of 5,775,	58		
Reactance loss = $I.S.$ = 3½% of 5,775.		202	
Hysteresis loss = 1½% of 102,			1.5
	4,967	3,205	103.5
Line.			
Resistance loss = $I.R.$ = 103.5 × 5.72,	592		
Reactance loss = $I.S.$ = 103.5 × 6.62,		685	
$\sqrt{(5,559)^2 + (3,890)^2} = 6,785 =$ volts at terminals of step-up transformers.	5,559	3,890	103.5
Step-up Transformers.			
Resistance loss = $I.R.$ = 1% of 6,785,	68		
Reactance loss = $I.S.$ = 3½% of 6,785,		238	
Hysteresis loss = 1½% of 103.5.			1.5
$\sqrt{(5,628)^2 + (4,128)^2} = 6,980 =$ volts at generator.	5,627	4,128	105.

The energy *E.M.F.* between any one line and the neutral at the generator end is seen to be 5,627, and the volts consumed by the reactance of the system, 4,128. The total volts required at the generator terminals are found to be 121 per cent of the voltage at the secondaries of the transformers, reduced to the line voltage, — i.e., with 10,000 equivalent volts between the lines at the transformer secondaries, the pressure at the generator must be 12,100 volts. The current delivered by the generator to the line is 105 amperes, and is 3 per cent more than the current in the secondary circuits. The effect of the transformer core losses is the same as if a corresponding current was consumed by lamps or other apparatus connected across the mains. The volt-ampere output of the generator is 125 per cent of the apparent watts at the receiving end. The power factor of the entire system is found to be about 80 per cent.

Simple Wiring Formulas. — A simple and sufficiently accurate determination of the sizes of conductors, voltage drop, and distribution of currents, in any direct or alternating-current system, can be made from the general formula based on Ohm's law, modified by the use of the proper constants. The former formula and constants will be found especially useful and convenient for this calculation:

$$\text{Area of conductor, Circular Mils} = \frac{D \times W}{P \times E^2} \times K$$

$$\text{Volts loss in lines} = \frac{P \times E}{100} \times M$$

$$\text{Current in main conductors} = \frac{W}{E} \times T$$

D = Distance of transmission (one way) in feet.
W = Total watts delivered to consumer.
P = Per cent loss in line of W.
E = Voltage between main conductors at receiving or consumer's end of circuit.

228 POLYPHASE APPARATUS AND SYSTEMS.

SYSTEM.	VALUES OF K.					VALUES of T.			
	PER CENT POWER FACTOR.					PER CENT POWER FACTOR.			
	100	95	90	85	80	95	90	85	80
Single-phase	2,160	2,400	2,660	3,000	3,380	1.052	1.111	1.172	1.250
Two-phase (4-wire)	1,080	1,200	1,330	1,500	1,690	.526	.555	.588	.625
Three-phase (3-wire)	1,080	1,200	1,330	1,500	1,690	.607	.642	.679	.725

Values of the constant, K, for any particular power-factor are obtained by dividing 2,160 by the square of that power factor for single-phase, and by twice the square of that power factor for three-wire three-phase or four-wire two-phase. The resistance of line wire is taken as 10.8 ohms per mil foot.

T is a variable, depending on the system and nature of the load, and equal to 1 for continuous current, and for alternating current with 100 per cent power-factor. Its value for two-phase and three-phase systems is .50 and .58 respectively, with 100 per cent power-factor.

M is a variable, depending on the size of wire, frequency, and power factor. It is equal to 1 for continuous current, and for alternating current with 100 per cent power-factor and sizes of wire given in the following table of wiring constants.

The values of M, as given in the table, are empirical. They are sufficiently accurate for all practical purposes, provided the displacement in phase between current and $E. M. F.$ at the receiving end is not very much greater than that at the generator; in other words, provided that reactance of the line is not excessively large, or the line loss unusually high. For example, the constants should not be applied at 125 cycles if the largest-size conductors were used, and the loss 20 per cent or more of the power delivered. At lower frequencies, however, the constants are reasonably correct, even under such extreme conditions. They represent about the true values at 10 per cent line loss, are close enough at all losses less than 10 per cent, and often, at least for frequencies up to 40 cycles, close enough for even much larger losses.

In using the above formulas and constants, it should be particularly observed that P stands for the per cent loss in the line of the *delivered power*, and not for the per cent loss in line of the power at the generator.

No. of Wire B. & S. G.	Area Circular Mils	Weight of Bare Wire Per 1,000 ft. Pounds.	Values of M.								
			30 Cycles.			60 Cycles.			125 Cycles.		
			Lighting Only. 98% P.F.	Motors and Lights. 85% P.F.	Motors Only. 80% P.F.	Lighting Only. 95% P.F.	Motors and Lights. 85% P.F.	Motors Only. 80% P.F.	Lighting Only. 95% P.F.	Motors and Lights. 85% P.F.	Motors Only. 80% P.F.
0000	211,600	640.73	1.26	1.27	1.24	1.64	1.85	1.85	2.44	3.06	3.14
000	167,805	508.12	1.20	1.17	1.14	1.49	1.63	1.62	2.15	2.62	2.67
00	133,079	402.97	1.15	1.08	1.05	1.39	1.46	1.42	1.92	2.25	2.29
0	105,592	319.74	1.10	1.00	1.00	1.30	1.32	1.28	1.73	1.96	1.99
1	83,694	253.43	1.06	1.00	1.00	1.23	1.21	1.16	1.57	1.74	1.73
2	66,373	200.98	1.03	1.00	1.00	1.16	1.11	1.06	1.44	1.54	1.53
3	52,633	159.38	1.02	1.00	1.00	1.11	1.04	1.00	1.35	1.38	1.38
4	41,742	126.40	1.00	1.00	1.00	1.07	1.00	1.00	1.26	1.26	1.22
5	33,102	100.23	1.00	1.00	1.00	1.04	1.00	1.00	1.19	1.16	1.11
6	26,250	79.49	1.00	1.00	1.00	1.02	1.00	1.00	1.14	1.08	1.03
7	20,816	63.03	1.00	1.00	1.00	1.00	1.00	1.00	1.09	1.01	1.00
8	16,509	49.99	1.00	1.00	1.00	1.00	1.00	1.00	1.06	1.00	1.00

APPLICATION OF FORMULAS.

SINGLE-PHASE SYSTEM. — 125 CYCLES.

EXAMPLE: 750 52-volt lamps, consuming a total of 45,000 watts. Ratio of transformation 20 to 1. Distance to generator, 2,500 feet. Loss in secondary wiring, 2 volts. Voltage drops in transformers, 2 per cent. Energy loss in line, 5 per cent of delivered power. Efficiency of transformers, $97\frac{1}{2}$ per cent.

Watts at transformer primaries
$$= \frac{45{,}000}{.98 \times .97\frac{1}{2}} = 47{,}100.$$

Volts at transformer primaries
$$= (52 + 2) \times 20 \times 1.02 = 1{,}101.6.$$

$$C.M. = \frac{D \times W}{P \times E^2} \times K = \frac{2{,}500 \times 47{,}100 \times 2{,}400}{5 \times (1{,}101.6)^2} = 46{,}500 \ C.M.$$

Next larger B. & S. wire
$$= \text{No. 3} = 52{,}633 \ C.M.$$

Loss of delivered power using No. 4 wire
$$= \frac{2{,}500 \times 47{,}100 \times 2{,}400}{52{,}633 \times (1{,}101.6)^2} = 4.4 \text{ per cent.}$$

Total volts lost in line
$$= \frac{P \times E}{100} \times M = \frac{4.4 \times 1{,}101.6 \times 1.35}{100} = 65.5.$$

Generator voltage $= 1{,}101.6 + 65.5 = 1{,}167.1.$

In a 60 cycle single-phase system, with the same conditions as in the above example, the values will be the same, with the exception of the volts lost in the line.

$$\frac{4.4 \times 1{,}101.6 \times 1.11}{100} = 53.8 = \text{volts lost in line.}$$

$1{,}101.6 + 53.8 = 1{,}155.4 = \text{generator voltage.}$

CALCULATION OF TRANSMISSION LINES.

TWO-PHASE SYSTEM. — 60 CYCLES. FOUR-WIRE TRANSMISSION.

EXAMPLE: 2,500 H.P. delivered, 5 miles, at secondaries of step-down transformers. Pressure between lines at receiving end, 6,000 volts. Energy loss in line and in step-down transformers (no step-up transformers), 10 per cent of delivered power. Efficiency of transformers, 97.5 per cent. Power factor of load, 80 per cent. Find size of conductors and voltage drop in transmission line.

Power delivered at step-down secondaries.

$$= \frac{2,500}{.975} = 2,564 \text{ H.P.} = 1,912.7 \text{ K.W.}$$

Energy loss in line = 7.5 per cent.

$$C.M. = \frac{5,280 \times 5 \times 1,912,700}{7.5 \times (6,000)^2} \times 1,690 = 315,940 \ C.M.$$

Three No. 0 B. & S. wires have an area of 316,776 C.M. The energy loss, using 3 of this size in parallel, making a total of 12 No. 0 B. & S. wires in all, is:

$$\frac{5,280 \times 5 \times 1,912,700}{316,776 \times (6,000)^2} \times 1,690 = 7.48 \text{ per cent.}$$

Power lost in line

$$= 2,564 \times .0748 = 195.8 \text{ H.P.}$$

Volts lost in line

$$= \frac{P \times E}{100} \times M = \frac{7.48 \times 6,000 \times 1.28}{100} = 574.$$

∴ Generator voltage = 6,574.

Current in line

$$= \frac{W}{E} \times T = \frac{1,912,700}{6,000} \times .625 = 199 \text{ amperes.}$$

The current is, in fact, slightly greater, as no account has been taken of the hysteresis current in the transformers. This will increase the above result about 1½ per cent.

POLYPHASE APPARATUS AND SYSTEMS.

THREE-PHASE SYSTEM. — 60 CYCLES. THREE-WIRE TRANSMISSION.

EXAMPLE: Same conditions as preceding. Find size of conductors and voltage drop in transmission lines.

Power delivered to transformers

$$= \frac{2,500}{.975} = 2,564 \text{ H.P.} = 1,912.7 \text{ K.W.}$$

Energy loss in line = $7\frac{1}{2}$ per cent.

$$C.M. = \frac{5,280 \times 5 \times 1,912,700}{7.5 \times (6,000)^2} \times 1.690 = 315,940 \ C.M.$$

Three No. 0 B. & S. wires have an area of $316,776 \ C.M.$

For the three branches of the three-phase system 9 wires will be required.

Energy loss is $= \dfrac{5,280 \times 5 \times 1,912,700}{316,776 \times (6,000)^2} \times 1.690 = 7.48$ per cent.

Power loss in line

$$= 2,564 \times .0748 = 195.8 \text{ H.P.}$$

Voltage drop in line

$$= \frac{7.48 \times 6,000 \times 1.28}{100} = 574.$$

∴ Generator voltage = 6,574.

Current in line

$$= \frac{1,912,700}{6,000} \times .725 = 233.9 \text{ amperes.}$$

The hysteresis current will increase this result by about $1\frac{1}{2}$ per cent.

THREE-PHASE SYSTEM. — 60 CYCLES. FOUR-WIRE SECONDARY.

EXAMPLE: Required, the size of conductors from transformers to the distributing centre of a four-wire secondary system for lights and motors. The load consists of four

CALCULATION OF TRANSMISSION LINES. 233

16 H.P., 200 volt induction motors, and 750 half-ampere 15 c.p., 115 volt lamps. Length of secondary wiring from transformers to distribution centre, 600 feet. About 15 volts drop on lighting circuits from transformers to distributing centre. Efficiency of motors, 85 per cent. Five volts drop on circuits from distributing centre to motors. Voltage at distributing point between main lines is 205. Current in main lines for motors is

$$\frac{4 \times 15 \times 746 \times .725}{.85 \times 200} = 191 \text{ amperes.}$$

Current for transformers from lamps is

$$\frac{(750 \times .5 \times 115) \times .607}{200} = 131 \text{ amperes.}$$

Total current from transformers is

$$131 + 191 = 322 \text{ amperes.}$$

For motors,

$$191 = \frac{W}{205} \quad .725. \quad W = 54,000.$$

For lamps,

$$131 \times \frac{W}{205} \times .607. \quad W = 44,240. \quad \text{Total watts} = 98,240.$$

Taking for trial two No. 0 B. & S. wires in parallel for each of the main conductors as preferable to one No. 0000, then

$$P = \frac{600 \times 98,240}{2 \times 105,592 \times 205^2} \times$$

$$\frac{1,200 \times 44,240 + 1,690 \times 54,000}{98,240} = 9.75.$$

Volts loss in lines

$$= \frac{9.75 \times 205 \times 1.32}{100} = 26.4.$$

Volts at transformers between main lines = 231.4.
Actual drop between main conductors and neutral to distributing point

$$= 26.4 \times \frac{115}{200} = 15.2 \text{ volts.}$$

The section of the neutral conductor should be about $\frac{131 \times 2 \times 105{,}592}{322} = 86{,}000 \; C.M.$ We may use 1 No. 1 B. & S. wire with a section of 83,694 $C.M.$ for the neutral.

MONOCYCLIC SYSTEM.—60 CYCLES. MOTOR AND LIGHTS ON SEPARATE TRANSFORMERS.

EXAMPLE: 1,500 half ampere 104 volt lamps. One 25 H.P. 110 volt induction motor; efficiency, 85 per cent. Distance from generator to transformer, 3,000 feet. Distance from transformers to motor, 100 feet. Loss in motor circuit, 2½ per cent. Loss of energy in transformers, 3 per cent. Loss in primary circuit, 4 per cent. Generator voltage, 1,040 at no load.

$$\text{Input at motor} = \frac{25 \times 746}{.85} = 21{,}940 \text{ watts.}$$

$$C.M. = \frac{100 \times 21{,}940}{2.5 \times 110^2} \times 3{,}380 = 245{,}000 \text{ No. 0000}$$

B. & S. wire = 211,600 $C.M.$, but as two No. 0 B. & S. wires will give the same loss, and $\frac{1.28}{1.85} = 69.2$ per cent as great a drop in voltage, they are preferable. Making each motor lead of two No. 0 B. & S. wires in parallel, then

$$P = \frac{100 \times 21{,}940 \times 3{,}380}{105{,}592 \times 2 \times 110^2} = 2.9 \text{ per cent.}$$

Volts loss to motors
$$= \frac{2.9 \times 110 \times 1.28}{100} = 4.$$

Volts at primaries of transformers for motors
$$= 1.05 \times 9 \times (110 + 4) = 1{,}076.$$

Volts on secondaries of lighting transformers
$$= \frac{1{,}076}{1.03 \times 10} = 104.5.$$

CALCULATION OF TRANSMISSION LINES. 235

Watts at primaries of motor transformers
$$= \frac{21{,}940 \times 1.029}{.97} = 23{,}200.$$

Watts at primaries of lighting transformers
$$= \frac{1{,}500 \times .5 \times 104.5}{.97} = 80{,}800.$$

Total watts delivered at transformers
$$= 23{,}200 + 80{,}800 = 104{,}000.$$

Power factor of load is
$$\frac{23{,}200 \times .80 + 80{,}000 \times .95}{104{,}000} = .91.$$

$$K = \frac{2{,}160}{.91^2} = 2{,}610.$$

$$C.M. = \frac{3{,}000 \times 104{,}000}{4 \times 1{,}076^2} \times 2{,}610 = 175{,}500.$$

Taking No. 000 B. & S. wire × 167,805 $C.M.$, then
$$P = \frac{3{,}000 \times 104{,}000}{167{,}805 \times 1{,}076^2} \times 2{,}610 = 4.19 \text{ per cent.}$$

Drop in primary circuit
$$= \frac{419 \times 1{,}076}{100} \times \frac{1.49 \times 80.8 + 1.62 \times 23.2}{104}$$
$$= 68.5 \text{ volts.}$$

Voltage between outside lines at generator
$$= 1{,}076 + 68.5 = 1{,}144.5 \text{ volts.}$$

Current in main conductors
$$= \frac{104{,}000}{1{,}076 \times .91} = 106.1 \text{ amperes.}$$

Primary teaser wire
$$= \frac{23{,}200}{104{,}000} \times 167{,}805 = 37{,}400 \; C.M. \text{ required.}$$

Use No. 4 B. & S. wire with a section of 41,742 $C.M.$

Graphical Illustration. — The curves on pages 236–239, Figs. 157, 158, and 159, have been calculated from the preceding formula and table of constants relating to the three-phase system only. They will be found useful for

236 POLYPHASE APPARATUS AND SYSTEMS.

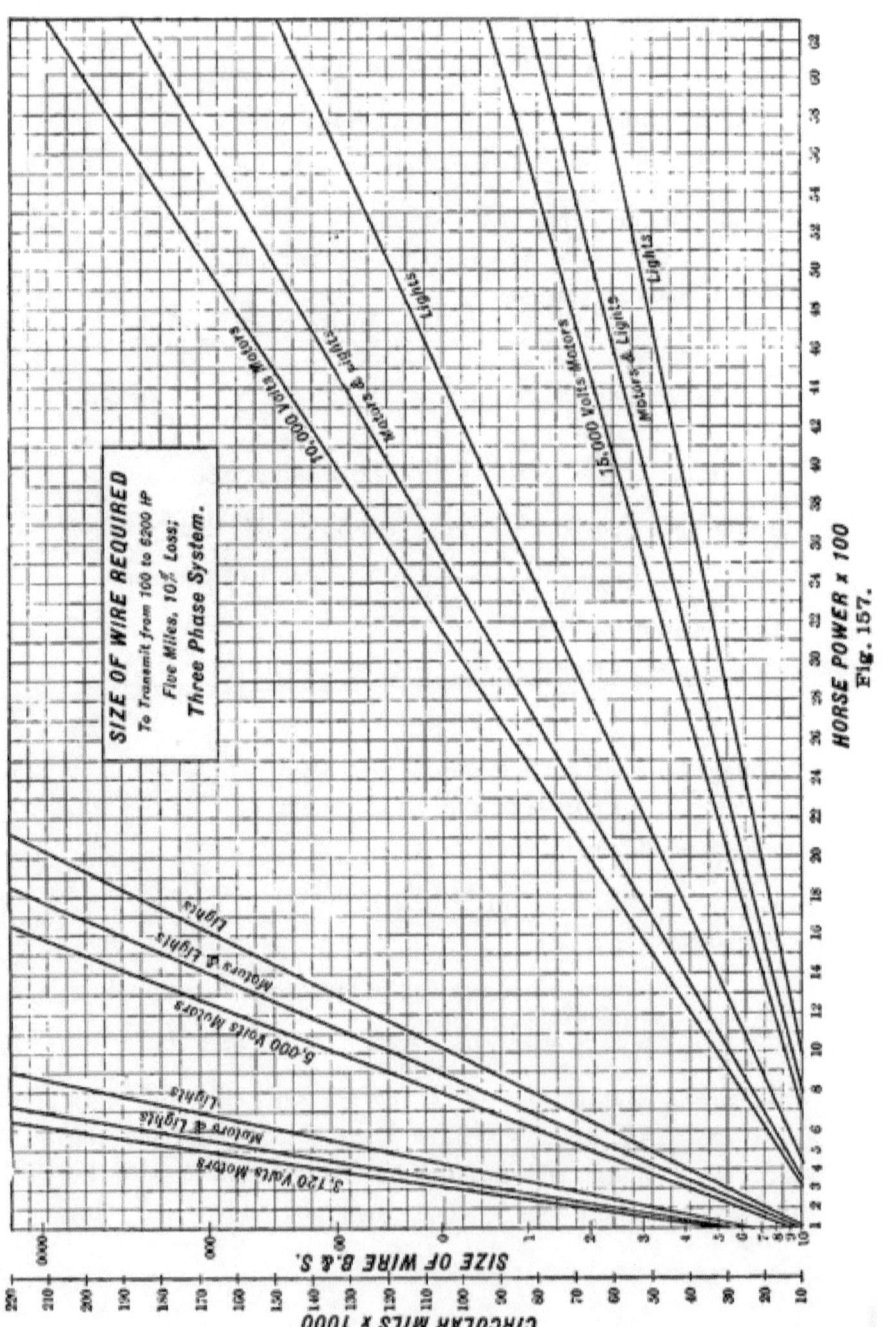

Fig. 157.

CALCULATION OF TRANSMISSION LINES. 237

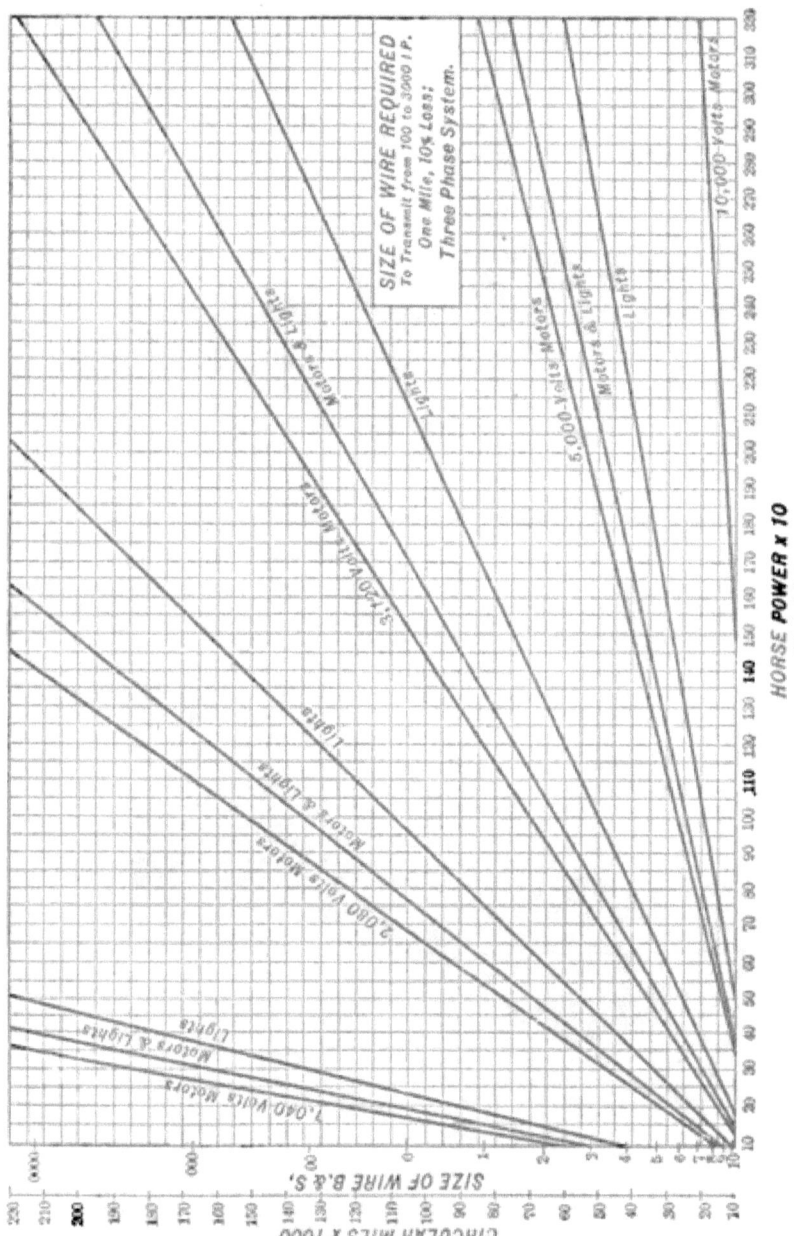

Fig. 158.

238 POLYPHASE APPARATUS AND SYSTEMS.

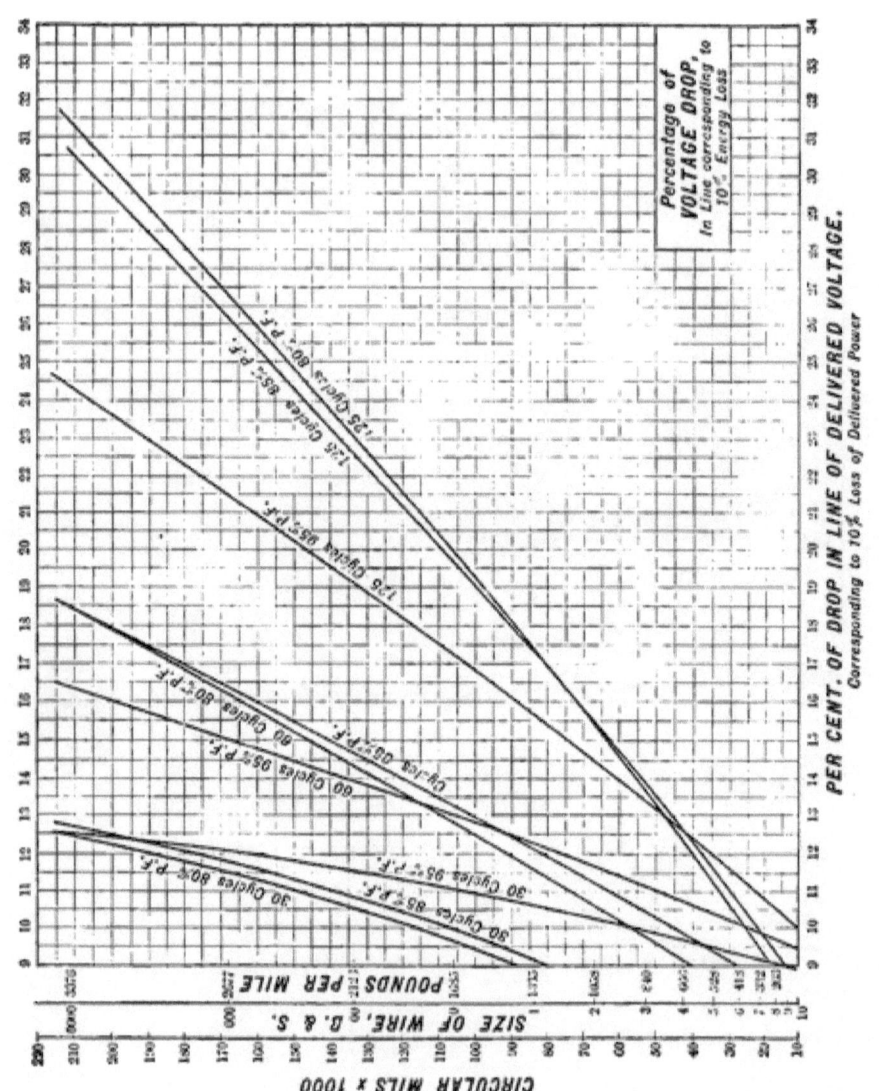

calculating and approximately determining the copper required for transmitting any amount of power any distance at voltages varying from 1,000 to 15,000.

For cases that fall outside the limits of the curves, the size of the wire may be found by applying the following rules:

With given power delivered, line loss, and voltage, the cross-section of the conductor will vary directly as the distance.

With given distance of transmission, line loss, and voltage, the cross-section of the conductor will vary directly as the power delivered.

With given distance of transmission, power delivered, and voltage, the cross-section of the conductor will vary inversely as the loss of energy in the line.

With given distance, power delivered, and line loss, the cross-section of the conductor will vary inversely as the square of the voltage.

The voltages are taken as those at the receiving end. The line loss has been assumed to be 10 per cent of the delivered energy. In plotting the curves the following power factors have been assumed:

For lighting load	95%
For mixed load of induction motors and lights . .	85%
For induction motor load	80%

To illustrate the use of the curves, find the size of the wire required to transmit 5,100 H.P., to be used for incandescent lighting, a distance of five miles, the current loss being 10 per cent, and the pressure at the primaries of step-down transformers, 10,000 volts. The curve (Fig. 157) shows that each of the three wires must have a cross-section of 120,000 circular mils. If the power delivered is to be consumed by induction motors, other conditions remaining the same, the conductor must have a cross-section equivalent to 170,000 circular mils each, or slightly larger than No. 000 wire. Or, supposing the wire to have been strung on the assumption that lights would be supplied, the line loss and pressure being the same as above, it will be seen that, if the load is changed to induction motors, only 3,600 H.P. will be delivered from these lines. This is a striking illustration of the decrease in the carrying capacity of the line, due to low power-factors, which load the line, and the generators as well, with so-called wattless current.

If the distance is raised to ten miles, the size of wire required for the same transmission is doubled in both the above examples. If the distance is increased to ten miles, and the energy loss reduced to five per cent, the cross-section of conductor will have to be made four times as great.

Three wires of about No. 3 size will transmit a lighting load of 5,100 H.P. a distance of five miles, the pressure being 15,000 at the receiving end. It will take three conductors of cross-section corresponding to a size between No. 1 and No. 2 to transmit the same power for induction motor use, and three No. 2 wires to transmit the same energy for a mixed load of lights and motors.

For determining the size of transmission lines with voltages of 5,000 and less, the curves in Fig. 158 will be found most convenient.

Fig. 159 represents the curves of percentage drop of voltage in transmission lines, at varying frequencies and power factors. The curves show the values of the constant, M, plotted from the table on page 238, and are based on 10 per cent energy loss in line.

A study of the curves shows some interesting facts.

When the transmission is effected at 30 cycles, it will be noticed that, for all commercial sizes of wires, the voltage drop is less with a load of low power-factor than with one of high power-factor. For illustration, assume that the transmission requires conductors of 120,000 circular mils each, the energy loss being 10 per cent of the delivered power. At 30 cycles, the drop in voltage is 10.1 per cent when the power factor is 80 per cent, 10.4 per cent when the power factor is 85 per cent, and 11.3 per cent when the power factor is 95 per cent. On the other hand, the same transmission at 125 cycles shows a higher voltage drop with low power-factors. The voltage drops 18.3 per cent with a 95 per cent power-factor, 21.2 per cent with an 85 per cent power-factor, and 21.7 per cent when the power factor is 80 per cent.

A curious condition exists at 60 cycles. The voltage drop is less with a power factor of 95 per cent, than when the power factor is 85 per cent; but an 80 per cent power-factor gives a drop approximately the same as that due to a power factor of 95 per cent. The curves also graphically illustrate the reduction in voltage drop to be gained by subdividing the conductors. A No. 00 wire, used in a 60 cycle transmission of power for induction motors, shows a drop of 14.3 per cent. By subdividing the wire into two No. 2 wires, and equivalent cross-section, the voltage drop is reduced to 10.6 per cent.

It will be seen, from the curves, that, by subdividing the conductor sufficiently, a wire of a size can be selected, which, for all commercial power-factors and frequencies, will transmit any amount of power, with a drop of voltage in the line actually less than the energy loss. This apparent anomaly is explained in Chapter I., under the paragraph, "Voltage Drop Due to Varying Power Factor."

242 POLYPHASE APPARATUS AND SYSTEMS.

Resonance Effect. — What is known as the resonance effect of a circuit is the rise of $E.M.F.$ at the far end, above that at the generator end. This phenomenon takes place when the natural period of discharge of a circuit is equal to the frequency of the generator $E.M.F.$ It is complete when the self-induction and capacity exactly neutralize each other. The charging current of the line, due to the capacity, then produces an $E.M.F.$ of self-induction equal to the generator $E.M.F.$

In transmission lines, where the inductance and capacity do not exactly neutralize each other, it is possible for partial resonance to be present. The circuit can be brought into complete resonance by the addition of a condenser or a reactance, according as it lacks the proper amount of either capacity or inductance. It is conceivable that an unexpected rise of pressure may occur of sufficient extent to destroy the insulation of line and of apparatus.

The rise of pressure due to complete resonance is limited by the ohmic resistance of the circuit. For this reason, and because practical transmissions of power are accomplished at a comparatively low frequency, the possible rise of pressure at the receiving end is not likely to be dangerously high.

For very long power transmissions, where resonance effects may be expected, it is desirable to employ generators producing an $E.M.F.$ wave which is sinusoidal. A distorted wave of $E.M.F.$ of the same period can be resolved into a number of simple harmonic components of a higher frequency. These higher harmonics have the same effect as an $E.M.F.$ wave of the same frequency and magnitude.

INDEX.

AIR blast transformers, 130.
Alternating circuit, flow of current in, 3.
 energy in, 10.
Alternations, 16.
Alternators (see Generators).
Ampere turns, rotary converter, 112.
Angle of lag, 11.
Apparent efficiency, 83.
 energy, 11.
 resistance, 14.
Arc lamps, on low frequency circuits, 209.
Armature, inductance, 34.
 induction motors, 60.
 multitooth construction, 34.
 reaction, 34, 35.
 resistance of induction motors, 60.
 unitooth construction, 33.
Auto converters for starting induction motors, 64.

BALANCED three-phase system, 187.
 two-phase system, 171–174, 176.
Blowers for cooling transformers, 132.
Breakdown point induction motors, 75–77.
 synchronous motors, 93, 94.

CALCULATION of transmission lines, constants for, 221, 224.
Capacity, 4.
 and magnetic reactance in same circuit, 8.
 of transmission lines, 224.
Charging current in transmission lines, 224, 225.
Choking coils for lightning arresters, 152.
Coefficient of self-induction, 4.
Combinations of circuits in polyphase systems, 166.
Compensators for induction motors, 64.
 synchronous motors, 97.
Composite winding of generators, 39.
Compounding of generators, 38.
Condensance, 8.
Condenser, use of, with induction motors, 86.
Conductors (see Transmission lines).
Connections of polyphase windings, 166, 180.
 delta, 168, 181, 182.
 interlinked, 167.
 ring, 168.
 star, 167.
 Y, 168, 181, 182.
Constants for line calculation, 223.
Converter (see Rotary converter).

INDEX

Cooling of transformers by air blast, 130.
   natural draft, 134.
   oil, 122.
   water, 127.
Copper, amount of, required with different polyphase systems, 214.
   losses in transformers, 136, 137.
Core losses in transformers, 137.
Cosine of lag angle, 11.
Counter E.M.F., 3.
Currents, alternating, definition of terms, 1.
Current, armature in rotary converter, 112.
   in synchronous motor, 100.
   lagging, 4.
   leading, 5.
   Wattless, 12.
Curve of E.M.F., 2.
   generator efficiency, 44.
   induction motor efficiency, 74, 86.
   transformer efficiency, 136.
   three-phase E.M.F., 180.
   two-phase E.M.F., 167.
Curves of line losses, 236, 237.
   voltage drop in transmission lines, 238.

Delta connection of windings, 161, 181, 182.
Distribution circuits, monocyclic, 197.
   three-phase four-wire, 184, 185, 190.
   three-phase three-wire, 176.
   two-phase four-wire, 173.
   two-phase three-wire, 176.

Efficiency generators, 44.
   induction motors, 74–86.
   synchronous motors, 92.
   transformers, 136.
Electrical resonance, 242.
Electromotive force, 2.
   impressed, 5.
   energy component of, 6.
   induction component of, 6.
Electromotive force, curve of, 2.
   three phase, 180.
   two phase, 167.
Energy apparent, 10.
   current, 12.
   loss in circuit, 13.
Engine, regulation for parallel operation of generators, 48.
Excitation, rotary converters, 111–114.
   synchronous motor, 99.
Exciting current of transformers, 137.
Exciter panel, 140, 146.
Exciters, capacities of, for generators and motors, 101.

Factor, induction, 11.
   power, 11.
Farad, the, 5.
Field induction motor, 68.
Field excitation, generator, 38.
   rotary converter, 111–113.
   rotary converter, effect on voltage, 110.
   synchronous motor, 99.
Flux, magnetic, 3.
Frequency changes, 163.
   choice of, 207, 212.
   definition, 16.
   effect of on parallel, 81.
   operation of generator, 209.
   high, 207.

INDEX.

Frequency, induction motors, 81.
   limit of rotary converters, 113.
   low, 209.

GENERATOR, armature construction, 20, 33.
   armature inductance, 35.
   armature reaction, 35.
   armature windings, 33.
Generators,
   conditions effecting cost of, 57.
   efficiency, 43.
   electro-motive force, 34.
   elementary forms, 17.
   field excitation, 34.
   inductor type, 27.
   losses, 43.
   methods of driving, 50.
   monocyclic windings, 196.
   parallel running, 46.
   revolving armature type, 18.
   revolving field type, 21.
   speed, 45.
   speed regulation of engine for driving, 48.
   three-phase windings, 180–182.
   two-phase windings, 166–168.
Geographical illustrations of line losses, 236, 237.
   voltage drops, 238.
Grounding of lightning arresters, 154.

HARMONIC motion, simple, 2.
Henry, the, 4.
High voltage generators, 33.

IDLE currents (see Wattless current).

Impedance, 7.
Impressed E.M.F., 5.
Inductance, 3.
Induction, 4.
   compound E.M.F., 6.
   factor, 11.
Induction motors, 60.
   condensers for, 86.
   construction of primary and secondary, 68.
   efficiency, 83.
   frequency, 81.
   initial voltages, 83.
   low inductance type, 77.
   methods of starting, 61.
   monocyclic, 203.
   principles of operation, 60.
   power factor, 83.
   single phase, 87.
   speed regulation, 78.
   starting torque and current, 72.
   transformer capacities for, 84.
   variable armature resistance type, 62, 67, 76.
   voltage, 82.
   wiring for, 83.
   with short-circuited armatures, 63, 67, 76.
Inductive loads, 83–100.
Inductor generator, 27.
Insulators, 156.
   glass, 156, 158.
   porcelain, 156.
   provo type, 158.
Iron losses, generators, 43.
   transformers, 137.

LAG, angle of, 11.
Lightning arresters, 149.
   G. E. type, 151.
   installation of, 152.

INDEX.

Lightning arresters, protection, 146.
   Wurtz type, 150.
Line (see Transmission lines).
Line constants for power transmission, 224.
   protection from lightning effects, 149.
Lines of force, 3.
Load, maximum induction motor, 76, 77.
   synchronous motor, 93.
Long distance power transmission by three-phase system, 190.
   by two-phase system, 170–173.
Losses in generators, 43.
   induction motors, 85.
   transformers, 136.

MAGNETIC circuit, inductor generator, 28.
   revolving field generator, 23.
Magnetic field induction motor, 60.
Magnetizing current, 75.
Measurement of power in monocyclic circuits, 204.
   three-phase circuits, 186, 187.
   two-phase circuits, 176.
Mesh connection (see Ring connection).
Monocyclic system, 194.
   distributing circuits, 197.
   features of, 194.
   generator armature connections, 196.
   measurement of power in, 204.
   motors for, 203.
   transformation to three-phase, 201–203.
   transformer connections for motors and lights, 200.

Motor connections in three-phase system, 184, 185.
   two-phase system, 170, 171, 177.
Motor generators, 165.
Multiphase (see Polyphase).

NEUTRAL point in three-phase system, 180, 182, 185, 187.

Ohm's law, modification of, in alternating current circuits, 3.
Oiled cooled transformers, 122.
Oscillatory character of lightning discharges, 152.
Output maximum of induction motors. 76, 77.
   synchronous motors, 93.

PARALLEL running of generators, 46.
Periodicity (see Frequency).
Phase displacement (see Angle of lag).
Phase transformation, 171.
Polycyclic System, 193.
Polyphase circuits, various connections of (see Two-phase, Three-phase, and Monocyclic systems).
   currents, 166.
   systems and combinations, 166.
   transformers, 120.
Power factor, 11.
   induction motors, 83.
   rotary converters, 116.
   synchronous motors, 102.
   voltage drop due to, 13.
Power measurement, monocyclic system, 204.
   three-phase system, 187, 188.
   two-phase system, 176.

INDEX. 247

Power transmission, long distance by three-phase system, 190.
    two-phase system, 170, 173.
Primary of induction motor, 60–68.
Prime movers for driving generators, 50.
Pressure Regulators, 160.
    polyphase type, 160.
    single-phase type, 160.
    Stillwell type, 161.
Punchings, generator armature, 33.

Radiating surface of transformers, 121.
Ratio of transformation of rotary converters, 110.
Reactance, 7.
    of transmission conductors, 224.
Reaction, generator armatures, 35.
Rectifiers, 162.
Regulation, inherent of generators, 42.
    of transformers, 138.
    speed, of induction motors, 78.
    of synchronous motors, 92, 93.
Resistance apparent, 14.
    copper conductors, 224.
    virtual, 9.
Resonance effect, 242.
Reversing induction motors, 68.
Ring winding, 168.
Rotary converters, 106.
    armature connections, 107.
    armature reaction, 113.
    general features, 106.
    limit of frequency, 113.

Rotary converters made from direct current generators, 106.
    parallel operation, 119.
    power factor, 116.
    ratio alternating to direct current voltage, 110.
    starting and running, 118.
    types and uses, 111.
    voltage variation, 114, 115.
Rotor of induction motor, 60–68.

Secondary systems of distribution, monocyclic, 197.
    three-phase four-wire, 183–185.
    three-phase three-wire, 181–184.
    two-phase four-wire, 173.
    two-phase three-wire, 176.
Self-induction, coefficient of, 4.
Simple harmonic motion, 2.
Sine wave, 2.
Single-phase induction motors, 87.
    synchronous motors, 93.
    wiring, 98.
Skin effect, 10.
Slip of induction motors, 61.
Speed control of induction motors, 79.
    effect of, on cost of generators, 57.
    regulation of engines for parallel running, 48.
    variation of induction motors, 78.
Star connection of windings, 168, 181.
Starting current induction motors, 61, 72, 73.
    synchronous motors, 95.

Starting of induction motors, 61.
    rotary converters, 118.
    synchronous motors, 95.
Starting torque effect of voltage on, 75, 76, 94.
    of induction motors, 72, 73.
    of synchronous motors, 93.
Static transformers (see Transformers).
Synchronizing devices, 154.
Synchronous motors, 92.
    advantages of, 92.
    field excitation, 99.
    methods of starting, 95.
    monocyclic, 94.
    power factor, 102.
    speed, 92.
    torque and output, 93.
    used as condensers, 104.
    voltage, 94.
Temperature of transformers, 122.
Theory of action of induction motors, 60.
Three-phase circuits for power distribution, 190.
    curves of E.M.F., 180.
    four-wire system, 185.
    long distance transmission circuits, 192.
    motor connections, 184.
    three-wire system, 199.
    transformer connections, 181.
Three-phase system, 180.
    measurement of power in, 186.
Torque diagram of induction motors, 73.
    starting of induction motors, 72.
    starting of synchronous motors, 93.

Transformation of phases, 171.
Transformer connections, monocyclic, 200.
    three phase, 181.
    two phase, 170.
Transformers, 120.
    air blast type, 130.
    efficiency, 135.
    losses, 135.
    natural draft type, 134.
Transformers, operation of air blast, 132.
    polyphase, 120.
    regulation, 138.
    self-cooled oil type, 122.
    water-cooled oil type, 127.
Transmission lines, calculation of, 221.
    capacity of, 224, 225.
    charging current in, 224, 225.
    inductance of, 224, 225.
    resistance of, 224, 225.
    voltage drop in, 221, 226, 238.
Two-phase four-wire system, 173.
    generator armature connections, 168.
    interlinked windings, 167.
    separate windings, 167.
    three-wire system, 176.
    to three-phase, 171.
    transformer connections, 170.
    unbalancing, 177.
Two-phase system, 166.
    relations of E.M.F. in, 166.

Unit of capacity, 5.
    of self-inductance, 4.

Voltage drop in transmission lines, 221, 226, 228.
Voltage, effects of on output of induction motor, 82.

INDEX. 249

Voltage of synchronous motor, 94.
Voltage of induction motor, 110.
　relation of line to induced E.M.F. in three-phase generators, 36.

WATER wheels as prime movers, 47, 51, 54.
Wattless current, 12.
Wattless or magnetizing current in induction motor, 85.
　transformers, 139.
Wattmeter for measuring power, in monocyclic circuits, 204.
　three-phase circuits, 187.
　two-phase circuits, 176.

Watts apparent, 11.
Windings generator armature, 33.
　interlinked, 167.
　monocyclic, 196.
　three phase, 180–183.
　transformers, 166.
　two phase, 167.
　primary of induction motor, 68.
　secondary of induction motor, 68.
Wiring formulas, 227.
　application of, 230.

Y connection in three-phase system, 181, 182, 186.

www.ingramcontent.com/pod-product-compliance
Lightning Source LLC
Chambersburg PA
CBHW031731230426
43669CB00007B/313